Leadership in a Changing World

Leadership in a Changing World

Dynamic Perspectives on Groups and Their Leaders

Edited by
Robert H. Klein, Cecil A. Rice, and
Victor L. Schermer

LEXINGTON BOOKS

A division of
ROWMAN & LITTLEFIELD PUBLISHERS, INC.
Lanham • *Boulder* • *New York* • *Toronto* • *Plymouth, UK*

LEXINGTON BOOKS

A division of Rowman & Littlefield Publishers, Inc.
A wholly owned subsidiary of The Rowman & Littlefield Publishing Group, Inc.
4501 Forbes Boulevard, Suite 200
Lanham, MD 20706

Estover Road
Plymouth PL6 7PY
United Kingdom

Copyright © 2009 by Lexington Books

British Library Cataloguing in Publication Information Available

Library of Congress Cataloging-in-Publication Data

Leadership in a changing world : dynamic perspectives on groups and their
    leaders / edited by Robert H. Klein, Cecil A. Rice, and Victor L. Schermer.
        p. cm.
    Includes bibliographical references and index.
    ISBN-13: 978-0-7391-2396-6 (cloth : alk. paper)
    ISBN-10: 0-7391-2396-3 (cloth : alk. paper)
    ISBN-13: 978-0-7391-3253-1 (electronic)
    ISBN-10: 0-7391-3253-9 (electronic)
    [etc.]
    1. Leadership. I. Klein, Robert H. II. Rice, Cecil A. III. Schermer, Victor L.
    BF637.L4L393 2009
    303.3'4—dc22   2008040460

Printed in the United States of America

™
♾ The paper used in this publication meets the minimum requirements of
American National Standard for Information Sciences—Permanence of Paper
for Printed Library Materials, ANSI/NISO Z39.48-1992.

We dedicate this book to all leaders and their followers who strive to maintain insight, compassion, accountability, and respect for all.

Contents

Part II: Case Studies

Foreword

Joseph V. Montville

The introductory chapter of this collection underlines a fundamental and enduring problem of leadership studies in the social sciences and the humanities. Most of the scholars and journalists who write about leadership still do not really understand some of its most important dimensions. It is remarkable—if not stunning—that, as the editors indicate, most of the articles in the January 2007, Special Issue of *The American Psychologist* on Leadership used the model of the individualistic "rational actor." In my earliest days as a newly minted political psychologist, I characterized this attitude as "resistance to knowing." By contrast, the editors and authors in this volume believe that leadership is co-created between those individuals who aspire to or are recruited by their communities, large groups, and nations and who interact with them in a sometimes creative and sometimes destructive process of psychodynamic negotiation.

There are numerous business schools and graduate programs that purport to teach leadership skills. Indeed, it is a lucrative activity that may very well improve the skills of otherwise competent individuals for high-level management positions. The best of them learn how to deal constructively with peers and subordinates and manage relationships for the greater productive good of the corporation or other hierarchically structured organization that they may serve. But this is not "leadership" in the terms upon which the authors herein are focused. With the notable exceptions of Richard Billow's broad-stroke portrait of "modes of leadership"; Jean Chin's insights into gender, diversity, and leadership; and Peter Gumpert's excellent discussion of corporate management, the authors, for the most part, care about leadership in the context of life and death, of the interests and welfare of large identity groups and nations. Their subject is historic trauma, the collective sense of justice denied, the enduring wounds to the feeling of worth inflicted in modern times or in the past. Leaders in this context are those that help the healing of historic hurts to the nation or in the worst cases exploit the enduring resentments of their followers to strengthen and secure their leadership positions. In the latter case, leaders such as these—Hitler, Pol Pot, Robert Mugabe, Slobodan Milosevic, Idi Amin, and Saddam Hussein stand out—drag their countries to near ruin as they literally hang on to power for dear life.

In my exposure to the broad sweep of academic research or political commentary on the behavior of individual leaders interacting with large groups or nations, I have been in a state of constant chagrin at the avoidance by most scholars and analysts of the tools of dynamic psychology. It is not as though I have a dog in the fight between those social scientists who utilize psychoanalytic psychology, in Freud's terms, as an instrument of research, and those who do not. My academic work was in Middle Eastern regional studies and comparative politics, all historical and descriptive.

Depth psychology came to me personally and as an avocation through the intimate connection with a family member's psychoanalysis and the tutoring of a next-door neighbor in Washington, DC, who was an MD analyst. In the process of learning about the impact of wounds of the past in my family life and assaults on identity and the sense of self worth, I not only got some grasp of a personal crisis but also of the dynamics of Iraqi identity conflicts and politics. My Foreign Service career had started in Baghdad and extended to the broader Arab-Israeli arena of conflict with subsequent service in Lebanon, Libya, and Morocco. I became by chance a dynamically oriented political psychologist.

In the mid- and late 1970s back in the Department of State in Washington, I fell in with several psychiatrists who were members of the American Psychiatric Association's committee on psychiatry and foreign affairs. They were politically sophisticated and either practiced or very much admired dynamic analytical approaches to identity conflicts, and they were determined to use their skills to advance the Middle East peace process. I was a country desk officer and regional policy adviser in the bureau of Near Eastern and South Asian affairs and, later, chief of the Near East division in the bureau of intelligence and research. Showing wisdom for which I will always be grateful, my supervisors permitted me to moonlight with an APA committee as it organized small, intense five-day workshops in Europe, Egypt, and the United States with Israelis, Egyptians, and Palestinians from the West Bank and Gaza, including psychiatrists as well as journalists, military and intelligence officers, ex-cabinet ministers, and academics.

We listened and learned, mediated, encouraged, wrote assessments, published papers, and established research centers at the University of Virginia and Harvard. Some of us spun off to apply our dynamic approach to the psychology of the U.S.-Soviet relationship at Esalen Institute in Big Sur, California, in the early and mid-1980s. The great and beloved Erik Erikson and his wife, Joan, were the centerpieces of the Soviet work at Esalen. Vamik Volkan, prominent in the present collection, and the late John E. Mack were key actors in these efforts. Leaders and leadership were always on our minds, but the social and political context within which leaders worked was always paramount.

These slivers of autobiography in a foreword are perhaps unorthodox. But I want to make the point that dynamic psychology was a basic tool in a very pragmatic approach of academic and clinical professionals—and one career diplomat—in trying to understand and prescribe therapeutic initiatives in interactions among nations that had been warring and whose citizens and soldiers had been dying and continued to die. The strengths, weaknesses, and idiosyncrasies of political leaders of the Israelis, Egyptians, and Palestinians were discussed, but our subjects for analysis were peoples, their histories, their memories, their self-concepts, and their esteem needs.

In fact, we were developing a new concept of leadership in distressed nations and states that came from political, academic, artistic, and religious sectors of the communities who could bring much greater moral authority to the leadership function of their peoples than most formal officials— leadership in literally showing the way. Some of us called this "track two diplomacy," a method of identifying and encouraging nonofficial leadership where political officials could not really lead or where, for group psychodynamic reasons, they strongly need the unofficial leadership help.

It's a pity and a shame that so many leaders and academic specialists in leadership do not understand how it works in co-creation with followers. I hope they will read this collection of articles and essays, learn, and change their ways. Lives are at stake.

Acknowledgments

While a book is, of course, the work of specific editors and authors, it is also the co-creation of a broad network of those who inspire, encourage, and support the work. As editors of the current volume, we think of our own relationships with leaders in our own field of group psychotherapy and psychoanalysis who served as role models, were sometimes friends, and made a difference in our thinking about and understanding of the leadership process itself: These include but are not limited to Drs. Gunther Abraham, Yvonne Agazarian, Max Day, Earl Hopper, Howard Kibel, Marty Livingston, Norman Neiberg, Malcolm Pines, John Romano, Scott Rutan, Leonard Salzman, Roger Shapiro, Sheryl Somerville, Walter Stone, and Gerda Winther, all of whom come to mind as colleagues who have crafted strong and positive leadership roles. We think too of those beloved colleagues who have passed on so recently that our grief is palpably felt even now: Drs. Anne Alonso, Toby Chuah-Feinson, Gene Eliasoph, Lamis Jarrar, and Patrick de Mare. All these leaders have taken strong stands regarding scholarship, treatment, and the conduct of our fields of endeavor, and their convictions have paved the way for lasting improvements in the collective work of our professions. Further, they have led with the insight, wisdom, and humanity that it is the goal of this book to engender more widely among leaders in all walks of life.

Regarding specific scholarly influences, special acknowledgments are due Vamik Volkan and Jerrold Post (both of whom contributed chapters to this book), as well as Warren Bennis, Otto Kernberg, and Pierre Turquet, who have stood at the forefront regarding applications of dynamic and group psychology to the critical problems of large groups and society. Similarly, of course, we are indebted to all our chapter authors not only for their pioneering work but also for the richness of their ideas and the time and effort they devoted to reflection and writing for the current endeavor. In October 2007, the editors convened a Think Tank on Leadership at the Washington Square Institute in New York City. Its purpose was to flesh out ideas that might prove useful in this book and other endeavors. Participants included Drs. Richard Billow, Jean Chin, Peter Gumpert, Susan Gutwill, Howard Kibel, Margaret Postlewaite, Karen Saakvitne, and Hala Taweel. We are grateful to them for their ideas and reflections.

Family members and friends form a network, which makes possible all our life activities. Klein is especially grateful to his wife, Serena-Lynn Brown, and his daughter, Sasha, for their unwavering love, support, and patience, and to his dear friend Marsha Block from whom he has learned so much of lasting value. Rice is grateful to his wife, Shirley, a partner and lover for a lifetime, his daughter Cathy, and his grandsons Benjamin and Ryan whose short lives have enriched his own. Schermer is grateful to his dear friends Tom Lawton, Janine Carazo, Ronald Dombroski, Michael Ricci, and Bill Wolf as well as his cousins, Joan and Gil Trachtman, for constant reminders of the inestimable value of enduring friendships and family ties. He also thanks his boss, Dr. Jane McGuffin, for her flexibility and generosity regarding his clinic schedule that allowed him to move forward with the book.

Finally, we thank our publisher, Lexington Books, their representative Joseph Parry, and our ever-patient and efficient editor and proofreader, Kathleen Paparchontis, for the resources and support we needed to accomplish our tasks and for easing the way to their completion.

> Robert H. Klein, Orange, Connecticut
> Cecil A. Rice, Needham, Massachusetts
> Victor L. Schermer, Philadelphia, Pennsylvania
> July 2008

Introduction: Co-creating In-depth Leadership for a New Millennium

Robert H. Klein, Cecil A. Rice, and Victor L. Schermer

WHY ANOTHER BOOK ON LEADERSHIP?

There are scores of books—scholarly, practical, and popular—on leadership. Nearly everyone has something to say about what makes for good and bad leaders as well as what explains and how to solve the problems that leaders face. Moreover, expert consultants are available to leaders in every walk of life. And political and corporate leaders are frequently scrutinized in the media and the popular culture. So why produce still another book on the subject? What new ground could it possibly cover?

The most important answer to this question is that the global problems that call for effective, visionary, and ethical leadership are approaching critical mass. The short- and long-term mismanagement of our environment, work worlds, economies, political situations, cyberspace, care priorities, family lives and values, natural disasters, and capabilities for mass destruction threatens life as we know it and the well-being of millions. Therefore, it is imperative that humanity return to the leadership drawing board to seek new and creative understandings of leadership—or the negative consequences could be of a magnitude and scope never before anticipated. At the outset of the New Millennium, the world is changing fast on a global scale. Something must be done to point it in the right direction, and the place to begin is with those who exercise the most power, authority, and influence, namely our leaders.

The second reason for a new look at leadership issues is that, as Bennis (2007) argues, cherished assumptions about how leaders are created and how they best do their jobs seem to be falling apart under our collective noses. And many are speculating—but few are seriously studying and

1

investigating—what new assumptions and paradigms would best replace the old ones.

In the most familiar timeworn paradigm, which has prevailed for more than five centuries, since the Renaissance focused upon the individual as initiator of change, leaders were seen to be persons who emerged from well-honed traditions (e.g., royalty), difficult trials (e.g., military leaders), or notable achievements (e.g., artists, scientists) into positions of influence, authority, and power. Their actions were perceived to be based on reason, ambition, and the dictates of conscience. In other words, their decisions and conduct appeared to result from conscious deliberation, the awareness of contingencies, and the interests of the various parties involved. That is, leaders were looked upon as individuals who possessed characteristics that were well suited to make conscious, "rational" decisions in their particular sphere of influence. (By "rational," we will of course mean based upon some attempt at reasoned-out thought, whether correct or not and whether or not influenced by strong emotions, sentiments, and affiliations.) Whether Elizabeth I, Napoleon, Lincoln, Churchill, J. P. Morgan, Hitler, Gandhi, or Stalin—and for whatever good or ill each of them did—that is how we have regarded leaders and sought to understand their qualities and actions, partly to "learn lessons" that might help future leaders do better. This notion of the leader as a consciously reasoning and influential decision maker has held sway to the present day. For example, in a recent Special Issue of *The American Psychologist* (see Bennis 2007), the majority of the articles reviewing aspects of the literature on leadership used this individualistic model of a "rational self" in its various empirically based forms.

The other side of the leadership equation—the ability to attract and influence followers—was again accounted for on the individual basis of the leader's particular power base, charisma, and/or ability to transform the motivations and ideologies of large numbers of people. Leaders were seen to possess the capacity to establish followers by either getting them to submit through power and control or to idealize and identify with the leader and his avowed purpose. So another set of assets was required of leaders: power, influence, charisma, and other traits that attracted or commanded followership. Followers, for their part, were less successful or more passive agents who were led to submit and produce the actions their leaders required. When they refused to comply, conflict, rebellion, or revolution occurred. Out of these rebellions, democracy and negotiation evolved as ways to promote a degree of equality and choice within society and the sociopolitical matrix.

This view of the leader as a self-contained ego making conscious, rational choices based upon "real world" contingencies and possessing power and influence has remained to this day the predominant mode of thinking about leaders in both the social sciences and the humanities. This is true despite over a century of newer "modern" and "postmodern" paradigms in which unconscious, social, and evolutionary forces are held to prevail over individual consciousness, choices, and will. Yet the premodern paradigm has remained true during an era in which mass psychology easily and tragically won out over individual rationality in two world wars, a cold war, segregation and oppression of minorities, recurrent ethnic conflicts, and imminent destruction of the global environment.

THE CO-CREATION PARADIGM OF LEADERSHIP

During the twentieth century, the potential for an alternative or complementary view of leadership did emerge, one that has great explanatory power but which has not yet been given the full attention it deserves in a rapidly changing, often volatile world. It is the notion that leaders, seemingly conscious and powerful "deciders," are in reality the product of two sets of forces: (1) deep unconscious conflicts within themselves but outside their awareness and (2) human interactions ranging from the early mother-infant pair and family environment to massive social movements, all of which combine to "co-create" leaders. That is, leaders' actions are significantly affected by their own unconscious motivations and the somewhat capricious "will" of the group or society. In this view, the leader is not a "rational animal" or "man on the mountain" standing above the masses. Rather, the leader is a member of a group—or, more accurately, numerous groups, both large and small—who, in part, receives, contains, and carries out the often unconscious intentions of the group in an ongoing dialogue that includes a partial merger of selves and identities and a mutual interplay among needs, defenses, desires, and fantasies. As Benjamin Disraeli once said, "I am their leader. Therefore, I must follow them." This view does not totally deconstruct the more traditional view of the leader as a "powerful, decision-making individual" but stands in a complementary relationship to it. That is, leaders are *both* autonomous cutting-edge individuals and, on another level, mere actors in a drama co-constructed by the group—or society-as-a-whole.

The latter perspective, in which *the group "co-creates" leaders and followers who, in a mutual, reciprocal interchange, serve conscious and unconscious purposes for the group,* is the paradigm advocated in this book. The significance of this viewpoint is not that it is new (traces of it can be found in the work of Plato, Aristotle, and the Greek tragedians; and Freud and Jung articulated its broad outlines nearly 100 years ago) but that ignoring it is a major reason why contemporary leaders have such difficulty addressing the consequential complexities of the New Millennium. To give but one example, taken up by Jerrold Post in this volume, modern terrorism cannot be addressed only by understanding and undermining terrorist leaders such as Osama Bin Laden. Terrorist candidates are emerging in large numbers in regions like the Middle East and Asia because the society in various ways provides breeding grounds—largely within families and neighborhoods—for hatred and martyrdom, which develops in childhood interactions and becomes florid in the ideologies of adolescence and young adulthood. In other words, as Post perceptively notes, understanding both normal and "pathological" leadership requires as well a grasp of the emotional and developmental lives not only of the leaders but also of the followers who will co-create the leadership that actualizes their collective identities. The chapters of this book exemplify contemporary situations where this dynamic "co-creation" is present at both conscious and unconscious levels.

Avolio (2007), in the above-referenced *American Psychologist* edition on leadership, offers the only one of five state-of-the-art position papers/literature reviews in which interpersonal and group systems are given priority in leadership theory and research. According to Avolio, "one might conclude that leadership studies had traditionally focused too narrowly on a limited set of elements, primarily highlighting the leaders yet overlooking many other potentially relevant elements of leadership such as the follower and context" (p. 25). He goes on to consider the various contextual elements that call for further study, such as, quoting Stodgill (1974), leadership as a "relation that exists between persons in a social situation," culture and history as contexts for leadership, and the relationship between the individual and the group-as-a-whole. Alvolio, however, employs a social psychological rather than a psychoanalytic frame of reference, and therefore neglects the unconscious and developmental aspects, which the current editors and chapter authors believe is critical in understanding co-creative relational processes. It is a premise of this book that a full comprehension of the "co-creation" of leadership by the group requires an understanding of the deeper, often unconscious, levels of motivation and conflict co-occurring in both the individual and in the multiple group systems in which all human life is embedded. We argue that leadership cannot be reduced to cognitive rational decision-making and/or behavioral contingencies.

The depth psychological relational paradigm we are advocating did not spring up out of nowhere. It has a hundred-year history within psychoanalysis and group dynamics as they developed, somewhat in tandem. A historical review will be helpful in orienting the reader to the more contemporary views articulated in this volume. This review will necessarily be selective with an emphasis on a few key historical figures and those aspects most relevant to the chapters of this book. Ashbach and Schermer (1987), DeMare (1972), and Gibbard, Hartman, and Mann (1974) provide fuller explications of these and related developments.

HISTORICAL OVERVIEW OF CONCEPTS
RELEVANT TO CO-CREATION OF LEADERSHIP

Partly because the conflicts in Europe and the horrors of World War I troubled him, Freud, who had hitherto focused on clinical issues regarding individual patients, became interested in the psychology of groups and mass behavior. In *Group Psychology and the Analysis of the Ego* (1921), he hypothesized a "natural continuity" between the dynamics of the individual and those of groups. He advanced a theory to explain "the psychology of groups on the basis of changes in the psychology of the individual mind" (Freud 1921, pp. 67–68).

Freud viewed the leader as a father figure whom the members idealized and with whom they identified. Paradoxically, his approach was not group-centered, but rather self-centered, emphasizing the followers' narcissistic basking in the leader's aura of power and authority. He saw two mechanisms operating in the members' relation to the leader: (1) "identification of the member's ego with an object" and (2) "replacement of the ego ideal by an object" (Ashbach and Schermer 1987, p. 4). In the first instance, members idolize and adopt the leader's characteristics, as, for example, African Americans identify with the ideals and aspirations of Martin Luther King, Jr. In the second, which is more primitive or regressive, the members project parts of their own selves into the leader (and then reintroject or identify with what is projected) in hopes that the leader will contain, express, and/or enact them on a larger, more powerful and influential scale. Thus, Germans projected into Hitler their need to scapegoat Jews and other minorities for their nation's grievous failings and losses and conversely introjected Hitler's grandiosity into themselves during his rabble-rousing demagoguery. This further allowed the self-proclaimed "Fuhrer" to genocidally carry out their aggressivized fantasies while they (the followers) seemingly looked away or were presumably "just following orders." The combined mechanism of identification and projection was subsequently termed "projective identification" by Melanie Klein (1977), when she recognized a similar, though perhaps less malevolent, pattern of defense in both children and adults in psychoanalytic treatment.

Projective identification is one of the main psychological mechanisms whereby members of a group or society co-create their leaders by placing split-off parts of themselves into the leader for containment and enactment. Thus, for example, the Palestinians idealized Yassir Arafat as a rescuer of his people (identification), but he also served as a container and proxy for aggressivized "bad" parts of the collective self of Palestinians who felt persecuted and hateful toward the Israelis. Curiously, Israelis and pro-Israelis in the West also projectively identified this "badness" into Arafat in a different way and began to think of him as the personification of evil rather than a struggling leader of his traumatized nation. Arafat "accepted" and "contained" these projective identifications as parts of himself so that he increasingly opposed Western interventions and failed to control the actions of terrorist groups in Palestine. The theory of projective identification suggests that if the Israelis and the Western world had aligned more with Arafat's role as a figure of idealization and identification for the aspirations of his people, he might have been more cooperative. As it happened, he became so "demonized" that he spent the end of his life confined by Israeli soldiers to a small office enclave surrounded by blighted areas of destruction. The persecutory conflicts of many decades of Arab-Israeli history, which have historical roots going back centuries, were phantasmagorically contained in that little space, but the belief that confining and isolating Arafat would help resolve the conflict was ultimately proven to be false because the dispute has continued well beyond Arafat's demise.

Identification and projective identification thus act like a "double helix" of a partial merger of leaders and their followers so that, in an almost trancelike state of the group where the differentiation between them is vague and unclear, they co-create self-concepts, motivations, ideologies, and agendas of a mutually reinforcing nature. These co-creations become exaggerated, larger-than-life caricatures that do not easily permit modifications based upon reality.

Freud's follower and later adversary, Jung, was also interested in group psychology and used the terms "collective unconscious" and "transpersonal psychology" to refer to hidden "shadow" levels of group relations. Jung (1968) regarded both good and evil motives as resonating in the group in the form of cultural myths that were passed from generation to generation. (In the present volume, Volkan, who is not a Jungian, nevertheless emphasizes that myth and ritual, transmitted across generations in the form of "chosen glories" and "chosen trauma" of victory and defeat, perpetuate and fuel recurrent hostilities between feuding ethnic groups.) While Freud (1927) saw social behavior as a collective defense against the instincts of sex and aggression, Jung (1968) regarded collectivism both as a "mask" or disguise of our basic nature and as a ritualistic expression of that nature. Jung regarded leaders as carriers and exemplars of "archetypal" myths, including "the myth of the birth of the hero" (Campbell 1949). History suggests that this transformational aspect of leadership, which Nietzsche (1969), for example, espoused, can have both positive and disastrous consequences. The danger is that the leader's charismatic and transformational attributes can easily represent to the "masses" a "magical" solution to human dilemmas, a poor substitute for the individual growth and development each follower must pursue to become a whole person.

During World War II, therapy groups were frequently used to treat "shell-shocked" traumatized soldiers, and a number of major developments in group psychology emerged during and after that time. One of the most significant of these was fostered by Wilfred Bion, who conducted hospital treatment groups as a British Army psychiatrist and later became a psychoanalyst who had a major influence upon both group dynamics and psychoanalytic theory and practice. Bion (1959) extended Freud's lines of investigation of groups, but, emphasizing the work of Melanie Klein on "object relations theory"—the study of interpersonal and social relations vis-à-vis their mental representations and the unconscious—portrayed still more primitive "psychotic-like" layers of group behavior, what he called the "basic assumption states" (BA) of dependency, fight/flight, and pairing.

For Bion, the primitive, unconscious components of group interaction occur anonymously and reflexively (without individual responsibility and conscious thought) by the very act of coming together in groups. The group-as-a-whole is the primary phenomenon, and roles such as leader and follower evolve in the process of defense against the psychotic anxieties evoked by participating in group life. (That is, even before the "co-creation" of leaders and followers, the creation of the group mentality itself occurs.) Furthermore, group formation is predicated on shared unconscious beliefs. In BA dependency, the group assumes that an omniscient, omnipotent leader will give them unending care and healing. In BA fight/flight, the group believes there is an enemy within or outside the group and attempts to rid the group of the badness or flee from it, so that group paranoia and scapegoating emerge with little attempt at or tolerance for rational thought. In BA pairing, the group unconsciously selects a couple to represent its hope and to enact its wish for magical, transformative, utopian leadership. All of these basic assumptions are rooted in fantasy and defense, so the group must ultimately grasp its own dynamics through self-introspection to achieve a "work group" that is oriented to reality and the task at hand.

Bion's pioneering observations led to the ongoing study of group dynamics at the Tavistock Institute in London and subsequently at the A. K. Rice Institute in the United States. In both instances, conferences, which included both small and large group interactions, led to many observations and inferences about social behavior. In the present volume, Gumpert's discussion of the psychoaffective problems related to a corporate expansion and establishing a new division within a company makes rich use of the "systems" orientation of the A. K. Rice Institute (Miller and Rice 1967) and of Bion's understanding of primitive defense mechanisms in groups. Systems thinking allows for many levels and possibilities for co-creation of leadership because a leader may be established within a small group, a subgroup, the overarching large group or society, or even at the boundaries between groups. Former President Jimmy Carter emerged as the leader of a subgroup (governor of Georgia) and then a large group (president of the United States). Later, he became a highly successful (boundary) mediator between conflicting groups, earning the Nobel Peace Prize. Interestingly, his intervention in the Israel-Palestine dilemma has proved more controvertial than his other efforts, with issues of mistrust perhaps reflective of some of the leader-group problems explored in this book.

One of the authors in the present volume, Vamik Volkan, has also worked frequently as a mediator between conflicted ethnic and national groupings. His chapter illustrates some of the thinking he uses in his "hands-on" work, which includes insights about large group dynamics as well as the leader's management or mismanagement of his or her own narcissism and grandiosity. In its most sublimated form, narcissism can help a leader manifest and realize the highest ambitions and ideals for his group. Volkan cites the founder of modern Turkey, Kemal Atatürk, as an example of such healthy narcissism at the service of society.

Paradoxically, narcissism is a social process, because, as Kohut (1977, p. 32) has suggested, the narcissistic self requires a "selfobject" (a significant other who is experienced as an extension of the self) for mirroring and idealization. Karterud and Stone (2003) argued that the group itself can serve as both a supraordinate self and a mirroring or idealizing selfobject, thus facilitating a form of "co-creation" of leadership and followership in which the group and leader sustain and transform the selves of the members or followers. This is, for instance, manifestly true of that idealized "sceptered isle" called England, where the people have in the course of the twentieth century and before suffered the rebellion and secession of many countries that were once part of its Empire, a massive, prolonged air attack on their capital, and the death of a Princess (Diana) who had come to represent (via projective identification) the vulnerable humanistic simplicity and altruism of the people. Yet, within their own worlds and within certain parameters, English men and women retained much of their self-esteem and values, sustained by the mirroring and idealization of their country's traditions and a wise Queen Elizabeth II, who set aside her personal ambivalence toward Diana when she realized the need of the masses for empathy with their grief.

In this book, Benson applies Kohut's theory of the self to the prolonged conflict between the two factions in Northern Ireland that has recently been considerably resolved via a peace process in which mortal enemies came together to work out their differences. Benson documents how the leaders' success in maintaining the allegiance of their constituencies during a time of change depended on their ability to empathize with and attune to the emotions of their people in a manner similar to the way a mother tunes in to the needs of her infant. Empathy, highlighted by Kohut (1977, pp. 252–61) as a prime ingredient in the therapist's listening process, is thus seen to have great value for leaders in all walks of life.

Important contributions to understanding the nexus between leadership and culture were made by Erik Erikson (1968) via his studies of identity formation through the life cycle of all individuals, and specifically of great leaders such as Gandhi (1969). Identity refers at one and the same time to what makes us unique and what makes us similar to others. In that sense, each person's "who I am" is a "co-creation" of self and group, both individuated-autonomous and also part of the whole. In the present volume, Green, in "What the I May See: Leadership, Identity, and Representation," suggests that the success of leadership in the New Millennium depends on the leader's ability to manage the complex and multiple identities of his constituents across global boundaries continually reset by the Internet, migrations, and shifts in power and ideology. Green, who has served as a long-time consultant on the A. K. Rice staff, also expands the concept of identity to include a group systems vantage point, showing how identity has components of the private self, interpersonal relations, and the large group mentality. He also posits a higher psychospiritual dimension of identity, implied in Erikson's work, that transcends cultural identity to include the universally human element. The Dalai Llama, who is both a spiritual teacher and leader of the Tibetan people in exile, is an exemplar of leadership at a high, spiritual level. The recent uprising of Tibetan Buddhists under Chinese rule presented a challenge to him to maintain his allegiance to them while advocating peace and universal love. Instead of taking sides, he seems to have partly transcended this difficult dilemma by calling for an international investigation of the Tibetan problem.

Erikson showed that leaders are often honed in a trial by fire, what he called an "identity crisis" in which the sense of self and its primary identifications are seriously challenged and undergo transformations to survive. Through this identity crisis, the potential leader may become a "vessel" or container for a set of beliefs and values that propel the group or society to new attainments, whether for good or ill. The leaders' identities and destinies become intertwined with those of their followers. This degree of bonding and identification resembles the primal unity of mother and infant, such that the mother responds to the infant as a part of herself. Only a minority of leaders relate in this passionately merged way. On the positive side, one can cite the great Mahatma Gandhi as well as his biographer Erik Erikson, who underwent an identity crisis about his origins and religion and later became a leader among psychologists, playing a role in creating a significant revolution in the social sciences. On the negative side, the young Hitler underwent an identity crisis, which led to an equation of his own fate with that of Germany. Curiously, the Enron disaster also involved the false equation of the identities of the leaders and followers and the corporate identity. Enron employees had invested large portions of their retirement plans in Enron itself, unwisely tying up their own fate with that of the company. They trusted their leaders to the point where the latter had no accountability. Finally, when the leaders failed, the entire company collapsed and so did the employees' life savings. The cause of this catastrophe lay ultimately in the sociopathic values of the leadership, who adopted the credo of Machiavellian self-interest and sacrificed truth to the appearance of success. But the co-creation paradigm would suggest that most Enron employees had projectively identified illusory hopes into their leadership, placing themselves in an insecure position and needing to unconsciously avoid and deny the corrupt actions in their midst.

It is not incidental that the influence of leadership—constructive or destructive—is profoundly a function of values. Values are a crucial part of the identity that links leaders and their followers. In the present volume, Billow makes this plain in "Modes of Leadership: Diplomacy, Integrity, Sincerity, and Authenticity," where he emphasizes the importance of emotional truth as it manifests itself in the relationship between therapist and group members. Experiences such as Enron suggest that the healing and compassionate values of the psychotherapist, in particular the qualities of integrity and authenticity, could represent a buffer of survival and quality for organizations and societies under pressure to compromise important values and priorities.

One of the points of this book is that leaders in all spheres can learn valuable lessons from the experiences of group therapists who work with groups of a most intimate, personal, self-disclosing nature and, because of this, must be highly attuned to their patients and are also bound by a strict set of ethical principles. Many of the chapter authors are seasoned group therapists, and others have applied the knowledge base of group therapy to their work in other domains. Because the reader may wonder about the relevance of group psychotherapy to leadership in other contexts, it behooves us to articulate the basis of addressing leadership from the vantage point of what is essentially a healing art that is only peripherally concerned with social, political, and economic issues. Because most group therapists spend part of their education by participating in training groups—groups convened for the purpose of experiencing and learning about group dynamics—we include such groups as well. And for a small but important cadre of group therapists, training in individual psychoanalysis is an important part of their education and must be included in the mix.

LEARNING FOR LEADERSHIP IN GROUP PSYCHOTHERAPY, TRAINING GROUPS, AND PSYCHOANALYSIS

At the most general level, it is key to learning for leadership that therapy and training groups represent a cross between the controlled experiments of social psychology and the less-structured development of naturally occurring groups. Like the former, the members are screened and selected for a specific purpose, they meet at assigned times, they have a specific agenda, and they have a set of rules that members are expected to follow. Like a field researcher, therapists keep a part of themselves separate from the group and strive to observe it in an objective manner. Audio and video recording, one-way mirror observation rooms, and supervision sessions sometimes aid this objectivity.

At the same time, the therapy group is typically allowed to unfold in a spontaneous manner, sometimes (even) challenging the therapist's expectations, to elucidate group development and dynamics that are important to the patients' self-insight and recovery. The same applies to training groups, except that the emphasis on treatment is altered to promote an understanding of the group process and one's role in it. It is perhaps a conceit of group therapists and trainers that all leaders should experience a semi-controlled training group such as theirs for the insights it would give them. Some might even advocate for a personal psychotherapy or psychoanalysis as part of leadership education, so that the dictum "Physician heal thyself" could apply to leaders as well. Though many leaders would balk at such requirements, it is undeniably true that participation in a therapy or training group, not to mention leading one, is a valuable way to learn about what transpires in groups and what makes for effective leadership. Importantly, some business schools and schools of international relations now include group dynamics training as part of their curricula (e.g., the Yale School of Management and the Wharton School at the University of Pennsylvania).

Another important asset of therapy and training groups in leadership studies is that they focus on the subjective, emotional levels of experience, both at conscious and unconscious levels. We often neglect these dimensions in leadership training because of the "rational self-interest" and behavioral contingencies models that are commonly used to understand and explain leadership. All too often what happens is that leaders in all walks of life become so caught up in practical matters and in their own careers that they lose touch with the sometimes turbulent emotions and subjective perceptions of their employees and clients that may have a powerful influence on outcomes. Knowledge of leadership from the standpoint of the subjective feelings and personal concerns of the "followers" has repeatedly proven its practical value, but it too often occurs in hindsight. Outstanding leaders, however, always take the pulse of their people. Group therapy and training is one of the best ways to learn how to take this pulse, while at the same time monitoring one's own pulse in a variety of situations.

"Empathy" or "trial identification" is a type of listening process that is familiar to psychoanalysts and other nondirective therapists and facilitates access to the subjective, experiential dimension of leadership and groups. The listener, as it were, puts himself in the shoes of the speaker and introspects about what it is like to experience self and world from the latter's standpoint.

In addition, some business people and salespersons also have a degree of acquaintance with what psychoanalyst Theodore Reik (1948) called "listening with the third ear." Several elements of this way of "hearing" the underlying emotionally toned messages can be of great use to leaders. One is a neutral, nonjudgmental stance. Drawing conclusions and taking sides interfere with hearing what is being said and what is beneath it. The second is a general suspension of "memory, desire, and understanding" (Bion 1970, pp. 41–54), an emptying of the mind akin to the Zen Buddhist way of meditating, which creates a high degree of receptivity to the experience of the moment and which can lead both to new awareness and transformation. The third is what Freud (1912) called "evenly hovering attention," in which one detects clues, images, metaphors, and "slips" that betray deeper layers of meaning and intent. And fourth, once again, is listening with empathy, which means putting oneself into another's shoes and resonating with what he or she might be experiencing in the moment. These four modes of listening seem to complement and support one another and all require openness to new experience, what Green, in this volume, calls the "third space."

Many of the insights on leadership presented in this book derive from the authors' ability to listen in such a manner to the deeper levels of individual and group experience. Gumpert's understanding of a corporate dilemma stems partly from "hearing" the underlying anxieties of executives and managers who typically cover over their fears and personal agendas to focus on "goals and objectives." Benson conducted many therapy groups in Northern Ireland during both the civil war and the peace process. His inferences about attunement and misattunement between leaders and followers come not only from following the news stories but also from seeking to understand his own personal reactions and those of his group members, who constitute a segment of the followers on both sides of the conflict. Volkan's understanding of "chosen" trauma and his observations about narcissism derive in part from empathic attunement to the personal trauma of his psychoanalytic patients. Billow's emphasis on the importance of truth, integrity, and authenticity in leadership is the result of meticulous monitoring of his "countertransference" reactions to his group members, which requires a high degree of self-honesty. Unlike some traditional practitioners, Billow also believes that the therapist should authentically disclose some of his inner reactions to the group. Leaders often struggle with what and how much to reveal about themselves to their constituency and under what circumstances. Billow's observations could be helpful in sorting this out.

Thus, a thesis of this book, manifest in diverse ways among the authors, is that such a therapeutic or psychoanalytic listening process furthers the "co-creative" paradigm of leadership and its potential utility in solving contemporary leadership dilemmas. Such listening enables one to tap into the beating heart of the problem and the feelings that fuel it, moving beyond the cognitive and behavioral "contingency" self-interest model to the awareness of the emotions, fantasies, and defenses that "co-create" our collective lives. For leaders to listen to their groups in deep, revelatory, and transformational ways that show empathy and compassion for their followers (and even at times for their enemies) is no easy task, but it may mean the difference between success and failure in a challenging world where people all too often fear not being heard, understood, and cared about.

Tenets of the Co-creation Paradigm of Leadership

Knowledge and understanding are not static, but evolve and change as new data and concepts emerge. What we call the co-creation paradigm has undoubtedly changed from the time Freud and Jung first articulated it to a point where it contains remnants of their ideas but incorporates nuances they did not know about. For example, rapidly accumulating knowledge of the earliest mother-infant interactions (Stern 1985) as well as the attachment process (Bowlby 1969; Wallin 2007) has shown that the individual mind/brain and social interactions are far more intertwined and interdependent from birth than anyone believed only twenty or thirty years ago. The brain develops in ways that allow for language and intersubjectivity to permit "mentalization" (Fonagy, Target, Gergely, and Jurist 2002) of attachments and separation. Conversely, social interaction, primarily between mother and infant, can affect developing brain structures and functions. Furthermore, we now know that the infant is not merely a passive recipient of caregiving, but rather *initiates* social activity in the earliest days of life, to the extent that T. Berry Brazelton, one of the foremost authorities on the mother-infant relationship, once said that "babies are competent executives." This suggests that some quasi-leadership skills are acquired very early in life and that the formative relationship to the mother may have a great deal to do with who becomes a leader and what kind of leader (s)he becomes. The co-creation of leadership begins at birth, and the earliest attachments, and how secure or insecure they are, affect how leaders and followers interact.

Partly as a result of such research findings regarding the earliest interactions and development of the infant and child, and partly because of ongoing challenges to the "reductionism" (Amacher 1965) of Freud, who, having been trained as a neurologist, explained all mental phenomena in terms of biological drives, we now have arrived at a depth psychology that gives equal significance to internal and external forces and influences and in which individual personality and social interaction are seen to be closely interwoven.

This shift in psychoanalytic thought, reflecting broader changes in modern philosophy and psychology, has led to what we call the "intersubjective" and "relational" perspectives. Intersubjectivity (Stolorow, Atwood, and Brandchaft 1994) views the therapist and patient, mother and child, or any configuration of two or more persons, as empathically intertwined, so that subjectivities emerge in their interactions. Relational psychoanalysis, as Mitchell (1988) articulated, points to the social matrix as fundamental and holds that all interactions are mutual and reciprocal so that one always must take into account all the participants in any relationship. These two perspectives are increasingly viewed as overlapping, and many of the newer insights emerging in the field of psychoanalysis are ultimately formulated in intersubjective and relational terms. It is easy to see that the "co-creation" paradigm of leadership advocated in this volume has close ties to the intersubjective and relational perspectives. However, neither the book's editors nor chapter authors are so aligned with these viewpoints that they are not open to other points of view as well.

Despite or because of the expansion of knowledge about the earliest human interactions and the relatively new emphasis on relatedness and attachment in psychoanalysis, an invariant set of principles comprise a co-creation paradigm of leadership and leadership studies. Thinking about the overall picture, we can perhaps state the following as fundamental tenets of such a paradigm:

1. Leaders are not simply individuals who possess the requisite skills, motivations, and personality traits, but rather they assume their duties out of complex necessities generated by groups. (A classic historical example is Harry Truman, who never considered himself presidential timber but became a powerful and memorable leader when the torch was passed down to him.) The process of human interaction (socialization, acculturation, group formation, bonding) is in fact the primary phenomenon. Leaders are not so much preselected by fate or genetics as the myth of the birth of the hero would have it; rather, they emerge from an interpersonal collective and transpersonal process. That leaders possess certain traits or a destiny that make them powerful, effective, and/or influential (which has been the focus of many leadership studies) results at least in part from the needs and dynamics of the evolving group and, as Chin reminds us in this volume, the broader sociocultural context. At a certain point prior to the primary elections in New Hampshire, the stoical Hillary Clinton became briefly tearful and overwhelmed during her meetings with the populace, and stated "I found my voice." Indeed that was also the "voice of the group," which needed to know that Senator Clinton had an emotional and feminine side.

Furthermore, we all have many groups and subgroups of influence that are "nested" (Agazarian and Gantt 2005, p. 165) within and around one another, so leadership roles are influenced and in turn influence multiple groups and subgroups. These groups change and are influential throughout life, and the most important ones become "groups of belonging," whether family, institution, or nation, and are instrumental in the formation of identity (Rouchy 2002). Few individuals become leaders in most or all of the groups to which they belong. In addition, many leadership positions—whether parent, senator, prime minister, CEO, or scout troop leader—are time limited. The temporality and circumstantiality of leadership further highlights how it is a function of context and coincidentally suggests that leader-follower relations invariably contain an emotional element of loss and mourning.

2. Leaders and followers are in interdependent mutual relationship with one another and by definition cannot exist without each other. This applies as well to their respective tasks, roles, identities, and other factors. To study leaders independently of followers is an artificial, arbitrary truncation of the phenomena, just as to study a baby without including its mother would risk serious reductionism.

To understand leaders and hold them responsible without taking into account their followers is all too common and can lead to fundamentally incorrect assessments and actions. One costly example of such fallacious reasoning was George W. Bush's decision to invade Iraq based on his belief in Saddam Hussein's malevolence and possible possession of weapons of mass destruction. If Bush had considered Saddam's role, however tyrannical, in maintaining stability in a country with conflicting Sunni, Shiite, and other factions, he might have foreseen the resultant insurgency that would keep the war going for five or more years. Instead, he maintained the illusion that the war would be won and democracy prevail when Saddam's regime was toppled, a mistake that has had serious consequences ever since. Power is a relational dynamic between leaders and followers, not just a sword wielded by a single individual. In a way, President Bush "bought into" Saddam's menacing attitude rather than taking into account the long history of factionalism and religious strife endogenous to Iraq and the Middle East.

3. Leadership is ultimately not a *person* but a *function and a process* that influences both leaders and followers to formulate and carry out the goals and objectives of the group-as-a-whole. This function and process can be assumed not only by individuals, but also by teams, other small groups, whole populations, subgroups, and even by inanimate entities such as billboards, flags, music, literary genres, and so on. One could think of leadership as exchanged by a relay stick that is passed around the group according to a set of explicit or implicit rules, as is the case among Native Americans who use the "talking stick" when meeting in groups. Therefore, leadership requires a *systems* understanding (Agazarian and Gantt 2005) regarding how it is dispersed and carried out by the group-as-a-whole.

It may seem a subtle point, but when we attribute leadership to an individual, we are in fact personifying a function and a process. Group functions and processes cannot be seen or touched and therefore need *representation* in the form of personifications (Foulkes 1983). Leaders are often symbolic representatives of executive functions sanctioned and carried out by the group. One reason Eisenhower was such a successful commander was that he realized what he represented to his soldiers, and he was able to powerfully influence them by personifying their ideals rather than "micromanaging" his officers.

4. Some components of leadership are outside of awareness of the leader and/or followers. These can be either *non*conscious (outside the field of perception) or *un*conscious (repressed or otherwise defended against, avoided, etc.). In other words, both sociopolitical forces and their own inner complexes influence leaders and followers without their knowing it. Seemingly, rational self-interest, goal setting, and so on are processes that occur in the context of a background matrix of dynamics, meanings, and contingencies unknown to the parties themselves.

For example, while many feel that Mikhail Gorbachev was one of the greatest leaders of the twentieth century, he eventually yielded his power not because of his inadequacies as a leader but because the political climate of the then Soviet Union insisted on a transition to nationalism, westernization, and capitalism, and Gorbachev was conservative in those respects. It is also possible that Gorbachev had emotional complexes that limited his tolerance for such a radical change in the society. In any case, it was not only by rational choice but also because of political necessity as well as Gorbachev's own unconscious complexes that he left office.

Unconscious forces often manifest in group psychotherapy. For instance, a male co-therapist successfully co-led a group of predominantly female patients for more than a year, when the members grew hostile toward him, favoring the female co-therapist, and he was ultimately compelled to resign from his role. What had happened was that under his co-leadership, the female members had developed enough trust to begin to deal with their difficulties with men but had not matured sufficiently to reconcile their differences with them. Instead, they extruded the male therapist. Reciprocally, the male therapist had personal "countertransference" problems dealing with women's anger because of childhood trauma related to his mother and so was unable to withstand and contain the aggression directed against him. These eventualities were neither intended nor foreseen.

ORIENTATION TO THE CHAPTERS

Having presented some of the basic tenets of this book, the purpose is now to guide the reader in approaching the subsequent set of independent and diverse writings by those whose understanding of leadership is informed, each in his or her own way, by a co-creative understanding of leadership. A brief summary of each of the subsequent chapters of the book may further help the readers orient themselves and see the connection to the central themes stated above. Part I is devoted to broader considerations and concepts, while the remaining chapters focus on specific instances or "case studies" that exemplify the co-creation paradigm within specific real-life leadership dilemmas. The reader should note the diverse ways in which the authors understand the co-created relationship between leaders and followers, with differing emphases and understandings. Here are the authors and their brief synopses of their chapters.

Richard M. Billow: "Modes of Leadership: Diplomacy, Integrity, Sincerity, and Authenticity"

Billow, a psychoanalytic group therapist, approaches leadership with his own relational thinking about interface between the leader and the group. In Billow's (2003) model, the therapist moves from an opaque, neutral stance to a degree of equality and mutual self-disclosure with the group. Therefore, his or her qualities of character and relationship to the group become increasingly important to therapeutic outcomes. Further, the intersubjective and relational perspectives assume that unconscious motivation and communication are always operative in the leader-group reciprocal interaction.

Billow's understanding of groups emphasizes "truth" as a primary value supporting group development. By this, he means emotional truth as elaborated by Bion (1970, p. 7) as self-awareness or insight. Unfortunately, many political and corporate leaders equivocate regarding the importance of such truth in human affairs, although experience shows that avoidance and denial of emotional truth can lead to the instability and downfall of a marriage, family, corporation, or even an entire civilization, as the example of the Roman Empire seems to suggest.

Billow sees *diplomacy, integrity, sincerity*, and *authenticity* as the leadership characteristics that facilitate the maintenance of emotional truth in the group. *Diplomacy* is concerned with establishing and maintaining relationships and alliances. *Integrity* resides in the leader's moral and ethical principles, with respect to his or her professional, political, ethnic, and religious affiliations. *Sincerity* is the mode that conveys the leader's positive emotionality. *Authenticity* bears upon how the leader approaches and avoids truth, whereby communications are mediated by appreciation of the dimensionality of emotion, the influence of the irrational and unconscious, and the inescapability of social role. Billow illustrates these four relational attitudes in action with respect to situations that arise in group psychotherapy, and he concludes on another note with a political illustration from George W. Bush's presidency, appropriately recognizing that "judging" Bush is largely a subjective matter, influenced by the observer's own political interests and orientation. That said, Billow suggests how diplomacy, integrity, sincerity, and authenticity operate or fail to operate in the relationship of powerful political leaders to their groups.

Zachary Gabriel Green: "What the "I" May See: Leadership, Identity, and Representation

Green is a seasoned group dynamics consultant who is especially interested in the problems and issues of minorities as well as conflict resolution and healing global strife. In this chapter, he rethinks and expands the notion of identity to include the leader-follower relationship and the group-as-a-whole from a systems theoretical and co-creation point of view. He considers that identity is a complex phenomenon manifesting at the individual, interpersonal, group-as-a-whole and transpersonal levels. In so doing, he reformulates the functions of leadership at each level. He defines the leader's multiple dimensions of identity as follows: (a) *Isolarity*, that is, leadership as "Individual." It is the "within" search for identity where one discovers the multiple persona and is challenged to manage the competition for dominance within oneself; (b) *recognition*, that is, leadership as association, the search for a contextual identity with or against others; (c) *discrimination*, namely, leadership as preference and prejudice, distinguishing "my group" from the "other group" in terms of identity; (d) *dominance*, that is, leadership as Will to Power; (e) *integral* leadership as interdependent and recognizing the limitations of dominance; (f) *transformation*, specifically, leadership at the level of authentic transformation for an individual, group, or society where new creations can emerge; and (g) *transcendence*, or leadership as One, a deep transformation in consciousness whereby recognition of the other is known to be recognition of oneself and one's own identity. Green's understanding of identity is systems oriented, is at the cutting edge of psychological theory, and will likely influence identity studies for some time to come because it takes into account the intensely interactive state of the world as humankind engages the New Millennium and its rapid technological, political, economic, and ecological changes.

Jean Lau Chin: "The Dynamics of Gender, Race, and Leadership"

Chin, a scholar, researcher, and university administrator, explores the issues of gender and race as they apply to leadership, concerns that become of increasing importance as women, for example, break through the glass ceiling to assume equal and multiple roles in society and as the commingling of diverse racial and ethnic groups becomes commonplace. According to Chin, today's leaders need to deal with heterogeneous and diverse contexts, but despite these social changes, are still influenced by traditional monolithic notions of leaders and leadership. Dimensions of diversity, for example, race, ethnicity, gender, disability status, sexual orientation, religious preference, have not been sufficiently incorporated into understanding leadership skills, traits, and leader-follower interactions or in the role context plays in defining leadership style and conferring leader status. Chin seeks to address some of these leadership shortfalls by focusing on the leadership concerns of women in particular.

Chin argues that to address gender and minority issues, today's leaders need to be *visionary, inspirational, authentic,* and/or *transformational.* Transformational leadership style has been identified as syntonic with women's connectedness and interpersonal orientation. In studying diverse women leaders, Chin suggests that feminist women often embrace leadership styles that are value driven, ethics based, and/or social change oriented, that is, transformational. Her own and others' research also found these women generally prefer using a collaborative process, empowering followers, and promoting inclusiveness, that is, an egalitarian model of leadership reflecting their desire to level power dynamics inherent in the leader-follower relationship.

Vamik Volkan: "Some Psychoanalytic Views on Leaders with Narcissistic Personality Organization and Their Roles in Large-Group Processes"

As a psychiatrist and psychoanalyst who has also played a role in "track II diplomacy" (nongovernmental facilitation of international peace and conflict resolution), Volkan has a unique and insightful "binocular" perspective on leaders from both the consulting room and the world stage. In this chapter, he examines the unconscious dynamics of the relationship between the leader and his constituency (the large group), beginning with George W. Bush's response to the 9/11 terrorist attacks. Volkan's position is that the leader's personality, understood at a depth psychological level, profoundly influences the proximal society where he exercises power and sometimes the world-at-large. He emphasizes the leader's narcissism and uses the analogy of a "baked apple pie," where a small bad piece of the pie whose taste is contaminated needs to be isolated from the tastier good part. Similarly, the leader must sustain his sense of power and grandiosity from the part of himself that feels depleted or inadequate. This parallels the need of the society to isolate or eliminate the bad elements or enemies within and without. The leader and populace engage in interactions to support these respective agendas, often utilizing "chosen glories" and "chosen traumas" (historical victories and defeats) to justify their positions. Volkan offers several examples and then cites Kemal Atatürk as an example of a leader with "healthy narcissism" who led his country to a better condition and position in the world. Volkan focuses on the leader's personality but shows how the leader co-creates change, for good or ill, in an ongoing dialogue with his followers and other large societal groups.

Harold S. Bernard and Robert H. Klein: "The Co-creation of Current and Prospective Political Leadership in America: 9/11, the Bush Years, and the 2008 Race for the Presidency"

This chapter provides an insightful analysis of contemporary American leadership since 9/11 from the co-creative dynamic framework. Bernard and Klein emphasize the influence of traumatic anxiety on leaders vis-à-vis their followers, emphasizing that 9/11 has become a national "chosen trauma," that is, Volkan's notion that significant collective trauma creates a legacy of regression, polarization, and resentment in the minds of the populace. When this occurs, the tendency is to think in more primitive, black and white ways. There is less tolerance for nuance and ambiguity. Careful analytic thinking and well-tempered judgment diminishes. Raw, unfiltered emotions tend to hold sway. Further, there is a felt need to effectively counteract the deep sense of humiliation, the underlying loss of self-esteem, and the disturbing influence on the collective sense of national identity that the nation suffered as a result of 9/11 and its aftermath.

Bernard and Klein elaborate on the implications of such developments for American politics, suggesting that mutual projective identifications among leaders and followers co-created a set of perceptions and emotional climates that affected decision-making, voting, and other aspects of the political process at the time of writing their chapter, namely, April 2008. This chapter is especially time bound in that the presidential nominations and elections will have occurred soon before the publication of this book. Therefore, the reader will have the opportunity for hindsight "quarterbacking" and be able to see how the dynamics Bernard and Klein elaborate did or did not play out in subsequent events.

A key concept Bernard and Klein use is Lakoff's (2002) notion of "contextual framing," asserting that the language chosen in the political arena has great influence over how the phenomenon in question is perceived. Once a conceptual framework is established, it defines the terms of the debate, a particular example being the "war on terrorism," which constitutionally is not a war because Congress has not declared such a war. The phrase has been extensively used, however, to create a climate of support for the Iraq War and other measures, such as random telephone tapping and torturing prisoners of "war" allegedly to combat terrorism. Contextual framing is useful in understanding how various projective identifications are "spun" into a web of misunderstanding that co-creates what may masquerade as objective perceptions and rational decision-making.

Peter Gumpert: "Managing Systemic and Leadership Problems in a Corporate Setting: A Case Study"

Gumpert, a business consultant who also has served in other contexts as a group trainer and therapist, addresses a real-life dilemma of a business firm that echoes many of the difficulties we see today in the corporate world as different value systems collide. He uses an organizational systems understanding of the group akin to the A. K. Rice model (Miller and Rice 1967), in which there are reciprocal exchanges among various hierarchical levels of an organization, whether it be the individual personality, a subgroup, a department, a corporation or institution, and so forth. The leader is seen as a functional or dysfunctional entity within other systems and subsystems of mutual influence. For example, one of Gumpert's assumptions about corporate leadership states: "The personal characteristics of top leaders, middle managers, and informal leaders influence the way the organization functions and can have substantial effects on its performance." Another is, "Both systems and leaders can exert forces on the group or organization that are cohesive (tending to bring people together) or alienating/isolating (tending to move members apart or into opposition)." In the first of these, individual personality is the salient variable, while in the second, the cohesiveness of the group is primary. Gumpert uses the psychiatric classification of personality disorders and clusters to suggest that certain types of disruptive personality types are present in today's corporate boardroom.

As part of his discourse, Gumpert presents a microanalysis of the pervasive problems brought about by the "bottom line short term results" philosophy that has dominated the corporate world in the modern era and was at least partly responsible for such disasters as Enron and Bear Stearns. He explores the part hidden agendas and alliances play as well as the organizational narrative and history. Finally, he offers his recommendations for preventing self-defeating patterns of coping and relating in the corporate world.

Hala Taweel: "Lessons in Leadership and Conflict Resolution: Working with Palestinians and Israelis in a Conjoint Educational Effort"

Dr. Taweel is an educator from Palestine who came to the United States for her own higher education while retaining a passion for better conditions in her homeland and for improved Arab-Israeli relations. She and a group of friends at Harvard University were moved to organize the University of the Middle East project, aimed at bringing together Israelis, Palestinians, and students from other Arab nations. Considering Taweel's own history, in which her mother was imprisoned by Israelis, as well as the potential for sudden flare-ups between groups of Israelis and Arabs, the risks of such a project would seem insuperable, and yet it turned out to be an ongoing success, despite the difficulties that frequently arose.

In her chapter, Taweel attempts to extrapolate from her experience as a leader of such an endeavor what might be useful for leadership in the ongoing Arab-Israeli conflict and other situations where there is intense conflict between groups. She addresses the following questions: Can leaders in a "changing world" detach themselves from political realities on the ground? Can they keep working with the "other" even during a state of war? Should leaders put their identity, feelings, and political affiliations on hold and act normally in a situation that is anything but normal? And how do these factors shape the leader one becomes?

Taweel provides a moving and detailed narrative of her own and the collective experience of the participants. She understands it in terms of the biographies of the participants as well as the nature of the interactions among the faculty and students of the newly co-created university. She notes that: "The founders were a passionate group of individuals brought together by the simple and powerful idea just noted. They had diverse backgrounds, political affiliations, and experiences of moral suffering in the face of conflict, as well as a love of adventure. The Oslo agreements, which offered hope for durable peace in the Middle East, helped stimulate this visionary group of graduate students in Boston . . . Not surprisingly the project faced problems from its inception. These included the deteriorating political situation in the Middle East, the failures of the Oslo agreement and subsequent Palestinian-Israeli negotiations, the suicide bombings in Israel, the repercussions of Sharon's election, the second Palestinian Intifada followed by the bombings of Ramallah and Gaza, the war in Iraq, the events of 9/11, the election of Hamas, the war between Hizbullah and Israel and the loss of hope on both sides. Tense moments arose when the UME leaders and students experienced the loss of loved ones during bombings in Israel or those related to the Israeli invasion of the West Bank and Gaza proved difficult to both students and leaders. Factors as varied as political views, interpersonal relations, management styles, gender, and age differences exacerbated these conflicts."

The working relationships and harmony achieved under these recurrent and trying circumstances were not only intended to be useful to the students. The hope was that the students, themselves school teachers in Israel and the Arab nations, would somehow positively influence the new generations of those they teach toward reconciliation and peace. This model of "seeding" positive change has great potential for facilitating social change, an approach that is receiving increased attention in a variety of international and ethnic conflict situations.

Jerrold M. Post: "When Hatred Is Bred in the Bone: Terrorist Group Dynamics and the Psycho-cultural Foundations of Contemporary Terrorism"

Post is a psychiatrist and professor of political psychology with a psychoanalytic and group systems orientation who consults for U.S. government departments and whose expertise is frequently called upon by the mass media. He studies pathological leaders and their spheres of influence and pursues in-depth analysis of terrorists as part of the worldwide effort to defuse such acts of violence. In his chapter, he suggests that one should understand terrorism not only in terms of its leaders but also in terms of the actual and potential followers who are drawn into participation in terrorist activities. His interviews of such individuals suggest that they are not diagnostically pathological in the psychiatric sense. Rather, throughout their development, their families and communities have fostered particular ideologies, attitudes, and emotions that lead them to be attracted to the violence and martyrdom implied in terroristic acts against those they perceive as real enemies.

Post introduces his analysis with two principles articulated by major international organizations convened to study and cope with terrorism. These premises, consistent with the co-creation paradigm are: (1) Explanations of terrorism at the level of individual psychology are insufficient in trying to understand why people become involved in terrorism; and (2) It is not individual psychology, but group, organizational, and social psychology, with a particular emphasis on "collective identity," that provides the most powerful lens to understand terrorist psychology and behavior.

Post's insights are based on his meticulous ongoing studies of the minds of the terrorists whom he interviewed in depth. They represent a major contribution to understanding the psychological roots of terrorism, and they show that while the terrorist mentality is deep seated, it is largely the outcome of interpersonal and group experiences in the child, adolescent, and young adult. Therefore, it may be possible to defuse terrorism before the "at-risk" individuals join the organizations that enact such atrocities.

Jarlath F. Benson: "The Northern Ireland Conflict and Peace Process: The Role of Mutual Regulatory Symbiosis between Leaders and Groups"

Benson is a psychotherapist in Northern Ireland who has personally experienced both the civil war, often called "The Troubles," and the peace process, and also empathized with his patients in the Belfast area in their traumatic anxiety and suffering over the violence and continual disruptions caused by the conflict, which influenced directly the lives of all the citizens. Benson discusses the interdigitation of leaders and the respective communities they led during Northern Ireland's recent civil war and subsequent peacemaking. He argues that leaders were effective to the extent that they and their communities could maintain "mutual regulatory symbiosis," by which he means that "leaders and their groups will create, select and relate to each other . . . on the basis of emotional resonance and attunement." This enables the group and leader "to participate in each other's state of mind, reflect what they care about most deeply, and thereby predict what they will do and say."

Benson illustrates his thesis with a rich variety of recent historical events in Northern Ireland, some resting on much earlier history. These include the leadership of Gerry Adams, Ian Paisley, and many others. In addition, he notes and illustrates that when leaders get too far ahead of their groups and lose their resonance with those groups, the groups eject them. Though Paisley was very effective in maintaining resonance for many years with the church he founded and with the political party he founded, he lost his resonance with his church when, because of the peace process, he shared power with McGuinness—one of his most potent enemies during The Troubles. His church felt betrayed and removed him from their ranks.

We, the editors, are confident that by accompanying these authors on their forays into the sometimes-thorny thickets of leadership, in several of the most difficult situations that occur in our changing world, you are going to experience a rich and seminal array of concepts, examples, and issues about leadership in the contemporary world. We hope you find them interesting and fruitful and that you will continue in your own groups the dialogue that they have begun.

REFERENCES

Agazarian, Y., and S. Gantt. "The Systems-centered Approach to the Group-as-a-Whole." The Group-as-a-Whole: An Update (Vol. 1) Special Edition of *Group. Journal of the Eastern Group Psychotherapy Society* 29(1) (March 2005): 163–85.

Amacher, P. *Freud's Neurological Education and Its Influence on Psychoanalytic Theory. Psychological Issues,* 4, 4, Monograph 16. New York: International Universities Press, 1965.

Ashbach, C., and V. L. Schermer. *Object Relations, the Self, and the Group.* London: Routledge, 1987.

Avolio, B. J. "Promoting More Integrative Strategies for Leadership Theory-building." *American Psychologist* 62(1) (Jan. 2007): 25–33.

Bennis, W. "The Challenges of Leadership in The Modern World: Introduction to the Special Issue." *American Psychologist* 62(1) (Jan. 2007): 2–5.

Billow, R. M. *Relational Group Psychotherapy: From Basic Assumptions to Passion.* London & New York: Jessica Kingsley Publishers, 2003.

Bion, W. R. *Experiences in Groups.* London: Tavistock, 1959.

———. *Attention and Interpretation.* London: Tavistock, 1970.

Bowlby, J. *Attachment and Loss.* 2 vols. New York: Basic Books, 1969.

Campbell, J. *The Hero with a Thousand Faces.* Bollingen Series XVII. Princeton, N.J.: Princeton University Press, 1949.

DeMare, P. B. *Perspectives in Group Psychotherapy: A Theoretical Background.* New York: Science House, 1972.

Erikson, E. *Identity, Youth, and Crisis.* London: Faber and Faber, 1968.

———. *Gandhi's Truth: On the Origins of Militant Non-violence.* New York: W.W. Norton, 1969.

Fonagy, P., M. Target, G. Gergely, and E. L. Jurist. *Affect Regulation, Mentalization, and the Development of Self.* New York: Other Press, 2002.

Foulkes, S. H. *Introduction to Group-Analytic Psychotherapy.* London: Karnac, 1983.

Freud, S. "Group Psychology and the Analysis of the Ego." In *The Standard Edition of the Complete Psychological Works of Sigmund Freud*, vol. 18, pp. 67-143. London: Hogarth Press, 1921/1961.

———. "Recommendations to Physicians Practicing Psycho-analysis." In *The Standard Edition of the Complete Psychological Works of Sigmund Freud*, vol. 12, pp. 109–20). London: Hogarth Press, 1921/1961.

———. "The Future of an Illusion." In *The Standard Edition of the Complete Psychological Works of Sigmund Freud*, vol. 21, pp. 3–58. London: Hogarth Press, 1927/1961.

Gibbard, G., J. Hartman, and R. Mann, eds. *Analysis of Groups.* San Francisco: Jossey Bass, 1974.

Jung, C. G. *Memories, Dreams and Reflections.* Edited by A. Jaffe. New York: Random House, 1961.

———. *Man and His Symbols.* New York: Dell, 1968.

Karterud, S., and W. Stone. "The Group Self: A Neglected Aspect of Group Psychotherapy." *Group Analysis* 36(1) (2003): 1, 7–22.

Kohut, H. *Restoration of the Self.* New York: International Universities Press, 1977.

Klein, M. "Notes on Some Schizoid Mechanisms." *Envy and Gratitude and Other Works 1946–1963.* New York: Delta, 1977.

Lakoff, G. *Moral Politics: How Liberals and Conservatives Think.* 2nd ed. Chicago: University of Chicago Press, 2002.

Miller, E. J., and A. K. Rice. *Systems of Organization: Control of Task and Sentient Boundaries.* London: Tavistock, 1967.

Mitchell, S. *Relational Concepts in Psychoanalysis.* Cambridge, Mass.: Harvard University Press, 1988.

Nietzsche, F. *Thus Spoke Zarathustra: A Book for Everyone and No One.* Translated by R. J. Hollingdale. New York: Penguin Books, 1969.

Reik, T. *Listening with the Third Ear: The Inner Experience of a Psychoanalyst.* New York: Grove Press, 1948.

Rouchy, J. C. "Cultural Identity and Groups of Belonging." *The Implications of Multicultural Diversity and Ethnopolitical Conflict for Working with Groups.* Special Edition. *Journal of the Eastern Group Psychotherapy Society* 26(3) (Sept. 2002): 205–18.

Stern, D. *The Interpersonal World of the Infant: A View from Psychoanalysis and Developmental Psychology.* New York: Basic Books, 1985.

Stodgill, R. M. *Handbook of Leadership: A Survey of Theory and Research.* New York: Free Press, 1974.

Stolorow, R. D., G. E. Atwood, and B. Brandchaft, eds. *The Intersubjective Perspective.* Northvale, N.J.: Aronson, 1994.

Wallin, D. J. *Attachment in Psychotherapy.* New York: Guilford, 2007.

I

CONCEPTS AND THEORIES

1

Modes of Leadership: Diplomacy, Integrity, Sincerity, and Authenticity

Richard M. Billow

"Tell the truth, but tell it slant," wrote the poet Emily Dickinson. "The truth must dazzle gradually, or every man be blind" (1960, pp. 506–7). By this, she meant that we have limited capacity to tolerate truth. Individuals, groups, and organizations of all sizes need truth for security and growth. However, truth may be premature, incomplete, or not relevant to the immediate situation; truth may hurt, mislead, or obstruct. The leader has the special role of managing truth: evaluating and responding to the truth needs of the individual, group, and organization.

The leader has available four modes of engagement: *diplomacy, integrity, sincerity,* and *authenticity*. They inform the struggle to seek, confront, or modify ("slant") truth. These are strategies of discourse (Austin 1962) or relational modes of speaking and listening, influenced, of course, by the intersubjective processes of group and organizational life (Billow 2003). The leader monitors discourses for truth through the lens of subjectivity and responds to various aspects of interaction that often are subtle and out of interpersonal awareness. Consensus among the participants concerning these modes—what is said or what is meant—may be absent, and the significance debatable. Finally, the effects of the modes of engagement—how truth is reached, delayed, modified, forestalled, or even avoided—are not always immediate or readily visible.

I propose that all interventions are captured under one of these overlapping rubrics; the four modes are exhaustive but nonexclusive. They supply conceptual references for the interactional stance one has adopted, allowing the leader to be more aware of what he or she is doing and why. Although the illustrative examples are based on my study of and experience with conducting long-term psychoanalytic group psychotherapy, I believe the modes are generalizable to all leadership situations.

DIPLOMACY

Diplomacy is concerned with establishing and maintaining relationships and alliances. Interpersonal relations entail negotiating the not always resolvable divergences of interests and goals and also between what can be known and what is safe to communicate. Diplomacy respects the motivations, affiliations, and beliefs among different people and subgroups and the roles they occupy. It may involve keeping channels of communication open so that the players can continue a search for communal or at least livable truths. Rather than one version of truth dominating another, differing positions of truth may compete—revealing their various strengths and weaknesses in capturing aspects of reality. A creative synthesis may emerge.

Though ideally, empathic and truth-seeking needs of different constituencies will come to support one another, versions of truth, and even the need for truth, may continue to vary or even clash. Issues of power now come to the fore along with the leader's authority and status in the group or organizational culture. Still, to some extent, power is shared, albeit unequally. If power were not shared, there would never be a need to be diplomatic. Even when the leader arrogates all power, the need to be diplomatic resides in the reality that over time power must be shared. In being diplomatic, leadership is strategic: influencing the group or organization not to express its power in forms of retaliation.

In the diplomatic mode, a leader situates certain truths and not others as primary or ideal. Certain truths may be emphasized and explored, while others are minimized, shaded, or withheld. Diplomatic interventions are not always popular or balanced evenly among all participants. In the following example, functioning as the leader of a psychotherapy group, I experienced turning against my own constituents and favoring a new member.

Case Example: Responding To Different Truth Needs

Claire, in her early thirties and engaged to be married, recently joined our group but now had second thoughts. "Everyone here has children or is planning to. I don't want any; you're going to think something is wrong with me." Her declaration stirred interest and an incipient interrogation. "This is what I feared, that I would have to explain myself."

I too was interested in exploring the meanings behind Claire's decision, but there was truth in her apprehension, and I felt it important to call attention to it. "Yes, no one would question why one of us would want to have a child. 'Childless' seems to define something negative." Claire felt the support of my intervention, but several of the women took issue. "I feel you [the therapist] are suppressing me. I just want to learn about Claire. Should I feel uncomfortable if I talk about being a mother and how wonderful it feels?"

Claire reassured the second speaker that she loved children and enjoyed hearing about them. But she was stung by the accusation of suppression that she felt was directed to her: "I don't want to suppress you . . .," and she broke off, near tears but also frozen with her own anger.

Again, I heard truth in Claire's ostensible misidentification. The first speaker was angry with Claire for her position: announcing yet refusing to explore her decision. The first speaker's anger toward me for defending Claire, in effect, redirecting the conversation, was justified. I matter-of-factly acknowledged both standpoints, neither of which seemed untenable. Claire was not willing to have a child or to talk about it at this time. She had declared her turf, and I secured her right to it. I suggested that perhaps more than one person was angry, with me particularly. My summary statement served its purpose of cooling the situation sufficiently, and the session proceeded with relatively peaceful coexistence.

Discussion. The strategy behind my assertion of power and authority was to forestall an open confrontation between a prematurely interpreting group and a member who would secede rather than abdicate a position of refusal, therefore, to prevent a fissure in developing group cohesiveness. In my evaluation, at this stage of the initiation of the new member, to identify the mutual hostility but not encourage its exploration was important. In taking an active stance and a clear position *vis-à-vis* differing truth needs, I could deflect some of the anger to a safer target: me.

THE DIMENSION OF SELF-INTEREST IN DIPLOMACY

The interests and goals of the leader group may not be entirely congruent with those of some or even all of the constituencies, and they may be partially or entirely self-serving (as in issues of salary and benefits, fee, vacation schedule, etc.), without necessarily being false or against the group's welfare.

Case Example: Disentangling Leader-member Entitlements

"How are you contributing to the group?" I asked Randy, cutting short his recount of an ongoing struggle with his wife involving his noncooperation with routine household tasks. "Maybe they [other members] can relate to their issues," Randy offered unconvincingly. Another man rejoined sarcastically: "It doesn't relate to me, I take out the garbage and don't have to be asked." Ignoring the group's resonance, Randy continued. I interrupted again: "Randy, you're making yourself the butt of the group, it's not good for you, and it's not good for the group. Isn't this what you do in your marriage?"

He launched once more into his story, and I said he had to stop and respect my leadership. "But no one else is complaining, Rich [the therapist]. You're making me angry." I responded: "I understand that, but you'll have to control yourself and give other people a chance to talk." Randy: "You don't talk this way to other people." "I don't have to," I countered. Randy: "All you care about is your group, the big bucks." "Not 'all,' but some," I acknowledged, "I care about the group, and I care about supporting myself, now let's move on."

Discussion. "Diplomatic" is not synonymous with "nice," supportive, or nonconfrontational. In the psychotherapy situation, the leader safeguards the group's emotional and interpretative impetus. Whereas I was willing once again to address Randy's entitlements (Billow 1997, 1999a, 1999b) and also acknowledge the truth in his identifying mine, my primary motivation was to "govern" the group system. My principles and practices served strategic purposes in the service of the group but also were self-serving, expressing my values and to some extent satisfying my own aesthetic, emotional, intellectual, and fiscal needs.

THE ROLE OF FALSITY

We make distinctions between factual truth and emotional truth. At times, one may be valued over the other. For example, in most exchanges between people, emotional truth and understanding between them is more important than exact attention to facts. But if a point of fact is crucial to understanding, then the factual truth comes first. Emotional truth implies a degree of tactfulness: factual truth does not.

Perhaps alluding to diplomatic communications, Samuel Butler (1912/1951) penned, "Truth does not consist in never lying but in knowing when to lie and when not to do so." We may be honest but merciless, and one must be careful how to ask for or volunteer truth when it can be hurtful. Questions do not always seek truthful answers, and even when they do, minimization, shadings of feeling and meaning, even white lies, lubricate and may make possible beneficial social relations. Straying from what is exactly true and completely honest is not necessarily malicious, self-serving, or harmful to others. In the following example, I sorrowfully came to understand the depth of Butler's pithy statement.

Case Example: Diplomatic Falsity

"Rich, I better see you. I've been too embarrassed to come to group or make an individual appointment. I've been going for tests. I'm sorry to have to say this—they put me on Aricept and Namenda."

It was terrible news, although I was not surprised. At age fifty-seven, my father was a practicing physician who could no longer tell time. I was intimately familiar with the trajectory of Alzheimer's. Dorothy had been complaining of memory problems for more than a year. Her individual sessions were marred by references to group members with "what's her name? I can't remember." I had ceased attributing dynamic significance to her lapses. And now the medical data were emerging. "What should I do," she asked. "I guess I better go back and say good-bye."

"Do you want to leave?" I asked.

"No, not at all. I just feel I can't participate like the others."

"So what else is new?" This had been a typical complaint of Dorothy, who was a Midwesterner in a group with many members who were, in her words, "sophisticated New Yorkers." But my communication was not honest because I believed that there was something "new" in her difficulty, which I ignored, and chose to mislead her.

Dorothy: "That's true."

Therapist: "Why don't you take your time and decide what feels comfortable for you. Would you like to stay?"

Dorothy: "Of course."

Therapist: "So stay."

Dorothy: "I don't want to appear 'out of it.'"

Therapist: "Me either!" I interjected playfully. But, fearing what I believed to be the inevitable *sequelae*, I added seriously: "If you lose interest in the group or feel that you're not connecting and we can't do anything about it, I'll help you leave."

Dorothy: "I'd hate that to happen."

Therapist: "Me, too."

Discussion. I misled, evaded, and encouraged and participated in collusion against factual truth. My pragmatic goal: to respond to what I felt was Dorothy's need (and perhaps my own) to feel comforted and cared for. I could tolerate the truth, but I felt it was in her best interest to forestall pointless pain so that she could continue to benefit from group membership and the stimulation and support it provided. Dorothy had the freedom to make her own choice: when to embrace factual truth.

INTEGRITY

In engaging from a mode of *integrity*, salience resides in the leader's moral and ethical principles in reference to his or her professional, political, ethnic, and religious affiliations. *Integrity* would seem to present little ambiguity concerning truth and falsity because the leader may refer to and rely on a clear set of conventions. But as I will emphasize, integrity involves strength and consistency but also flexibility; it emerges not only from principles but how they are applied.

Integrity without judgment, self-examination, and relatedness is not sufficient, and can be, in fact, inappropriate and even damaging. Integrity may manifest as rigidity, blindness to personal contingencies, and even be of questionable moral value. Though integrity denotes being true to one's principles, such principles may be false, that is, ill chosen, ill applied, or wrong. As the "Mayfair Madam," Sydney Biddle Barrows (1986) acknowledged, "I ran the wrong kind of business, but I did it with integrity."

INTEGRITY AND SELF-KNOWLEDGE

Samuel Johnson (1759/1985) clarified that "integrity without knowledge is weak and useless, and knowledge without integrity is dangerous and dreadful." For any leader, *self*-knowledge is important; for the clinician, it is the lens through which one evaluates emotional truth and falsity and responds to the contributions of others. In the following example, the group therapist Jerome Gans (2006) carried out a painful introspection so that he could function with thoughtful integrity rather than moralistically. Gans first came to understand the truth that he, too, had an unethical part of his personality.

Case Example: Understanding One's Own
Conflicts Regarding Integrity

A group member: "My wife's insurance is paying for my therapy, but it doesn't take effect until April. Could you bill the insurance company for eight sessions in April rather than the four we met in March and the four we met in April?" At one time Gans would have quickly responded, "No," motivated by unspoken moral outrage: "Who does he think he's dealing with, asking an ethical guy like me to participate in such underhanded shenanigans?" (2006, p. 22).

Gans concurrently worked at a facility where many of the medical staff were double-billing their patients and finding other ways to inflate income. He found himself tempted, "frightened by the intensity of my own greed and the seeming ease with which I could rationalize it away" (2006, p.

21). Getting in touch with his own fraudulent impulses provided crucial self-knowledge and stimulated curiosity about the member, rather than an internal rush to judgment.

Gans linked the request with traumatic incidents of corruption in the patient's family history. When the patient brought up his request again, Gans responded: "How could you ever win with a request like that? . . . If I do not comply with your request you will probably be annoyed with me, and if I do, you will have a corrupt therapist" (2006, p. 22).

Discussion. Had Gans not understood his urge to react moralistically, his engaging from a position of integrity would have been premature and defensive. Hiding behind a screen of integrity is hypocritical; whereas engaging with integrity may include temporarily laying aside certain ethical or moral truths in the service of developing meaning. A harder-won emotional honesty may emerge for all participants, the "sinners" and the "sinned against."

INTEGRITY APPLIED "SYSTEMATICALLY"

Embedded in the complexities of every psychological situation are ethical dilemmas: dimensions of truth and falsity, both bold and shaded, exist in leader and the constituency. In the following example, a leader found herself caught between conflicting systems of ethics, her loyalty to the group member and respect for his confidentiality, and what she interpreted as state-mandated legal procedures. In retrospect, neither system captured the nuance of the psychological situation in which the therapist as well as the group and the member and his wife were embedded.

Case Anecdote: A Leader's Problematic "Will to a System of Integrity"

Scott occupied many group sessions vilifying his wife, who had been, and possibly continued to be, unfaithful. Now he reported an incident in which his wife, tussling with their adolescent daughter over control of the television remote control, left a bite mark on her arm. The next day, the therapist telephoned and requested that Scott appear immediately in her office. She explained: "I was troubled all night by what I heard, and I think I might be required to call Child Protective Service to report abuse."

Scott became enraged and could hardly respond. "My wife and daughter have a great relationship! You know that! She's not an abusive mother. You must hate her as much as I do!" He stormed out of the office: "I don't think I can come back to the group."

Although often reticent and even secretive about group, Scott·shared this incident with his wife, who responded sympathetically. At the same time, she empathized with the therapist who said: "I'm sure I don't have the best reputation with her" and encouraged him to return to group and attempt to work it out. This did not entirely please the husband, who, while mollified toward the therapist, now had to present a different view of his wife to his group. For, even when hearing falsities about herself as an unfit mother, she had remained steadfast, empathic to her accuser, and loyal to her husband and his need for therapy. To reconcile with the wife—and with the group and its therapist—all would have to inspect Scott's mantle of moral outrage—his "truth" and how he misused it.

Discussion. Cohen and Schermer (2002) described the "moral order" of a group, referring to its norms, values, beliefs, and ambience, which supplies a context for each member's group self and the group's collective conscience and ego ideal. The leader most often personifies this ideal and, due to tendencies in one's personality as well as to projective pressure, may reflexively take on a moral mantle. Rulebooks are ever present, symbolic, but also real. They guide but also may mislead. We are all susceptible to a "law and order" mentality and must assess our urges for fairness and "equal treatment for all" and wishes to advise and protect. Nietzsche (1889/1980) advised vigilance regarding orthodox adherence to text and the chimerical safety of dogma: "I mistrust all systematizers and avoid them. The will to a system is a lack of integrity."

SINCERITY

Sincerity is the mode that conveys the leader's positive emotionality. "One cannot both be sincere and seem so," Andre Gide (1902/1996) averred. He meant that *sincerity* is categorical—either you are or not. In my conceptualization (based on Melanie Klein's psychogenetic metapsychology), sincerity derives from the developmental stage of idealization, preceding the full-fledged "depressive position." In this phase, others are capable of being recognized and preserved mentally as loved objects. However, splitting rather than mature thinking remains prominent as a mode of organizing experience ("either/or," "good/bad" thought and feeling).

I contrast the mode of sincerity with that of authenticity, described in the next section, which represents achievement of the depressive position. The hallmark of the depressive position is not only the capacity to love but also to experience ambivalent feelings yet maintain a balanced and humane outlook. Authenticity involves mental integration of conflicting feelings, thoughts, wishes, and motives, directed to loved objects and also competitors and even, enemies. Translated into Bion's (1961) group terminology, sincerity remains linked to the "basic assumption" mentality while authenticity encompasses "work group" thinking as well.

Freud (1921/1961) attributed the formation groups to a biological need to love and to be in harmony with others: "A group is clearly held together by a power of some kind: and to what power could this feat be better ascribed than to Eros, which holds together everything in the world" (p. 92). Writing on the analyst's stance toward the patient, which also applies on the leader's stance to the constituents, Racker (1968) concluded, "to understand, to unite with another, and hence, also to love, prove to be basically one and the same" (p. 174). In "uniting" with the other (and by the extension, the group or organization), the leader bonds via the preverbal, empathic level characteristic of early, infant-mother mutual idealizing exchanges.

Sincerity is communicated by and also between and under the leader's words. It may be felt and conveyed immediately, activated by the leader's interest and compassion. It may be ongoing and constant, amplify over time, or be withdrawn. However, we may think we are being sincere without being so, for changes in feelings often precede awareness, yet are obvious to others. A leader's sincerity may be perceived as lacking or insufficient to meet the relational needs of the group, organization, or a particular member.

SINCERITY MAY REPRESENT
A LEADERSHIP ACHIEVEMENT

In writing of group psychotherapy, Yalom (1995) stressed that "underlying all consideration of technique must be a consistent, positive relationship between therapist and patient. The basic posture of the therapist to a patient must be one of concern, acceptance, genuineness, empathy" (p. 106). I stress that any leader may adopt this attitude without sincerely loving in a manner the relational context requires. In the following case example, I cared; I offered good enough interpretations, and the patient reported "getting better." All was true, but none of this satisfied a particular developmental need to be idealized: considered as special, attractive, delightful.

Case Example: Insufficient Sincerity

June (age 61) lamented to her group: "I don't feel you are excited to see me. People are delighted to see each other, but no one is delighted to see me." June was the respected "senior member," a slight limp from childhood polio added to her gravitas.

"You are 'soo' reserved," a group member responded truthfully, while a chorus of others added, ineffectively, "We care for you."

The theme emerged in her individual psychotherapy. June: "I'm feeling blank, nothing. Weekend was pretty good, the kids brought the grandchildren, but not that exciting. I never have enough time. Always a stack of work on my desk, this committee and that. I can't enjoy myself because I think about all I have to do."

I reminded her of her feeling that I, and her group too, did not enjoy her. "Yes, it is not that you don't like seeing me. But I guess I feel most people could take me or leave me." I asked whether she *believed* that I did not enjoy her, as well as *felt* it. She considered the question and decided that she really believed it. "It's a matter of caring, you don't care that much. My parents took care of me, maybe overprotected me when I got polio, but never made me feel pretty and that I could have that kind of effect on them."

"So that's what you want!" I replied, and then brought us into a truth of our heterosexual adult life: "You want me to find you sexually attractive." June did not directly respond, but I believe she had allowed me to offer and herself to receive a sexual thought. She ended the session without her usual tense facial expression and its trace of bitterness. I sensed that we both felt more relaxed and connected to each other.

Discussion. Beauty and its appreciation exists in every person, no matter how stifled by social forces or physical limitation. In Stephen Sondheim's musical play, *Passion*, a handsome visitor, Giorgio, arouses in the ailing and homely Fosca a love that proves irresistible, and he ultimately yields without regret. We cannot love, or love sufficiently, or effectively, without reciprocity of feeling, real or imagined. I, or our group alone, could not reignite June's libido from its embers. She too had to supply energy. Like Fosca, June took the chance to reconnect to her desire, especially her desire to be desired. She became more appealing when I could feel her as emotional and interested in being experienced as sexual. Derivatives of erotic feelings are natural and expectable, an enjoyable aspect of bonding with others and, at times, a dimension of sincerity.

RUPTURES IN SINCERITY

We cannot will our feelings and are rarely pure of heart and mind. Feelings spring from sources other than Eros and may conflict with leadership ideals and sincere intentions. The leader's love—openness to others, interest, concern, and enjoyment—are revealed in the subtleties of timing, tone, and cadence, which amplify, modify, or even contradict what is verbally spoken (Chused 1992; McLaughlin 1991). The sincere leader learns by ruptures, and when opportune, attempts to repair them.

Case Example: Competency Disguises a Rupture in Sincerity

After five years of intensive combined psychotherapy, the thrice-married Ralph began to grasp what I dubbed a "Fox News" dimension in his personality, a reference to the politically conservative American television network and their bullying commentators. But here he was again, bellowing and fiercely finger-pointing at Julie, a group member and wife-substitute, such that I had to intervene. In an attempt to exculpate himself, he reminded the group that he had not behaved this way in quite a while and that even his wife said he was better. That satisfied the members sufficiently to move on to other interactions.

Several weeks later, Ralph asked me in an individual session whether something had changed between us. "You seem a little different, not distant or uninvolved, but maybe more work focused or businesslike."

Associating to the incident in group and realizing the truth of his observation, I said: "I don't think I've recovered from the last 'Fox-News broadcast.'" My acknowledgment sounded to me defensively lighthearted, so that I added a corrective: "You're right. I don't feel the same way about you. I think you are going to have to repair our relationship."

"I apologized, what do you want! Now you're being hard-assed like Fox-News," he retorted.

I wondered whether I was abiding by the talion principle, paying back for what I had experienced as his hardness. I asked: "Did you apologize? It doesn't feel like one to me."

Ralph continued: "I checked it out with Julie after group, and we're okay."

"We're not okay, at least not yet," I acknowledged.

Ralph teased: "Oh, you're pouting. Just like my wife."

I did not try to hide my amusement and smiled. I offered him what I understood to be the current state of my feelings: "Your bringing this up might help. I don't know yet."

Discussion. It took a while to realize that something had come alive again in our relationship: my *sincerity*, and I liked the feeling. I even liked saying: "I don't feel the same way about you," which I recognized was true in my consciousness but no longer true in my unconsciousness. I had become one of Ralph's walking wounded, hurting from his ruthless treatment of Julie (and me, via my identification with her). Ralph felt my lack of involvement, and he pursued me, becoming playfully seductive, which apparently I needed to be able to love him again.

THE LIMITATIONS OF SINCERITY

Wilde wrote, "All bad poetry springs from genuine feeling" (quoted in Trilling 1972, p. 119). Sincerity is always simple, and sometimes simplistic. Consciousnesses of positive feeling and its public expression do not necessarily advance relationships. The target of our love may be unready, or undeserving, and in not moderating or holding our emotional response in thoughtful abeyance, we may distract or obscure that which is cogent. Sincerity has its risks. One can be self-deceptive and sincere, ineffective, inappropriately seductive, willful, misleading.

Case Example: Sincerity Has Unpredictable Effects

A senior therapist had established a warm working relationship with Helene, a patient in combined treatment. Helene had endured several miscarriages and, nearing forty years old, she feared becoming infertile. Being the trusted witness to Helene's travails, the therapist felt increasingly uncomfortable withholding her own parallel experience. At a moment she felt it particularly beneficial, she disclosed that she also had married in her late thirties and described similar difficulties in childbearing. Helene seemed reassured when the therapist revealed that she was the mother of two thriving teenagers.

Now, pregnant again and halfway to full term, Helene came into a group session announcing that the fetus had died, and she would have to have an abortion. The therapist cried along with the patient, which touched the members, who concurred that the therapist "really cared."

The therapist wondered was she crying for Helene or for her earlier self. She felt herself to be false, undeserving of the credit for "caring" because the group did not know of her own reproductive struggles and identification with Helene. And, in her atypical display of emotion, the therapist was concerned that she drew attention to herself, depriving the anguished Helene.

The patient had a different take; much later, Helene revealed apologetically that if she could not deliver a healthy child she would be a disappointment to the therapist.

Discussion. As leaders, no matter how sincere our feelings and intentions and how directly we express them, we cannot be fully aware or certain of our motivations, meanings, or interpersonal consequences. In expressing certain truths, we may omit others and falsify ourselves.

AUTHENTICITY

Whereas *sincerity* is categorical and simple, *authenticity* is dynamic and complex: tension exists between self-awareness and expression. Authenticity bears upon how the leader approaches and avoids truth in the context of frame, technique, and propriety. Appreciation of the dimensionality of emotion, the influence of the irrational and unconscious, and the inescapability of social role mediate communication.

In his monograph *Sincerity and Authenticity*, Trilling analyzed the differences between these terms. *Authenticity* suggests "a more strenuous moral experience than 'sincerity' does, a more exigent conception of the self and of what being true to it consists of, a wider reference to the universe and man's place in it, and a less acceptant and genial view of the social circumstances of life" (1972, p. 11).

Trilling's conceptualization implies that authenticity is difficult and remains ambiguous. It requires "strenuous" mental activity, an "exigent" (i.e., demanding) standard of being true and of representing truth. A "less acceptant" view of human interaction is requisite for authenticity: the recognition that neither leader nor constituent can simply love and remain sincere. Uncongenial circumstances of social life inevitably get stimulated by group and organizational processes and must become part of authentic experience.

REMORSE AND REPARATION:
THE PATHWAY FROM SINCERITY TO AUTHENTICITY

Interpersonal relations stimulate covetous, angry, and censorious feelings, thoughts, and behaviors, even toward those we love; so we feel guilt and sorrow (Klein 1975). The commitment to authentic leadership involves an act of reparation, efforts to repair the harm we have caused, both imagined and real. The leader moves from the mentality and mode of sincerity to authenticity as he or she tolerates the "depressive position." He or she thereby becomes informed by what Bion referred to as the "painful bringing together of the primitive and the sophisticated that is the essence of developmental conflict" (1961, p. 159). That is, authentic leadership involves synthesizing the irrational and rational, the narcissistic and socialistic, the blunt and cultivated aspects of our personality and of group and organizational life.

Case Anecdote: The Member's "Passion," The Leader's Reparation

Seth summoned courage to report that he had felt "ambushed" when I began the New Year with the announcement of a raise in group fee. "I had no choice," Seth protested. "It would be fairer if you had discussed it first in group." Other members disagreed: "This is what other doctors do." "It wouldn't make a difference, it is Richard's right to set the fee." "We don't have to stay."

I was surprised and became interested in Seth; he spoke up forcibly rather than being his usual agreeable self. He had made a fair point, and despite my support from other group members, I felt embarrassed and remorseful for hurting him. But I was also annoyed, as if he was being ungrateful for making so much of the issue. After all, my rates were not exorbitant and he was benefiting from my efforts. I knew that aspects of my conflictual response were "primitive" and irrational and that I needed to remain "sophisticated" as well. My act of reparation involved tolerating the mix of pleasant and unpleasant feelings toward Seth and supporting his efforts at being authentic (as well as my own). I responded by saying that I had not realized that he had felt ambushed and that I would do as he suggested next time, even if no one else seemed to care. Seth was delighted: "I didn't expect to be heard."

Discussion. In struggling toward a mutually authentic relationship, Seth had become less acceptant and genial. He now required others (myself particularly) to be more acutely reparative: anticipating and recognizing our effects on him and, thereby, modifying our behavior, no matter how we might feel or wish to behave in the interactive moment. Seth had become a person capable of expressing and integrating a range of emotional thoughts and, in so doing, contributed to the "passion" in our relationship and within the group.

THE ROLE OF "PASSION"

Whereas sincerity expresses love, authenticity strives for "passion," which represents the essence of the painful "bringing together [mental] process." Bion introduced the term *passion* and defined it ambiguously, but he was clear to mean something not limited to sensuous or sensual experience: "Passion is evidence that two minds are linked" (Bion 1963, p. 13). I take the term to describe the relational process of realizing and engaging one's basic emotions (and attendant fantasies and thoughts) as we link to our own minds and to the minds of others (Billow 2000a, 2000b, 2002, 2003). In this optimal situation of passion, a leader (including group members taking leadership opportunities) achieves the mental clarity and "moral freedom" (Racker 1968) to feel and to think—if not say—anything.

Etymologically, "passion" draws on its Latin derivation, meaning suffering or submission. Tolerating and trusting gut knowledge that arises partially from the primitive or irrational part of oneself is not easy. Meaninglessness and confusion are part of the relational process of leadership, along with the foreboding that the emotional emergent will be dreaded and resisted. In striving for passion, the authentic leader endures and encourages others to tolerate and suffer through the breakdown of preestablished emotional and cognitive attitudes and modes of functioning. Thus, while the leader supports the secure connections and bonding relationships characteristic of sincerity, he or she also disturbs them to drive change and stimulate creative growth.

THE INFLUENCE OF THE UNCONSCIOUS

Sincerity is spontaneous yet deliberate. Authenticity is mediated but, paradoxically, happens without full awareness or certainty. Words and actions are partially derivatives of an unfolding (and evolving) unconscious. Authentic communications represent the leader's most profound insights and powerful intentions. Yet, they remain only "best guesses" of what the leader feels, thinks, and decides is appropriate to express, to be reevaluated and revised over time and further experienced within the life of the group or organization.

THE INESCAPABILITY OF SOCIAL ROLE

"Every profound spirit needs a mask," Nietzsche asserted (quoted in Trilling 1972, p. 119). Leaders and constituents wear masks, that is, roles that are social and mutually contracted and that allow individuals to relate to each other in ways not otherwise possible. Within their respective roles, they participate in and bear witness to the struggle to develop and communicate truth.

Most prominent for an effective leader are "two faces" (Billow 2005), that of conservator and challenger of group process and organizational culture. He or she introduces principles and practices that normalize interpersonal relations and provide a sense of identity, regularity, and security. In this role, however, the leader risks generating an overly conformist "Establishment" (Bion's [1970] term), becoming too comfortable in a professional identity and in the overt and covert diplomatic alliances that compromise a group's creative potential. In the role as powerful agent of change, the leader encourages freethinking and intra- and intergroup challenge regarding group culture, process, and leadership—disturbing the very status quo that he or she works to establish.

EVALUATING GEORGE W. BUSH:
THE FOUR MODES APPLIED TO POLITICAL LEADERSHIP

President George W. Bush remains a controversial figure, stimulating polarized opinions. For my purposes here, I will refer to "Bushies" and "anti-Bushies" and red and blue states, respectively. This classification is not exact, as there are conservatives who object to Bush's exceptionist, interventionist foreign policy, as well as his domestic fiscal policies. Likewise, some liberals favor the war in Iraq. However, the two groups have differed markedly in their evaluation of Bush as a leader and in his relationship to truth.

Diplomacy

Bush's style of diplomacy eschews compromise. The "Bushies, applaud his confrontational, "meeting the enemy there rather than here," "with us or against us" style of engagement. He is the "decider" (his word), entitled to appoint officials who serve "at the pleasure of the president." He boldly asserts authority with tough rhetoric ("bring it on"), threats, ultimatums, and powerful follow-through. His "or else" to Saddam Hussein promised an action, soon delivered.

The "anti-Bushies" decry the president's refusal to engage in many traditional diplomatic maneuvers, such as talking and negotiating with one's enemies rather than name-calling ("the axis of evil": Iran, Iraq, and North Korea) and nurturing rather than alienating long-term allies ("old Europe"). They see Bush's diplomacy as self-serving, satisfying his allegiance to various special interests.

Integrity

Bush supporters perceive a man of integrity. Ethical, moral, and religious principles guide his political philosophy and decision-making. His belief in democracy, the sanctity of life, freedom from excessive government regulation, and Bible-supported (heterosexual) norms motivate how he engages, as in overthrowing an oppressive dictator, nominating conservative Supreme Court justice candidates, opposing stem cell research and abortion, and promulgating an anti-gay marriage stance.

Bush's antagonists decry an ideologically based, wrongheaded, and hypocritical assertion and application of moral and ethical principles. They characterize as antidemocratic and not humane Bush's incursion into civil liberties (increased surveillance), violation of international norms via the Patriot Act (suspension of habeas corpus and use of torture), neglect of the poor and disenfranchised (Hurricane Katrina and New Orleans), and obstruction of national and international attempts to address global warming (e.g., denial of California's right to regulate carbon emissions).

Sincerity

Some agreement between the "reds" and the "blues" exists in the evaluation of President Bush's sincerity. He is straightforward in articulating how he understands key concepts he favors: God, Jesus, freedom, democracy, life, and that which he sees as natural (heterosexual). Regarding advisors and to their advice, he remains steadfastly consistent and loyal (e.g., Secretary of Defense Rumsfeld, "'Heck of a job' Brownie" of Homeland Security, Attorney General Gonzalez, Putin of the Russian Federation), even when this is unpopular with constituents on the right.

To a significant extent, Bush's appeal rests in his sincerity. One knows how he feels and thinks and may predict how he will act on his convictions. To supporters, Bush's sincerity makes him affable and trustworthy. Adhering to stances unpopular with some conservatives, on immigration, budget deficits, and Iraq, is proof of Bush's sincerity and courage, and so admirable.

By dividing the world into simple categories, such as good/bad, Bush persuades constituents to love (and hate) accordingly. To opponents, sincerity makes him odious and dangerous. They judge that by idealizing certain people and certain ideas (e.g., "freedom" for Iraq, or stem cells), Bush detracts from and falsifies that which is cogent but more complicated.

Authenticity

Bush prides himself on being a categorical not complex thinker. No evidence exists in his history of "strenuous" mental activity (an indifferent student, failed businessman, casual governor). He values short work hours, physical exercise, and lengthy vacations, even in times of national and international crisis. For wisdom and direction, he relies on the Bible, "feelings of conviction," and the minds of others (a conservative brain trust, including Wolfowitz, Perle, Rove, and Cheney, and their military, legal, and industrial cohorts).

Bush denies making mistakes or wishing to have made different decisions; hence guilt and reparation are unlikely to impinge on this leader's consciousness. (We cannot know what impinges on his unconsciousness, for as a public, mostly scripted figure, we are not privy to derivatives that would be revealing. If consciousness and unconsciousness are dissociated, authenticity is obviated.)

The lines of "we" versus "they" are clear. For supporters, single-mindedness is one of the qualities that makes G. W. Bush a trustworthy and unifying leader. When choices are clear, and the demarcations between good and bad, right and wrong, are clear and simple, there should be no demarcation between modes of sincerity and authenticity.

For his detractors, Bush is guided by simple emotion and not by "passion," which involves tolerating and integrating a complex of tensions, even contradictory feelings and attitudes. They caution that a deliberate "go slow" reflective stance is not the same as "waffling" or being paralyzed by indecision or overanalysis. They note that to conclude that invading Iraq was going to be quick, cheap, and easy disregarded available but unwelcome information about the mental and emotional life of individuals and their ethnic, religious, and political subgroups: the complexities and ambiguities of truths of an alien society.

They see Bush as inauthentic—false and posturing—serving at the pleasure of the religious right, oil industry, and big business, and instituting a misguided war (aimed at Iraq rather than Afghanistan) based on lies (the existence of weapons of mass destruction) and wishful thinking. The president who is authentic must lead with "two faces," the reassuring, patriotic face of conservator of the republic and also the face of a leader who brings difficult truths to the public, and in making it think, secures the republic's vitality, perhaps even, its future.

Summary

In the leader's striving for authenticity, the modes of diplomacy, integrity, and sincerity also come into play. G. W. Bush believes his truths and, to this extent, he is sincere. Whether he has been sufficiently complex in his thinking, diplomatic, and ethical in his behavior remains controversial, polarizing the country into two camps.

CONCLUSION

Leadership involves holding the tension of truth as one understands it and deciding at what level—how, when, and how much—to convey truth, which individuals and their political states need to prosper and grow. *Diplomacy, integrity, sincerity,* and *authenticity* describe modes of relating to truth as well as to others. The four modes are navigated to cement bonding, build trust, allow relationships to evolve and resolve, and strengthen the abilities to think creatively and relate constructively to impasses and challenges. They represent the leader in interaction: how he or she approaches and avoids truth. In leading, significant truth about the leader also is revealed. These conceptual tools have been illustrated in a variety of group psychotherapy situations and in evaluating G. W. Bush in his role as president.

REFERENCES

Austin, H. *How to Do Things with Words.* Oxford: Clarendon Press, 1962.
Barrows, S. B. "'Mayflower Madam' Tells All." *Boston Globe*, September 10, 1986. [Quoted by Marian Christy].
Billow, R. M. "Entitlement and Counter Entitlement in Group Therapy." *International Journal of Group Psychotherapy* 47 (1997): 459–74.
———. "An Intersubjective Approach to Entitlement." *Psychoanalytic Quarterly* 68 (1999a): 441–61. Translated and reprinted in *Aperturas Psicoanalíticas* (http://www.aperturas.org), No. 6, 2000.
———. "Power and Entitlement: Or, Mine versus Yours." *Contemporary Psychoanalysis* 35 (1999b): 475–89.

———. "Bion's 'Passion'; The Analyst's Pain." *Contemporary Psychoanalysis* 36 (2000a): 411–26.

———. "From Countertransference to 'Passion.'" *Psychoanalytic Quarterly* 69 (2000b): 93–119.

———. "Passion in Group: Thinking about Loving, Hating, and Knowing." *International Journal of Group Psychotherapy* 52 (2002): 355–72.

———. *Relational Group Psychotherapy: From Basic Assumptions to Passion*. London: Jessica Kingsley Publishers, 2003.

———. "The Two Faces of the Group Therapist." *International Journal of Group Psychotherapy* 55 (2005): 107–87.

Bion, W. R. *Experiences in Groups*. London: Tavistock, 1961.

———. *Elements of Psycho-analysis*. London: Heinemann. Reprinted in: *Seven Servants: Four Works by Wilfred R. Bion*. New York: Aronson, 1963.

Butler, S. *Samuel Butler's Notebooks*. Boston: E. P. Dutton, 1912/1951.

Chused, J. "The Patient's Perception of the Analyst." *Psychoanalytic Quarterly* 63 (1992): 161–84.

Cohen, B., and V. Schermer. "On Scapegoating in Therapy Groups: A Social Constructivist and Intersubjective Outlook." *International Journal of Group Psychotherapy* 52 (2002): 89–109.

Dickinson, E. "Tell All The Truth But Tell It Slant." In *The Complete Poems of Emily Dickinson*, edited by Thomas H. Johnson. Boston: Little, Brown, 1960.

Freud, S. "Group Psychology and the Analysis of the Ego." In *The Standard Edition of the Complete Psychological Works of Sigmund Freud*, vol. 18, edited and translated by J. Strachey, 67–144. London: Hogarth Press, 1921/1961.

Gans, J. "My Abiding Therapeutic Core: Its Emergence over Time." *Voices* (Winter 2006): 14–29.

Gide, A. *The Immoralist*. Translated by R. Howard. New York: Vintage Books, 1902/1996.

Johnson, S. *The History of Rasselas, Prince of Abissinia*. England: Penguin Classics, 1759/1985.

Klein, M. *Love, Guilt and Reparation*. New York: Delacorte Press, 1975.

McLaughlin, J. "Clinical and Theoretical Aspects of Enactment." *Journal of the American Psychoanalytic Association* 29 (1991): 595–614.

Nietzsche, F. *Sämtliche Werke: Kritische Studienausgabe*, vol. 6, p. 63. Edited by Giorgio Colli and Mazzino Montinari. Berlin: de Gruyter, 1889/1980. [Twilight of the Idols, "Maxims and Arrows," section 26].

Racker, H. *Transference and Countertransference*. Madison: Conn.: International Universities Press, 1968.

Trilling, L. *Sincerity and Authenticity*. Cambridge, Mass.: Harvard University Press, 1972.

Yalom, I. *The Theory and Practice of Group Psychotherapy*. 4th ed. New York: Basic Books, 1995.

2

What the *"I"* May See: Leadership, Identity, and Representation

Zachary Gabriel Green

Leadership can be thought of as embedded in systemic processes whereby those who lead and those who are led exchange aspirations intrinsically and often unconsciously linked to identity. As such, leadership becomes operative in the space between people and process. It is a powerful reflection of the illusory but lived experience of shared, constructed characteristics (Derrida 1984). These characteristics are viewed as essential and grow to contain psychological and emotional importance that is recognized, celebrated, and protected by a group. Those who emerge in roles of leadership are those who best articulate and take actions that most mirror the needs of the group as it understands itself to be in a given moment (Burns 1978; Rioch 1975). A moment can be the minutes it takes to manage a crisis that draws people otherwise unconnected to action. A moment can also be an era, spanning millennia, where questions of fundamental belief about the nature of life are core.

Leadership is challenging when identity is operative because groups hold more than one understanding, experience, and exercise of who they are. As such, what we call intracultural conflict can be more accurately viewed as shattering the unanimity of the illusion of identity. Leadership that fails to recognize that some core who claim to share an identity will invariably feel alienated and betrayed by actions taken on behalf of the group refuses to face the harsh reality that representation of any group is a fluid process (Bion 1961; Kahn and Green 2004; Miller and Rice 1967). Living human systems are constantly changing. By the nature of life itself, the membership of the identity group changes in the face of the life-and-death cycle (Erikson 1980). What is viewed as essential also changes. Leadership that can represent, anticipate, and support these changes remains robust and resilient.

In contemporary Western society, leadership faces a fundamental challenge. The boundaries of what is considered essential have become fluid and beyond the capacity of any person or group to control. Identity can be exchanged and changed through encounters with some "other" globally through the Internet and other means and media. Those once accustomed to readily exercising the power and privilege to conserve ways of being are now watching their leadership and influence erode. New populations are finding ways to have their voice heard, thus challenging basic structures. From blogs to suicide bombs, from YouTube to a war on terror, from walls to block immigration to continental integration, leadership faces a new world order that has not yet defined itself. Leaders of this new world will need to reflect and integrate the dynamic, emerging nature of who we are all becoming (Heifetz and Linsky 2002, p. 208). This chapter begins to address the challenges inherent in this global, systemic process.

LEADERSHIP

When we consider leadership in terms of identity, it is easy to think that we are exploring an individual process. Such an error is common as leadership is often equated with a person in a formal role of leader (Burns 2003; Sorenson 1999). When we place leadership in identity terms, the nature of the construct broadens to include the implicit group or groups to which a leader belongs. As such, leadership and representation are closely related constructs. The group seeks a way for its voice to be expressed, reflecting its collective sense of "I am" and "We are." In this respect, leadership is the fluid representation and expression of the collective voice of a group embodied temporally in a person or smaller group of the whole. A president may be one expression in one context while a council of elders may be yet another.

Beyond person or process, leadership in this form is an ongoing, often unconscious, negotiation between the embodied leaders and their relationship to and with the identity group or groups they represent (Klein, Gabelnick, and Herr 1998; Turquet 1985). The identity group endures while those who hold leadership, regardless of how long they may rule or hold office, are limited by terms of service or length of life. Indeed, the influence of a particular leader may endure beyond their presence in the role. What is key conceptually is that the nature of the relation between the identity group and its need for a particular expression of leadership remains a function of that group (Rioch 1971; Wells 1990). Though this function may evolve, the identity group continues to seek to represent itself as it understands itself at any given moment. Also, the nature of the role may be fixed as in terms of office or number of members of a council.

Leadership itself is fluid, constantly moving with the boundary of the identity. For those who represent a group, a significant task is to meet the *adaptive challenge* that leadership related to identity presents (Heifetz 1994, p. 127). As no identity or identity group functions in isolation, there is a constant flow of transaction at its boundary. The group enjoys a domain of identity that includes those who identify with the group yet may not in any other way be members (Alderfer 1995, p. 204). Nothing precludes such identification or ways to prevent actions that are inconsistent with how the larger majority of the identity group may see itself. Where leadership comes into this picture is how to provide protection at the boundaries of the identity that does not alter the very nature of the perceived and lived values that draw a group together and name itself as one. Evidence of this process can be seen in the emergence of "homegrown terrorists" in the United Kingdom. Though it is possible that citizens of a nation would over time adhere more closely to the values of their adoptive land, the persona that are connected to other ways of knowing and being can easily be drawn into dominance. In the absence of shared characteristics celebrated with equanimity, the experience of oppression can lead to an explosive response whereby the adoptive identity is abandoned and denied in hopes that another salient one can provide solace and a consistent sense of belonging.

One example of this process is when a wave of violence struck Denmark in February 2008. Cars were burned and angry youths defiantly hurled bottles and rocks at police authorities in the capital, Copenhagen, over several nights. Officials stated they did not understand the unrest in largely immigrant neighborhoods as the government had made great efforts to integrate these populations into Danish culture. What these same officials failed to address was how the violence coincided with the reprinting of political cartoons depicting the prophet Mohammed in ways that many members of the Muslim community found offensive. The newspapers were marking the second anniversary of the first publication of these images to make a statement about the "absolute" sanctity of the freedom of the press. Though the first publication of the drawing sparked protests and deadly riots in many Islamic areas around the world, many Danish citizens and the government that supported the rights of the newspapers were largely incredulous if not defiant in the face of the reaction (Ahmed 2008).

In this scenario, two identities are pitted against one another. Immigrants to Denmark of Muslim faith likely recognize and value the choice involved in adopting a new land. The capacity to integrate the ways of the new culture becomes largely facilitated when there are few reminders of the marked differences between what is being adopted and what has been central to identity historically and culturally. In this instance, the Mohammed drawings placed Islamic immigrants in a position where they were inherently faced with a choice between who they understood themselves to be and who they chose to learn to be. It is no wonder that through the youths, where issues of identity are developmentally central, that such a question resulted in a violent reaction. Alignment of their immigrant identity with being "Danish" means acceptance of an alienating absolute, represented by the centrality of freedom of the press. Such an action creates a dissonance inducing collusion with the adopted culture and its call for primacy, if not dominance. The cost is rejection of deeply held religious convictions that are central to a historical and cultural identity core. The explosive response reflects what is often the impossibility for some to "hold" both realities and continue to function (Fitzgerald 1945). In this circumstance and others like it, a higher level of leadership is necessary. The challenge is for such experiences to be managed, understood, and approached in a manner that respects and holds all parties concerned (Rothman 1997).

Leadership is unable to provide such direction and holding in the face of assaults at its boundary fails (Hefeitz and Linsky 2002; Klein et al. 1998). The common source of such failures is a propensity to respond in known and characteristic ways. The delimiting manner of such a response is caused by the inability of those charged with leadership to recognize that what is being confronted is itself a new entity, no longer subject to react in once-effective ways. At a basic biological level, "super" bacteria and viruses now prove resistant to the same treatments that once wiped out others of a similar nature. The bacteria and viruses adapted to survive. In the larger human condition, identity groups face similar challenges. Historically, early encounters among different peoples during the age of discovery often meant exposure to diseases for which there was no resistance. Disease destroyed the first Jamestown colony. It is also believed that contact with conquistadors brought diseases to the Mayans that wiped out significant proportions of the population and spread to other indigenous populations throughout South America.

By analogy, the contact between peoples and the diseases that followed represented an adaptive challenge for which there were no resources to respond (Heifetz 1994, p. 29). Indeed, any experience at the boundary of two entities offers such a challenge. The failure to meet that challenge results in the collapse of the leadership. The contemporary equivalent is seen in reverse where European and North American countries attempt to strengthen their borders against different others who seek to immigrate. Though cast in the language of security, at a fundamental level of identity, what is being protected is the very sense of identity that many people fear could die off if the "other" is allowed free access to their land. Leadership that voices and champions the challenge of immigration is often rewarded as recent election results in European capitals suggest. Identity is symbolically protected from a foreign body crossing the boundary. Seeing those "others" who enter as potentially lethal "cells," entire populaces clamor for the illusion of safety that such leadership promises.

Adding to the complexity is the challenge of directionality in this anal-ogy. The foundation of effective leadership is to provide protection, order, and direction for one's group, and those who seek more stringent immi-gration policies meet this fundamental test (Heifetz and Linsky 2002, p. 168). From the perspective of those who seek life in new lands where the promise of opportunity abounds, leadership is in the form of personal au-thorization. Those who cross boundaries, literally and metaphorically, are those who provide the hope for a different way of knowing. They further represent the potential for a different quality of life for those they left be-hind but with whom they share salient identity. These boundary crossers challenge the dominant order and model a way for others of their group. Their actions are often at their own peril yet may serve as the source of inspiration. As such, boundary crossers meet the test of another kind of leadership (Kouszes and Posner 2002). Therefore, we are not left with an easy answer about how leadership and immigration policy (as only one example of global organizational change) is managed. Rather, we are faced with the more basic intersection of two valid models of leadership, each of which seeks to attend to the boundary of what we call identity.

IDENTITY

The classic definition of identity stemming from the work of Erikson (1980) describes how the individual derives a sense of self from the blend of a consistent self-view with an intersecting experience of sharing salient char-acteristics with others. Despite Erikson's recognition that identity develop-ment is a psychosocial process, it is largely from an individual perspective that identity is understood (Shotter 1992). The crisis of each of the Erikson stages of identity development involves interactions with others as a part of the necessary conditions for resolution along the continuum. These ten-sions are said to be present for age cohorts through early adulthood, which implies a group-level phenomenon. Nonetheless, it is not the interaction of the members per se that creates identity. More accurately, what is described is the common experience of development along the life cycle.

The major contribution by identity stage development theorists who built upon the work of Erikson is their collective offering of a fluid process subject to change over time and influenced by interactions beyond the self (Kegan 1982; Wilber 2000). What emerges is a more robust definition of identity that has four key components:

1. Intrapsychic sense of self, *intraidentity.*
2. Interpersonal recognition by an other, *interidentity.*
3. Identification with a group or groups of others, *identificity.*

4. Integral orientation to humanity and all sentient beings, *integral identity.*

Intraidentity

Intraidentity begins as an illusory experience (Chattopadhyay 1999; Pinderhughes 1971). There is a longing for an internal, consistent sense of self. The quest for a single "I am" is demonstrated more colloquially by the way that people choose to describe themselves in terms of salient manifest characteristics and desired enduring traits. More popularly, the descriptors in "in search of" personal ads and online profiles are crude but common examples of how intraidentity is expressed. Yet even in these examples, seldom can one characteristic or trait be used to provide a sufficient picture of the complete identity.

The anxiety about intense existential isolation calls for a powerful ego need to latch onto some self-definition to ward off the more perilous fear of disintegration (Krantz 1998). What we term psychosis is the lived experience of the gap between where one wishes to be and where one finds him- or herself. Unable to secure and sustain the illusion of a singular, unified, integrated self, psychosis provides a route for the anxiety and unreality of it all to find expression.

Those who are termed healthy only attend to the whisper that comes when the collective nature of the intraidentity makes itself known (Hesse 1925; Jung 1935/1984). What is often reduced to different levels of consciousness may be also understood as *multiple persona* (Assagioli 2000). Moving beyond the Jungian notion of persona but related to it, multiple persona is *not* dissociative identity disorder. Rather than representing split-off elements of consciousness that come to be adaptations to trauma, multiple persona are the ongoing, enduring, unconscious faces of the self that collaborate and compete for expression. Though the self is obliquely aware that there may be multiple persona operative, the need for the illusion of a unified identity feeds a quiet denial that keeps the self from collapsing into dissociation or decompensating into psychotic delusion (Assagioli 2000; Kegan 1998).

Multiple persona are the active response used to organize the internal world of the self and the response and defense against the impingement of external environments (Kafka 1989). Intraidentity is a part of a larger systemic, fluid process that forms real identity. It is the relationship across the boundary between intraidentity and interidentity. There is the role with:

1. *The self*—sustained by temporality, where only one persona can be/is typically expressed at one time.
2. *The immediate other (an other)*—the dominant, perceived to be most appropriate persona for the relationship—without "other" there is no

need for the external identity—level of need for real identity likely differs based on predisposition and internal capacity to manage anxiety, relationship to self, history, and experience.

3. *The group and/or groups*—necessarily an approximation of some normative expression of how the group is introjected. It is important to note that one need not share salient characteristics with a group. A form of identification with the group (Alderfer 1995) and wish for recognition/recognition without reciprocation/context in absence of the other can provide proxy. An example of this process is when a person is in an alien or foreign context and seeks to learn those social cues that are necessary to interact, if not "survive." The pace at which one can demonstrate adoption of identification through what becomes a detached but dominant persona that mirrors the foreign context is the degree to which safety of other persona can be gained.

4. *Humanity and sentient beings*—which has a quality of spiritual linkage and highly developed sense of consciousness. This level transcends salience and sentience and reflects an authentic integral experience (Wilber 2000). Such an experience is not easily experienced, achieved, or consciously witnessed (Kegan 1982). Such transcendence is itself fluid and subject to temporal expression and should not be confused with a state or stage of being. At most, it is a moment that the individual and a rare collective of humans may achieve.

Interidentity

Characterized by interpersonal recognition by an "other," *interidentity* is where the social construction of identity begins in the continuum (Shotter 1992). One school of thought suggests that authentic human consciousness arises from recognition by another human. Absent mutual recognition, there is isolation, alienation, and potential subjugation (Hegel 1977). Linked to the classic Eriksonian concept, interidentity is the element of the process whereby shared characteristics are experienced and differences emerge. The notion of "I am" is rooted in how mutual interpersonal recognition allows for a sense of self that stems from intraidentity and can be tested beyond a subjective reality (Assagioli 2000).

The challenge of interidentity comes in the degree of influence one has on another. Where the boundaries of intraidentity are more fluid, conditional, or absent recognition by an "other" can lead to a degree of collapse in the sense of selfsameness and the potential for subjugation. In extreme cases, the less fluid and thereby dominant "other" defines and alters the constructions of the intraidentity of the more fluid one. In other words, vulnerable people face the prospect of being defined and likely dominated by others. When introjection overwhelms more fluid boundaries, the very nature of identity shifts (Lawrence 1970). In cases where the interpersonal exchange leads to recognition by one party without reciprocal recognition, identity collapses. The party that recognizes without being recognized is dominated and loses the capacity to state "Who I am." This process is often a form of violence and places the dominated party in a position where the remaining shreds of intraidentity become suppressed into a preconscious realm difficult to access in the interpersonal moment.

Though described here as an interpersonal process, interidentity dynamics function more powerfully at the group and societal level. Most who develop intraidentity are able to find others with shared characteristics. When identity along these characteristics creates a group ethos, it is in the encounter with others who are "not me" that the potential for conflict emerges. Identity expands in recognition as well as in opposition to this other group. When there is mutual recognition at the group level, interidentity allows each to learn and function from their relative subjectivity, strongly bounded yet permeable in the encounter with the other group. Where the differences are marked and either group experiences threats to their intraidentity, conflict and the fight for dominance over definition of the shared space of constructed reality emerges (Shotter 1992; Smith 1989).

Though examples of this process are legion, the ones that dominate the international psyche include the experiences of those who are Palestinian, Kurdish, and Basque. In each instance, another more dominant power lays claim to the land these peoples see as linked to their identity. The land itself becomes the physical symbol of the boundaries of identity and becomes the proxy for the conflict over determining "me" and "not me." The level of violence speaks to an experience where growing numbers of people who share an identity choose a voice of leadership to represent them that speaks to liberation. The fight for the land is the fight for identity. The conflict serves to create also a source of opposition for dominant and the dominated to know more clearly who "they" are, one in terms of the other.

Identificity

In some instances, the shared characteristics with which one or a group may identify may be acquired. The concept of identificity, and the third point on the identity continuum, is the identity that stems from identification with a group or groups of others. Whereas interidentity arises out of the encounter with the other to create consciousness, identificity is the manner in which an individual or group appropriates identity. This process may include acculturation into one's own group, assimilation into another group, and/or identification with and practice reflective of another group (Shotter 1989). The latter of these processes, identification with another group, does not require direct contact or encounter with this group. Further, the "other" group with whom this identification occurs does not necessarily have knowledge of, nor controls through any degree of recognition, the manner of this identification (Kafka 1989; Smith 1989).

Identificity, in this respect, is a hallmark of a rapidly changing age of information technology and globalization. An individual can access other ways of being, other expressions of identity through the Internet. YouTube videos are but a small example of how windows into realities that "the others" live can be acquired without the reciprocal recognition of interidentity. Identificity can be experienced as an internal process by an individual or group until it makes itself known within the boundaries of an otherwise recognized social construction. At a facile level, identificity on a global scale can be seen in the presence of hip-hop culture among young people on nearly every continent. Fashion and music that was an outgrowth of gritty urban circumstances of African Americans is now adapted and appropriated as commerce among youths of Europe, Asia, Africa, and South America. Lyrical raps, baggy pants, and baseball caps are global phenomena, yet direct encounters between those who share in this identificity are often limited to music and videos.

At another geopolitical level, democracy movements, beginning with those crushed at Tiananmen Square in China and more recently in Myanmar, have at their root global communication through media that those in power cannot readily control. The failure to recognize that crushing identificity does not negate its importance as an element of identity. We only need to look to the liberation of South Africa, the response to the genocide in Darfur, and the international attention to global warming to see how virtual encounters lead to actions that change the boundaries of concern and thereby the boundaries of identity (Trist and Murray 1990).

Integral Identity

Integral identity is an elemental yet flowing nested expression of the self, groups, organization, cultures, and other human systems. It should not be confused with psychological integration or any other notion that points to unity of the psyche. More accurately, integral identity stems from the different potential layers or levels within us and within our groups that are used to meet and communicate with others. According to Beck and Cowan (1996) and other proponents of spiral dynamics on which many variants of integral theory are based, humans speak in the language of unfolding and overlapping memes. More than stages, these memes represent the historical evolutionary layers of human experience as well as the current continued source of conflict and tension in our efforts to understand each other across cultures.

At the level of integral identity, a form of thinking emerges where the capacity for holistic interaction with different others can be experienced.

In what is often termed second-tier consciousness (Wilber 2000, p. 25), the distinction and distance between "me" and "we" has progressively less relevance. More fundamentally, each person is understood to be an elemental, holographic representation of the whole of humanity. In short, we are reflections of one another and, by extension, are one another. Such thinking does not seek to negate or diminish the significant complexities inherent in the efforts of humans to live, love, and work with one another. What integral identity creates is the potential for such connections to be differently perceived, approached, and held.

The highest level of integral identity is what is often seen as transcendent and, thereby, rarely a known experience in the life of most humans. Yet, what the theory provides is a glimpse at a consciousness whereby all of humanity is deeply linked to one another, other sentient beings, and to the living nature of the planet. Our narrow conflicts over our differences serve, therefore, as our primary distraction from connecting to this consciousness, enabling us to find defended collective contentment with the familiar. As such, we are more likely to function in an unconscious realm, often known as first-tier thinking, characterized by ignorance of integral experience, perpetuated by projections onto one another, and reinforced by denial of other ways of knowing. In the end, integral identity remains elusive primarily because of our collective evolutionary limitations. At present, we may lack the capacity to move beyond being largely as we are. The unfortunate consequence is that we allow our ways of being to continue to masquerade as a preferred truth and reality (Wilber 2000, pp. 63–64).

REPRESENTATION

The relationship between identity and leadership can be found in representation. In many Western societies and others globally where elective representative forms of government are practiced, the link between leadership and representation appears to be obvious. In simple terms, it can be argued that those who are elected to office as "leaders" represent the people who elect them. Indeed, as a function of their roles, these officials speak on behalf of the people of that local district, or great state, or sovereign nation, or international body (Sampson 1993). In the simplest terms, the winner represents the identity.

When the electoral analogy is used to help define representation in terms of leadership and identity, we have a facile but incomplete picture. Temporally bound to terms of office, elections as representation are actually one of the better ways to see the illusory quality of identity and fluid nature of leadership. Once a constituency no longer desires a person or party to be its voice, the identity of the representation changes though the "leadership" role continues in the same manner as previously. The change in the person or party of the representative says more about the identity of the group than necessarily the person who relinquishes representation (Smith and Berg 1995).

In the analysis of victory and defeat on election days, media analysts turn to such categories as race, gender, age, party, and education to give meaning to the outcome. Such categories are treated as essential in the sense that they are presented as if to reflect some static and measurable aspect of the human condition. In other words, these crude analyses attempt to reduce identity into knowable terms. Yet, representation cannot be neatly summarized by percentage of voters.

Though representation is indeed intrinsically related to identity, it does not necessarily require selection or election to be operative (Smith and Berg 1995). Similarly and more to the point, most examples of representation do not involve choice. They are founded in delimiting self-attributions as well as equally selective perceptions and projections by others. Returning to the concept of intraidentity, the "who" we say we are may not match the representation we are invited, and at times chosen, to carry by the group (Turquet 1985). In this thinking, "the group" is any human collective that shares a view on an identity, defines it in their own terms, and makes attributions of characteristic traits onto itself or in contrast to itself; the classic "not me." If these processes were consistently conscious either on the part of the individual or the group, references to representation would not be the source of conflict that they are (Alderfer 1995; Rothman 1997). In this sense, representation is the potential clash between the intraidentity ideal, an interidentity negotiation, and the struggle for mutual recognition.

A young Asian female, for example, may accept a view from an "other" that she is this set of essential characteristics if and when it matches the same set as her intraidentity. When there is a match between the individual and the group, the manifest level of conflict is reduced, and this person *becomes* an embodied construction of a "young" and "Asian" and "female" representation. Paradoxically, whether the person accepts the attribution of essential characteristics or not, the representation process is practiced by the "other" (Smith and Berg 1995). This form of representation is the kind to which most people are subjected.

RELATION

In leadership terms, relational elements are key to the creation of identity. Absent the other with whom relational ties are formed, the processes that underlie leadership lack the means of expression. It is important to distinguish how that which is relational itself also takes on different expressions dependent on the theoretical orientation and the developmental nature of the analysis. In psychological fields and academic leadership, relational theory, while sharing characteristics also holds distinct differences.

From the perspective of psychological theory, relational theory is characterized by the quality of empathy between the patient and therapist. In this context, identity is explored through the lens of the relationship, where it is recognized that interaction shapes and forms the lived experience of both parties (Kohut 1971; Winnicott 1965). The construction of a self that emerges from such contact yields to the mutual influence of one to another, providing the basis for how interactions with others in the relational field of an individual are managed. This process operates at multiple layers or levels. The first is at the intrapersonal level where the relationship is between and among the multiple personas within the individual. As noted previously, these personas hold identity differently. While akin to dissociative pathological processes, multiple persona are those healthy efforts to organize identity for an individual to function well socially, professionally, and psychologically. The rapid, adaptive manner of this process allows for the illusion of internal coherence. At the interpersonal level, where relational theory from a psychological perspective is most manifestly operative, there is an exchange at the boundaries of identity in each interaction (Somé 1995; Wells 1990).

Relational leadership theory functions primarily at the group level of identity. This perspective offers the view of leadership whereby collective actions of people are aimed at creating common good (Komives, Lucas, and McMahon 1998). Derivative of transforming leadership theory that argues that leadership exists when there is moral foundation aligned with the higher values, relational leadership theory suggests that the purpose of leadership is to create conditions for these higher values to become lived realties (Burns 1978). The challenge such a theory presents is the presumption about what is in the common good. Intergroup conflict on identity is in part because of differing views on this very question.

In contrast, Wheatley (1994, p. 39) presents a different view that it is the relationship that creates the potential in human and natural systems for leadership to emerge. The potential of what may arise then influences identity. Linked to situational theory, identity groups may take on leadership based on what evolves in a moment (Rioch 1975; Sorenson 1999). There are distinctions to be made between different levels of identity that are a function of relatedness rather than relationship. Each suggests a different level and nature of bond. Relatedness is presence with another. More than proximity, relatedness implies exchange at the level of role rather than identity per se (Bazelgette, Irvine, and Quinne 2006). The degree of affective linkage is also temporal, lacking necessarily any sustaining quality beyond the moment of interaction. In contrast, relationship has affection as the distinguishing characteristic. More enduring than relatedness, relationship offers the catalyst through which identity becomes strongly experienced.

DEVELOPMENT PROCESS

Leadership and identity, in addition to being related constructs, can also be thought of in terms of a developmental process. This progression, while akin to the sequence found in Erikson's classic psychosocial model, represents an evolution of identity development theories (Nobles 1973) and advances in integral theory, particularly spiral dynamics (Kegan 1982; Wilber 2000). In this respect, the development process is not linear but rather a looping and revisiting dynamic whereby an individual and the groups from which identity arrives can all be in different phases of the process concurrently. When this developmental process includes the construct of multiple personas, the location of a single identity is neither fixed nor inherently completely measurable. Like efforts to account for the qualities of light as a point and a wave, doing both synchronously, is not currently possible (Wheatley 1994). Further, the act of observing and placing identity in terms of leadership in such a schema brings the possibility of identificity influences that seek to define the construct in terms of the observed and the representational lens brought to the observation which may, or more likely, may not match the intraidentity of the individual. With these caveats in mind, identity seeks leadership to give itself voice in the following ways.

Isolarity Leadership as Individual

Characterized by the solidarity and isolation of intraidentity, isolarity is the "within" search for identity. In this process, one discovers the multiple persona and is challenged to manage the competition for dominance within oneself. Absent sufficiently strong boundaries around the various personas, there can be tension between feeling alienated *from* and intruded *on* by others. Leadership within is essential to ward off the terror of psychic collapse into depression, dissociation, or psychosis (Palmer 1999, p. 58).

In the healthier, more adaptive side of isolarity, there is recognition that the personas are expressions of the self but with no particularly powerful attachment to any one dominant persona. This balance among the various personas allows for the optimal possibility for interpersonal connection and greater resilience when conflicts regarding recognition by "the other" inevitably emerge at later stages. It is through isolarity that "I am" emerges, becomes embodied, and lives.

Recognition Leadership as Association

Leadership at this phase stems from the search for a contextual identity in association with or against others. Marked by the movement from the intraidentity to interidentity, an individual and groups move from the struggle within and begin the search for mutual recognition. First, this recognition is likely to be sought and received from perceived similar others—those with whom salient characteristics are shared. The process continues to include recognition with and sometimes "against" the different other. In the latter process, the effort is to gain definition of identity in opposition to an "other." The classic "me" and "not me" duality is created (Foucault 1980; Rothman 1997).

The ability to gain recognition for the emerging identity while managing the presence of the "other" characterizes leadership in this phase. In contrast to isolarity, there is a sense that the consciousness gained from being in relationship with others broadens and deepens identity. Further, as a leadership process, the possibility of discovering similar others with whom a common identity can be formed and potentially directed makes recognition worth the effort and risk (Hegel 1977; Kegan 1998). The effort creates shared construction of reality. The risk allows the possibility that this core of similar others can have sufficient strength to ward off any "not me" other that may seek dominance. The failure of recognition is ultimately a failure of leadership that invariably brings some degree of conflict (Smith and Berg, 1995, p. 91).

Discrimination Leadership as Preference and Prejudice

At this phase of leadership, there is a need to to distinguish "my group" from the "other group" in terms of identity. Beyond a form of association that yields recognition to create consciousness of a group identity, discrimination begins as a benign process to define differences and preferences within the group. This process also has intraidentity antecedents that take the individual deeper into the identity. Those who become the voice of these preferences and differences that make one's group distinct from another hold the roles of leadership for the group (McIntosh 1988; Sampson 1993).

The encounter with other groups leads to conflict when preferences are not aligned. The lines that define these differences may also lead to lines that determine recognition between groups. At this level, failure of recognition creates constructions of "me" and "not me" that become more fixed. More than preferences and differences, the distinctions evolve into values, mores, and norms that delineate the boundary between one group and another (Brown 1978). At the more malignant level of this process, the voice of leadership for one group or another shifts the preferences into prejudices through which "the other" is seen. As such, a condition for continued membership in a group is implicitly and sometimes explicitly marked by adherence to a view of reality through a lens that denigrates the other (Skolnick and Green 2004, p. 122).

As an intraidentity process, this more malignant form of leadership related to identity can create a strong degree of conflict within an individual conscious of multiple personas (DuBois 1903). It is not only possible but also likely that one's membership in one group stands in direct opposition to membership in another. As such, it is not only the externalized other but the dislocated and possibly dissociated other within that must be managed. In this respect, the voice of leadership as preference and prejudice is not only embodied in those voices that represent the group but also is operative within an individual. One must then determine where the preferences in terms of lived experience come to be marked in any given context. Those unable to meet the challenge of this fluidity of identity remain in a constant debilitating dissociative state. The same process can have adaptive leadership potential when the dissociation is used to recognize and organize the personas (Jung 1970). The embodied construction supports leadership within the individual as well as potentially within given groups when clarity of boundary is held in differing contexts. A dominant voice tends to emerge in such cases to promote action and remain in relationship to others.

Dominance Leadership as Will to Power

As an intraidentity process, leadership at this phase is expressed through the dominance of one persona over others. The voice that dominates carries and characterizes the identity that is constructed and presented to others. It is also the persona that is taken to be "Who I am" in an illusory sense of integrated identity. This same will to power can be found at the interidentity level when one person seeks dominance over another (Chené 2000). The condition for recognition, one to another, in this frame depends on one party's willingness to accept recognition without balanced reciprocation. When moved to the group level, this process is one where leadership is characterized by the claim of victory and supremacy over another group. In some instances, this form of leadership may also require the other party to submit to some form of subjugation (Fanon 1952; Hegel 1977). Leadership in the group where recognition is accepted at an inferior level also "gains" the benefit of labeling the dominant other as oppressor. The pain of this process is real. People suffer. Yet, the leadership that emerges can claim to be the voice of the "liberator" that calls those who share identity to seek and mobilize its energy in a fight for freedom (DuBois 1903).

Leadership as will to power is temporally determined (Burns 1978; Jung 1970). In terms of intraidentity, a decades-long struggle may exist among

various personas over dominance. Harmony between the personas to support a more unified sense of identity largely depends on the ability for there
to be sufficient consciousness that permits shared expression of voice. At
the group level, the same processes may extend for decades and millennia.
Leadership driven by an intense will to power becomes a cultural artifact
that constructs identity in terms of dominance of some "other" (Chené
2000). The social construction of collective narratives that define the location of one group in terms of another supports the perpetuation of these
relative positions. Until a critical mass of one group or another shares persona with "the other" to bridge these differences, the voice of leadership as
will to power dominates (Sampson 1993; White 2005).

In the most pernicious instances, boundary rigidity keeps constructions
of "the other" intact as a form of group-level isolarity. Reality becomes the
lens through which the other is seen, rather than direct experience. The
leadership that perpetually emerges voices these narratives and continues
to hold these lenses up to those who share identity (Rothman 1997). An
embodied grasp to the will to power on behalf of their group does not
erode easily. A large amount of people who share characteristics within
an identity group must recognize the need for liberation over the need for
dominance. The challenge in this process is that power is often confused
and suffused with the sense of identity that is being expressed by many of
the group and voiced by its leadership. The process shifts when there is sufficient resonance among the people who recognize the erosion of the will
to power does not present an inherent threat to identity. Yet one only needs
to look to Cambodia under the Khmer Rouge or Uganda under Idi Amin
to see the extent to which such leadership has gone to stop this erosion
of the will to power. Such repressive regimes brutally restrain the reign of
liberation—for a period, from years to millennia. As such, the will to power
appears to "win" in these exchanges. Yet, in the course of human history,
the demand for freedom can outlive even the most oppressive systems. We
need only look at slavery, colonization, Soviet communism, and apartheid
as examples. Unfortunately, the scars of oppression are slow to heal and the
will to power often finds new morphed expression to continue its existence.
Now, human trafficking, exploitive labor practices, neonationalist conflicts,
and imbalanced trade policies replace their more pernicious forms of the
past. As a consequence for a significant proportion of the global population, liberation awaits its day anew (Bulhan 1985; Wilber 2000).

Integral Leadership as Interdependent

At the integral level of identity and leadership, there are processes that
recognize the limitations of dominance. The need to lord over others internally and externally gives way to a different form of recognition. The

perceived value of dominance evolves as the value and significance of mutual dependence with different others becomes a clear need. Acquisition of
a sense of identity embodied by accumulated resources through implicit
and explicit subjugation of the other erodes. A different form of isolarity,
born out of a subtle but stark realization that the nature of relationship was
through imposition of fear rather than mutuality of desire, causes dominance to fade in significance. Though elements of the individual and collective psyche grasp for the gratification that dominance once held, those
personas and those members of an identity group who can and do evolve
seek acknowledgment of the value of interdependence with the other (Kegan 1982; Miller 1985; Shotter 1992).

A form of interdependence characterizes the integral process of leadership
whereby there are recognizable but permeable boundaries between one and
the other identity. At the intraidentity level, personas once dominant yield
to those that seek to move in the direction of mutuality of recognition, first
within and then at the interidentity level. This acceptance of various personas without the corresponding need to have power over them allows for a
flow of identity and greater potential for connection to the other. Though
the distinction between "me" and "not me" persists, the relative scale and
nature of difference is reduced. Personas become nested, one to another, in
the form of an intermingling growth hierarchy wherein each persona needs
the other for a greater fullness of identity to be expressed (Kegan 1998, p.
108; Wilber 2000, p. 25). At the interidentity level, recognition is mutual.
The value gained by collaboration and the learning that comes from seeing
the relative values of other orientations to constructed reality expands the
understanding and practice of identity for all parties. Those who are able to
voice the delicate balance between holding a view and voice that articulates
the distinction of one identity group compared to another *and* the relative
value of "the other" without the corresponding denigration or dominance
take on leadership. This interdependent leadership benefits mutuality without the collapse into merger with the other. The benefit at the interidentity
level may indeed serve to create a third space that marks and holds the values and practices that stem from mutuality. This *third space* is neither one
nor the other persona nor one nor the other identity group. It exists in the
space between, where the interaction and experience of one another take
place (Josselson 1992, p. 240). It is a space of acceptance, exchange, and
work where leadership is expressed.

The *third space* is something with which we have great familiarity but may
be more accustomed to addressing as polarities in its more facile dualistic
form. Quite simply put, the *third space* is our experience when we encounter a new way of thinking that challenges our cherished assumptions. It is
encountered when we begin an authentically intimate friendship or form a
new, key professional relationship. We know this space when we begin life

in a new organization after years with another entity. Perhaps in its most profound form, it is the fundamental experience of immigrants, ex-pats, or international aid workers who live and work in different countries for an extended time. In each of these instances, a self that is known and familiar is placed in relationship to some other way of life and being.

Rather than the basic "me" and "not me" dichotomy, the *third space* begins as an additive experience of "me" and "also me." The "me" is our familiar way of knowing ourselves that comes before meeting that intimate friend, working in the new organization, or living in the other country. With these experiences, the "also me" is who we are becoming through this relationship. Initially this "also me" is more like a "not me" or "other me"—other persona, rather than an integrated and coherent part of "me." What makes *third space* thinking different is that it is a further departure from reductionistic duality. It moves beyond what is represented by "me"/ "also me" and "not me" descriptors. Yet, this basic bifurcation is needed to create a third way. What emerges is the birth of another experience. Visually it is projected off the "me"/"also me" continuum into space to form a plane of experience. The movement from linearity to dimensionality is the *third space*. It is more than the integration of "me" and "also me" in that it is the space of emerging leadership (Green and Elson 2007).

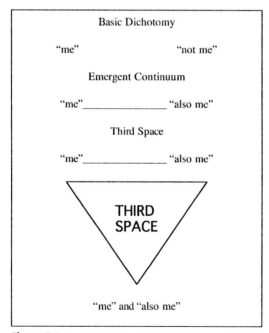

Figure 2.1

In the rhetoric of American politics, the split into so-called Red states and Blue states is a basic false "me"/"not me" dichotomy. It is used to divide, allowing for the continued illusion that one political experience is not contained in the other. Those who say that Americans are not Red states or Blue states, but the United States, are appealing to a way of thinking that reflects a third space (Obama 2006, p. 40). In a more basic fundamental way, children born of parents, one "black" and the other "white" were by law and custom taught or assigned to one racial identity over another. Indeed, in the southern United States under Jim Crow laws, a "single drop of Negro blood" defined identity (Branch 1988, p. 230). Only in recent years in the American context have these children been able to claim a different way of understanding and naming themselves, claiming for themselves a third space that includes both, and possibly multiple, racial and cultural legacies. Tiger Woods is but one prominent voice of this way of being.

The third space supports the emergence of new forms of leadership in that it dramatically shifts the range of how representation can be experienced, expressed, and understood. Its promise comes in how it fundamentally challenges the dualistic thinking and the dominance discourse it represents. In third space forms of leadership, there is more than a basic top-down hierarchy, there is a nested form where interrelationship and dimensionality can be explored. Networked leadership that garnered Nobel Prizes and brought forward the international campaign to ban landmines and current continued efforts to address the potential threat of global warming are but two examples of how third space thinking is becoming transformative (Green 2000).

Transformation Leadership as Emergence

Leadership as emergence is at the level of authentic transformation for an individual, group, or society. The mutuality of identity expands the third space, permitting new creations to emerge. At the intraidentity level, personas are organized in such a way that internal collaboration produces a variety of coherent expressions of self in the world. It allows for ease of connection with different aspects of identity without the sense of threat or conflict that could otherwise tear the person apart (Palmer 1999). In this orientation, "Who I am" is continuously balanced with "Who am I becoming." This thinking and being requires leadership within that values the emergence and respects the unique contributions to oneself made by the multiple personas, individually, collectively, and in various permutations of expression. At the deepest level, the very practices of the personas are transformed, and the approach to the world is characterized by a new view of what is and what can be (Bazelgette et al. 2006; Kegan 1998).

When leadership speaks in the language of transformation for identity groups, there is no need for will to power (Jung 1970). Mutual acceptance and the potential of love rule. The need for one another and the possibility of what one can be created with the other emerges as the primary currency through which relatedness is understood and expressed. This leadership seeks and inspires those of shared characteristics to their higher aspirations, which includes recognition of the inherent interdependence with others (Burns 1978, p. 117). Rather than foment fear of the other, the similarity of desires are found and promoted. Where there was once dominance and supremacy, leadership invites acceptance and equanimity. Such an orientation transforms the nature of the social construction of reality and the societal formation of identity. Indeed the world is seen, as Einstein once suggested, anew (Calaprice 2005).

Transcendence Leadership as One

Leadership as one likely transcends human experience (Kegan 1982, p. 229). At this level, intraidentity and interidentity are no longer important distinctions. What remains is identificity, but no longer identification with one persona or another or one identity group or another but with the world at large. What distinguishes this process from primitive merger is the leadership required to hold this space, which is paradoxically spaceless (Batchelor 1997, p. 77). A deep transformation in consciousness characterizes this level whereby recognition of the other is known to be recognition of oneself and ones own identity. Dissociations at the intradentity level and differences at the interidentity level are deeply illusory at this level. Nonetheless at the same time, there is profound recognition and empathy for the lived experience of others who are bound by these illusions (Campbell 1968; Chattopadhyay 1999). This level of leadership does not deny the embodied reality in which people live but seeks to liberate people from the contexts and conditions that too often are a source of suffering.

Implications

We enter an era where the complexity of identity and the rapid access to the experience of one another requires a new and different kind of leadership. The level of global connection and interdependence has perhaps never been more evident and visible to so many, yet conflicts over our differences, regardless of how minute, persist (Freud 1930). What is required is a leadership that invites a critical mass of humanity to a different kind of consciousness. In this respect, we are not referring to the higher consciousness movements commonplace in the late 1960s. Rather, what is suggested is a form of recognition where the humanity of others is more fully embraced and seen as consistent with "my own" and "our own." In this respect, what has been termed here as identificity means that many people who have never had direct contact with one another can enjoy and reflect on aspects of other beings. The challenge is to do so in a way that does not once again require others to be subjected to dominance and oppression.

Perhaps such thoughts represent unwarranted idealism that is inconsistent with the evolution of psychological thought or organizational theory, yet it is the capacity to think in this manner that may begin to yield a different way of being and the leadership that is necessary for the world to come. As one leader put it:

> I come from the East, most of you [here] are Westerners. If I look at you superficially, we are different, and if I put my emphasis on that level, we grow more distant. If I look on you as my own kind, as human beings like myself, with one nose, two eyes, and so forth, then automatically that distance is gone. We are the same human flesh. I want happiness; you also want happiness. From that mutual recognition, we can build respect and real trust of each other. From that can come cooperation and harmony.

—His Holiness the Dalai Lama
The Art of Happiness

REFERENCES

Ahmed, S. "'Terror Plot' to Kill Mohammed Cartoonist." http://edition.cnn.com/2008/WORLD/europe/02/12/denmark.cartoon/index.html (accessed March 21, 2008).

Alderfer, C. "Staff Authority and Leadership in Experiential Groups." In *Groups in Context: A New Perspective on Group Dynamics*, edited by J. Gillette and M. McCollom, 252–75. Lanham, Md.: University Press of America, 1995.

Assagioli, R. *Psychosynthesis: A Manual of Principles and Techniques*. New York: Penguin Books, 2000.

Batchelor, S. *Buddhism without Beliefs*. New York: Riverhead Books, 1997.

Bazelgette, J., B. Irvine, and C. Quinne. "The Absolute in the Present." In *Dare to Think the Unthought Known*, edited by A. N. Mathur, 89–118. Tampere, Finland: Aivoairut Publishing, 2006.

Beck, E. D, and C. C. Cowan. *Spiral Dynamics: Mastering Values, Leadership, and Change*. Oxford: Blackwell Business, 1996.

Bion, W. R. *Experiences in Groups*. New York: Basic Books, 1961.

Branch, T. *Parting the Waters: America in the King Years, 1954–63*. New York: Simon & Schuster, 1998.

Brown, L. D. "Toward a Theory of Power and Intergroup Relations." In *Advances in Experiential Social Processes*, vol. 1, 161–80. London: Wiley, 1978.

Bulhan, H. A. *Franz Fanon and the Psychology of Oppression*. New York: Plenum Press, 1985.

Burns, J. M. *Leadership*. New York: Harper & Row, 1978.
——. *Transforming Leadership*. New York: Atlantic Monthly Press, 2003.
Campbell, J. *Creative Mythology*. New York: Penguin Books, 1968.
Calaprice, A. *The New Quotable Einstein*. Princeton, New Jersey: Princeton University Press, 2005.
Chattopadhyay, Gouranga P. "The Illusion of Identity." *Socio-Analysis*, I, 1, Melbourne, 65–86, 1999.
Chené, R. "Teaching the Basics of Intercultural Leadership." In *Cutting Edge: Leadership 2000*, edited by B. Kellerman and L. Matusak, 124–28. College Park, Md.: Academy of Leadership Press, 2000.
Dalai Lama, and H. Cutler. *The Art of Happiness*. New York: Riverhead Books, 1998.
Derrida, J. "My Chances." In *Taking Chances: Derrida, Psychoanalysis and Literature*, edited by J. H. Smith and W. Kerrigan, 1–29. Baltimore: The Johns Hopkins University Press, 1984.
DuBois, W. E. B. *The Souls of Black Folk*. Chicago: A. C. McClurg, 1903.
Erikson, E. H. *Identity and the Life Cycle*. New York: Norton, 1980.
Fanon, F. *Peau noire, masques blanc*. Translated by C. Markmann. Paris: Editions de Seuil, 1952.
Fitzgerald, F. S. *The Crack-up*. Edited by E. Wilson. New York: New Directions Publishing, 1945.
Foucault, M. *Power/Knowledge: Selected Interviews and Other Writings 1972–1977*. Edited by Colin Gordon. London: Harvester, 1980.
Freud, S. *Civilization and Its Discontents*. Translated by J. Strachey. New York: Norton, 1930.
Green, Z. "Spirits of leadership." *Inner Edge* 3 (2000): 16–17.
Green, Z. G., and O. Elson. The Third Space: Identity, Potential, and Transformation. *Working paper*. Unpublished manuscript, 2007.
Hegel, G. *Hegel's Phenomenology of Spirit*. Translated by A. V. Miller. New York: Oxford University Press, 1977.
Heifetz, R. *Leadership without Easy Answers*. Cambridge, Mass.: Bellnap Press, 1994.
Heifetz, R., and M. Linsky. *Leadership on the Line*. Boston: Harvard Business School Press, 2002.
Hesse, H. *Damian*. New York: Harper and Row, 1925.
Josselson, R. *The Space between Us*. San Francisco: Jossey-Bass, 1992.
Jung, C. G. *Analytic Psychology: Its Theory and Practice*. New York: Village Books, 1935/1984.
——. *The Undiscovered Self*. New York: Mentor Books, 1970.
Kafka, J. S. *Multiple Realities in Clinical Practice*. New Haven, Conn.: Yale University Press, 1989.
Kahn, W., and Z. G. Green. "Seduction and Betrayal." In *Group Relations Reader 3*, 175. Jupiter, Fla.: A. K. Rice Institute, 2004.
Kegan, R. *The Evolving Self*. Cambridge, Mass.: Harvard University Press, 1982.
——. *In Over Our Heads*. Cambridge, Mass.: Harvard University Press, 1998.
Klein, E. B., F. Gabelnick, and P. Herr, eds. *The Psychodynamics of Leadership*. Madison, Conn.: Psychosocial Press, 1998.
Kohut, H. *The Analysis of the Self*. New York: International Universities Press, 1971.

Komives, S. R., N. Lucas, and T. R. McMahon. *Exploring Leadership*. San Francisco: Jossey-Bass, 1998.

Kouszes, J., and B. Posner *The Leadership Challenge*. San Francisco: Jossey-Bass, 2002.

Krantz, J. "Anxiety and the New Order." In *The Psychodynamics of Leadership*, edited by E. Klein, F. Gabelnick, and P. Herr, 77–107. Madison, Conn.: Psychosocial Press, 1998.

Lawrence, W. G., ed. "Exploring Individual and Organizational Boundaries: Bion's Contributions to Thinking about Groups." In *Do I Dare to Disturb the Universe?*, edited by J. J. Grotstein, 1–21. Beverly Hills, Calif.: Caesura Press, 1970.

McIntosh, P. "White Privilege and Male Privilege: A Personal Account of Coming to See Correspondences through Work in Women's Studies." Working Paper No. 189 from the Wellesley College Center for Research on Women. Copyright 1988 by Peggy McIntosh.

Miller, E. J. "The Politics of Involvement." In *Group Relations Reader 2*, edited by A. D. Coleman and M. H. Geller, 383–90. Washington, D.C.: A. K. Rice Institute, 1985.

Miller, E. J., and A. K. Rice. *Systems of Organization*. London: Tavistock, 1967.

Nobles, W. W. "Psychological Research and the Black Self-concept: A Critical View." *Journal of Social Issues* 29 (1973): 11–31.

Obama, B. *The Audacity of Hope: Thoughts on Reclaiming the American Dream*. New York: Three Rivers Press, 2006.

Palmer, P. *Let Your Life Speak*. San Francisco: Jossey-Bass, 1999.

Pinderhughes, C. A. *Racism: A Paranoia with Contrived Reality and Processed Violence*. Paper presented at the American Psychoanalytic Association, Washington, D.C., 1971.

Rioch, M. J. "'All We Like Sheep—'(Isaiah 53:6): Followers and Leaders. *Psychiatry* 34 (1971): 258–73.

———. "The Work of Wilfred Bion on Groups." In *Group Relations Reader*, edited by A. D. Colman and W. H. Bexton, 21–34, Sausalito, Calif.: GREX, 1975.

Rothman, J. *Resolving Identity-based Conflict*. San Francisco: Jossey-Bass, 1997.

Sampson, E. E. "Identity Politics: Challenges to Psychology's Understanding." *American Psychologist* (December 1993): 1219–30.

Shotter, J. "Social Constructionism and Realism: Adequacy or Accuracy?" *Theory & Psychology* 2 (1992): 175–82.

Skolnick, M., and Z. Green. "Diversity, Group Relations, and the Denigrated Other." In *Group Relations Reader 3*, edited by S. Cytrynbaum and D. Noumair, 129–43, Jupiter, Fla.: A. K. Rice, 2004.

Smith, K. K. "The Movement of Conflict in Organizations: The Joint Dynamics of Splitting and Triangulation." *Administrative Science Quarterly* (1989): 1–20.

Smith, K., and D. Berg. "Paradox and groups." In *Groups in Context: A New Perspective on Group Dynamics*, edited by J. Gillette and M. McCollom, 106–32. Lanham, Md.: University Press of America, 1995.

Somé, P. M. *Of Water and the Spirit: Ritual, Magic and Initiation in the Life of an African Shaman*. New York: Penguin Press, 1995.

Sorenson, G. "Taking the Robes Off: When Leaders Step Down." In *Cutting Edge: Leadership 2000*, edited by B. Kellerman and L. Matusak, 137–41. College Park, Md.: Academy of Leadership Press, 1999.

Trist, E., and H. Murray. *The Social Engagement of Social Science: A Tavistock Anthology.* London: Free Association Books, 1990.

Turquet, P. M. (1985). "Leadership: The Individual and the Group." In *Group Relations Reader 2,* edited by A. D. Coleman and M. H. Geller, 71–88. Washington, D.C.: A. K. Rice Institute, 1985.

Wells, L. Jr. "The Group as a Whole: A Systemic Socioanalytic Perspective on Interpersonal and Group Relations." In *Groups in Context,* edited by J. Gillette and M. McCollom, 51–85. Reading, Mass.: Addison-Wesley, 1990.

Wheatley, M. J. *Leadership and the New Science.* San Francisco: Berrett-Koehler Publishers, 1994.

White, M. "Michael White Workshop Notes on Narrative Theory." www.Dulwich centre.Com.Au (September 21, 2005) (accessed December 17, 2007).

Wilber, K. *A Theory of Everything.* Boston: Shambala Publications, 2000.

Winnicott, D. W. *The Maturational Processes and the Facilitating Environment.* New York: International University Press, 1965.

3

The Dynamics of Gender, Race, and Leadership

Jean Lau Chin

LEADERSHIP AND GROUPS

The nexus of most leadership theories is on the leader; these include trait approaches that identify leader characteristics, skills approaches that identify leader competencies, and process approaches that examine how leaders lead, for example, leadership styles. Others have emphasized the follower and the context; these include situational leadership and contingency approaches that emphasize the influence of contexts or situations on leadership style and path-goal theory that matches how various leadership styles interact with follower characteristics and work settings. The nexus of Leader-Member Exchange Theory (LMX) centers on the interactions between leaders and followers—the dyadic relationship is the focal point (Northouse 2004). This is similar to a group systems understanding of leadership taken by the editors of this book in which the leader is but a component of the structure and process of groups (Yalom and Leszcz 2005). Using a "group systems" understanding of leadership, the editors look at the emergence of relational interactions between the leader and the group being led and hold as a fundamental tenet "that *leadership, rather than exclusively an expression of an individual personality or a set of historical circumstances, is co-created in vivo; it is a function of the group, whether large or small, the individual, and their interrelationship*" (Klein, Rice, and Schermer 2008).

This shift from examining leadership traits and characteristics to examining the contexts in which leadership is exercised, and/or the relationship between the leader and the group being led, influences the types of questions we might raise about our understanding of leadership. If leadership is co-created in vivo with the group, and if it is to meet the needs of a changing world, it must be interactive, dynamic, and contextual. The identities of the leader and the group members need to be aligned; examination of contexts in which leadership is exercised needs also to include an understanding of group dynamics and the psychology of differences. Examining the co-creation of leadership in vivo with the group means examining the following questions about leaders and leadership:

- How do leaders emerge in groups?
- What types of leaders and leadership are needed for what types of groups in what contexts?
- How does a group's identity influence what its members expect and want from the leader?

These questions are important to answer a fundamental question: What is the type of leadership needed for a changing world?

Leadership in a Changing World

Today's world is changing rapidly; we now live in a global and diverse society. Technology, transportation, communication have brought groups and communities in close proximity across the world in time and in space; in fact, they often overlap and result in similar lifestyles globally. Countries and communities have become both more homogeneous and more heterogeneous. They have become more homogenous as the rapid import of foods and products bring fresh and foreign produce to areas where it is not their natural habitat; as multinational companies replicate their products throughout the world, for example McDonald's, Starbucks; and as economic trade brings an exchange of products to and from all parts of the world. They have become more heterogeneous at the same time, with the growing diversity of the national population not only in the United States but also in many other countries where the ascendance and visibility of minority groups create a challenge for national identity and the exercise of leadership. The migration of racial/ethnic groups has introduced fusion cuisine and multiethnic cuisine in major cities throughout the world reflects that diversity, for example, New York City, the Roppongi district in Tokyo, Japan.

Today's leader needs to deal with complex, heterogeneous, and diverse contexts. Despite these changes in society, we still hold monolithic notions of leaders and leadership in our theories and in our views of leaders. Dimensions of diversity, for example, race, ethnicity, gender, disability status, sexual orientation, and religious preference, have not been incorporated into understanding the complexity of leadership skills, traits, and leader-follower interactions, or in how contexts are important in defining leadership style and conferring leader status.

Northouse (2004, p. 3) defines leadership as "a process whereby an individual influences a group of individuals to achieve a common goal." House (2004, p. 2) defines leadership as "the ability of an individual to influence, motivate, and enable others to contribute toward the effectiveness and success of the organizations of which they are members." Similarly, Terry (1960, p. 5) defines leadership as: "the activity of influencing people to strive willingly for group objectives," that is, both leader and follower. Virtually all definitions of leadership share the view that leadership involves the process of influence, that all leaders have one or more followers (Vroom and Jago 2007) and that leadership is exercised in groups.

Dynamics of Gender and Race/Ethnicity

As the U.S. population becomes increasingly diverse, attention to the complex and multiple dimensions of diversity is essential to our understanding of leadership. Issues of race/ethnicity and gender invariably influence all aspects of our daily lives including the groups of which we are a part—whether these groups are family, workplace, community, or government. Women and individuals from diverse backgrounds are now filling leadership positions in all realms of society including political and religious leadership, corporate and community leadership (e.g., Meg Whitman, CEO of EBay; Andrea Jung, CEO of Avon Products; Nancy Pelosi, Speaker of the House of Representatives).

More women are now heads of state in countries around the world and CEOs of corporations—common definitions of formal leadership positions. Nonetheless, women and racial/ethnic minority groups are still underrepresented in U.S. leadership positions. We have yet to elect a woman as president in the United States although internationally, this has happened on all the continents beginning in 1940 with Head of State Khertek Anchimaa-Toka, People's Republic of Tannu Tuva in the Soviet Union; Acting Head of State Sühbaataryn Yanjmaa, Mongolia in 1953; Song Qingling, widow of Dr. Sun Yat-Sen, China in 1968; Executive President Maria Estella Martínez Cartas de Perón, Argentina in 1974; President Vigdís Finnbogadóttir, Iceland in 1980; Corazon Aquino, President of the Philippines in 1986, Asia's first woman president; Mary Robinson, President of Ireland in 1990; and Michelle Bachelet Jeria, President of Chile in 2006 (http://www.terra.es/personal2/monolith/00women2.htm). Nor have we elected a person of color as president despite the changing population demographics and the fact that persons of color lead countries throughout the world. The emergence of Hillary Rodham Clinton and Barack Obama as front-runners in the 2008 presidential campaign was a major turning point, as the first woman and the first black presidential candidates for the Democratic National Party.

How do we understand these questions as to why women and racial/ ethnic minority groups in the United States are underrepresented in leadership positions? How might we understand what groups want in their leader within political leadership and government? In examining the contexts in which such leadership emerges and is sustained, we might understand the dynamics of how gender and race/ethnicity contribute to leadership and the importance of diversity in defining leadership in a changing world.

How Do Leaders Emerge?

Research studies have examined how leadership emerges and then fades within different cultures and governments. Leaders can ascend to their positions by birth (e.g., monarchs), by seniority (e.g., elders of a tribe) and natural succession according to established rules, by rules defined by the institution (e.g., election in governments, promotions in corporations), and sometimes by the imposition of brute force (e.g., revolution). Leadership status can be conferred or taken. Throughout history, the impact of war, revolution, and conquering crusades has resulted in the forceful taking of leadership. Moreover, the ascendance to leadership positions has historically been male dominated—that is, patriarchal lines of succession and male CEOs. Presumably, they have embodied the ideal of the people. Although women comprise half of the population, we have been unable to see them as the embodiment of the ideal leader. The same has been true of racial/ethnic minorities in the United States. A known phenomenon is that of "passing," for example, where light-skined African Americans have been known to "pass" as white in their pursuit of economic and social mobility. It might also capture other characteristics of diversity as when Franklin Delano Roosevelt, the thirty-second president, needed to "pass" as ablebodied; though he was wheelchair bound, the media rarely had a picture of him in a wheelchair as if that would have diminished his status as a leader. In Asian history, Hua Mulan, better known as the Woman Warrior, had to disguise herself as a man, that is, to "pass" in order to go to war in place of her ailing father.

The ascendance to leadership status is not the same as exercising effective leadership. One way to measure leadership effectiveness is by the number of the followers. By this standard, Adolf Hitler would have been considered a very effective leader during his dictatorship; however, many will argue that his approach was defined as leadership by coercion and by his abuse of power. Another way to measure leadership effectiveness is to assess the extent of influence on the followers. Within organizational contexts, this could be defined as productivity where effective leaders generate higher productivity, lower costs, and more opportunities than ineffective leaders. Effective leaders create results, attain goals, and realize the vision and other objectives of the organization more quickly and at a higher level of quality than ineffective leaders. In political and public leadership, this influence might include inspirational, transformational, or charismatic styles that inspire followers to work toward a common goal.

However, it is unclear how dimensions of gender and race/ethnicity bias confound the evaluation of effective leadership and the conferring of leadership status. Eagly and Karau (2002) suggest that perceived incongruity between female gender role and leadership roles leads to prejudicial appraisals of women leaders, that is, women perceived as less favorable than men in leadership roles. Eagly (1987) also found that women leaders were evaluated differently and less favorably than men. These biases have also been identified by Dovidio and Gaertner (1996) in unintentional or unconscious discriminatory evaluations of racial/ethnic minority individuals because of underlying anxiety about race and ethnicity; this has been termed aversive racism. Steele (1997) found that diverse individuals might also underperform in situations where they are evaluated on a domain in which they are regarded, on the basis of stereotypes, as inferior—stereotyped threat.

Women and racial/ethnic minorities face barriers in ascending to leadership positions compared with men of comparable strengths and talents—a phenomenon often described as the glass ceiling. Now that more women are in such positions of leadership, Eagly and Carli (2007) have described this process as a "labyrinth." Once in these roles, women and racial/ethnic leaders in the United States have often been placed in double-bind situations or been victims of double standards used to evaluate their leadership.

Several examples might illustrate how we have evaluated the leadership of some significant women leaders throughout history. Empress Dowager Cixi from China was a powerful and charismatic figure who became the *de facto* ruler of the Manchu Qing Dynasty and ruled over China for forty-seven years, from 1861 to her death in 1908. She rose from being a concubine to empress and exercised almost total control over the court under the nominal rule of her son the Tongzhi Emperor and her nephew the Guangxu Emperor, both of whom attempted to rule unsuccessfully in their own right. Many historians considered her reign despotism, and attribute the fall of the Qing Dynasty, and therefore Imperial China, as a result of Cixi's rule (Wikipedia 2007). Cleopatra VII's reign in Egypt marked the end of the Hellenistic Era and the beginning of the Roman Era in the eastern Mediterranean. She was the last pharaoh of Ancient Egypt and a descendant of Alexander the Great who lived nearly 300 years before. Her patron goddess was Isis, and thus during her reign, it was believed that she was the reincarnation and embodiment of the goddess of wisdom. Cleopatra's story has fascinated scores of writers and artists through the centuries. Though she was a powerful political figure in her own right, it is likely that much of her appeal lay in her legend as a great seductress who was able to ally herself with two of the most powerful men (Julius Caesar and Mark Antony) of her time (Wikipedia 2007). Joan of Arc was a fifteenth-century national heroine of France. She was tried and executed for heresy when she was only nineteen years old; this judgment was overturned by the pope, and she was declared innocent and a martyr twenty-four years later. Her valor on the battlefield was renown in her attempt to recapture Paris and lead the troops to victory (Wikipedia 2007).

All three women leaders were noted for their uncharacteristic leadership. As women leaders, both Cleopatra and Empress Dowager Cixi emerged as leaders by seizing power, ascended to power through their seduction of men, and reigned because of their alliance with the men of their times; their route to power and leadership are generally viewed as invalid, tyrannical, and exercised in a masculinized context. Joan of Arc, on the other hand, was victim to charges of heresy and executed; she was not unlike the victims of the Salem witch hunts, in which women were feared and executed because their "mysterious powers" threatened the power of men. They were not accepted as leaders in a world that men ruled and dominated. In today's world, women leaders are often described by their clothing fashion in the media as if this were material to their leadership. Moreover, their depiction as being "feminine" is often a double-edged sword: to be "too feminine" is to risk being perceived as weak and emotional or as manipulative and devious when exercising leadership; whereas to be "insufficiently feminine" generally results in being labeled as masculine, abrasive, or pushy. In the U.S. Congress, when Nancy Pelosi was elected as House Minority leader in 2002, she became the first woman ever to head a party in either chamber of the legislature. In a *Boston Globe* column, McGrory (2002) wrote, "He is called the Hammer. She's a velvet hammer. He is Tom DeLay, the newly elected House majority leader, who is all coercion and threat. She is Nancy Pelosi of California, who is all persuasion and smiles." This description reflects the gender bias and differential language used to describe women leaders in masculinized contexts. Though pointing to Nancy Pelosi's collaborative and interpersonal strengths, it also reflects the tendency to "feminize" women leaders in ways that suggest weakness or to suggest incredulity when women behave as decisive and effective leaders.

What Types of Leadership for
What Types of Groups in What Contexts?

To examine leadership as the interaction between leader and follower in a group, we must ask what types of leadership are needed for what types of groups in today's global and diverse world. In a changing world, leadership styles need to motivate change and influence followers to work toward that goal; this often means that today's leaders need to be visionary, inspirational, authentic, or transformational in their styles. Authentic leaders are genuine people who are true to themselves and to what they believe in. They engender trust and develop genuine connections with others; they are more concerned about serving others than they are about their own success or recognition (George 2007). A transformational leadership style has also been identified as syntonic with women's connectedness and interpersonal orientation. In studying diverse women leaders, Chin, Lott, Rice, and Sanchez-Hucles (2007) found that feminist women often embrace leadership styles that are value driven, ethics based, and/or social change oriented, that is, transformational. The generally expressed preference was for using a collaborative process, empowering followers, and promoting inclusiveness, that is, an egalitarian model of leadership reflecting their desire to level power dynamics inherent in the leader-follower relationship. At the same time, many of these diverse women leaders felt constrained by the masculinized contexts in which leadership was exercised; they felt the need to use more hierarchical leadership styles to be effective, be viewed as decisive, or as exercising leadership rather than using a more collaborative process. As an aspirational goal, Porter and Daniel (2007) identify a feminist model of leadership that promotes values consistent with feminist principles and addresses: values, action-collaboration, learning, understanding of power, ethics, and social constructiveness (i.e., VALUES). Many feminist principles are also generic principles embraced in contemporary literature on leadership, consistent with transformational leadership styles, and authentic "in knowing who they are, what they believe and value" (Avolio, Gardner, Walumbwa, Luthans, and May 2004, p. 803).

Research has shown that women perceive a need to adapt their behavioral style so men do not feel intimidated (Ragins, Townsend, and Mattis 1998) and that a narrower range of acceptable behavior exists for female leaders than for male leaders (Eagly, Makhijani, and Konsky 1992). While self-reports of differences between men and women are common, few empirical differences have been found between women and men in the exercise of leadership (Eagly and Johnson 1990). "Transformational and authentic leadership are advantageous for leaders of both sexes; however, leadership remains a different experience for women and men" (Eagly, 2007, p. xviii).

The significance of this difference in experience for women and for racial/ethnic minority groups compared with white Anglo men even when they hold the same leadership position has not been well understood. Leadership theories have simply not incorporated the diversity of individuals, cultures, and groups in how they interact with the exercise of leadership. Moreover, the exercise of leadership has been shown to vary with the gender composition of the group. Consequently, the worldviews reflected in leadership theories reflect the limited views of their creators. For example, it was our concern with communism and its threat to democracy in the governments of world powers post-World War II that led to the study of democratic vs. autocratic leadership styles. Values of collaboration and empowerment emerged in theories of "shared power" and "servant leader" as the women's movement raised our consciousness about gender and racial/ethnic inequities and their exclusion from leadership roles. With changing population demographics and growing diversity, there is growing concern that leaders need to be inclusive as a dimension of their leadership styles and to empower their followers. Military groups have tended to demand their leaders to be more directive and commanding in presence while religious groups have tended to expect their leaders to be more inspirational.

Aligning Leader and Group Identity

If we look at what the group or followers want, we must also examine how the leader embodies what the group wants. This includes how the leader and group identity coalesce. From a group systems perspective, all communities, nations, and cultures operate as groups; identification of the leader(s) or conferring of leader status is but one dimension of their functioning. It is the commonalities among group members that make for group cohesion and identity. It is often the differences between groups that both consolidates group identity and builds cohesion of the "in" group. At the same time, it is the differences that lend themselves to creating the "out" group or marginalized groups—positions in which women and minorities have often ended up.

Though the leadership literature has discussed leader characteristics and traits, there has been little discussion of leader identity and how it connects with the identity of the group, its role in fostering group cohesion, or in enabling individuals to ascend to positions of leadership. As a race-based society, where corporations and their leadership are still largely dominated by Anglo, heterosexual, able-bodied men, diverse leaders who are different because of race, gender, or other factors face added stressors when ascending to positions of leadership. Often they are expected to behave according to stereotypic gender and racial norms, while being identified by their diversity status and having their competence and effectiveness defined by gender and racial/ethnic stereotypes.

Group perceptions about the identity of its leader and how a group should be organized often means having a white, male leader. A commanding presence, for example, is often viewed as being "tall." Though men and leaders are often admired for being assertive, the same behavior by women may define her as "a bitch," "a dragon lady," or as "acting like a man." The leader's identity is often expected to embody characteristics the group desires, especially when they view themselves as homogenous. Therefore, there is an added process for the group when a leader is perceived as being different from expectations. When the leader is different by virtue of gender or race/ethnicity, these characteristics are included in defining his/her identity and effectiveness as a leader. This is why women and racial/ethnic minorities make the news when entering positions of leadership. Not only do diverse leaders stand out as different, they also risk being viewed as deficient and weak as leaders, or ineffective and incompetent.

The image of Americans, or of any nation for that matter, as being homogenous has been largely illusory; yet, these illusory idealistic images have been perpetuated in the national psyche and in our expectations of our leaders. The melting pot myth reflects aspirations to create our national identity in the United States but had the adverse effect of disenfranchising those who did not melt because of racial and ethnic differences. From attempting to erase the cultural origins of all Americans using a melting pot metaphor to promoting patriotism and in pursuit of a national identity, we deluded ourselves into believing that there was a single ideal for both leader and follower, and in defining how the group ought to be organized, e.g., the image of "our forefathers." It is an oxymoron that persons of color rule governments throughout the world; yet, these same racial/ethnic group members have been excluded from positions of leadership in the United States.

As scholars of multiculturalism, it is now clear that individuals often embrace multiple and intersecting dimensions of identity related to race, ethnicity, gender, sexual orientation, and disability. Many now note that it is essential for us to move beyond single dimensions of identity in defining individuals, groups, and leaders and to examine these multiple and intersecting dimensions to obtain a more comprehensive understanding of how diversity contributes to leadership (Chin and Sanchez-Hucles 2007). Given the changing population demographics in the United States, can the perceptions and expectations of a leader's identity reflect this diversity? Are Americans now ready to follow and accept a Mormon, a Jew, a Black, or a woman as their leader? Have the results of the twentieth-century movements, that is, the women's movement, immigrant rights, civil rights, and human rights movements, changed enough of our national identity for us to become more diverse and inclusive in defining who may enter our positions of leadership? These issues are dimensions of leader identity now being raised in the 2008 presidential election.

Does Difference Make a Difference?

In looking at the experiences of diverse women leaders (Chin et al. 2007), we identified some challenges they faced as they negotiated their paths to leadership, which included added stressors of being expected to behave according to gender and race/ethnicity stereotypic norms and managing the work-family balance. Though research studies of leadership gender differences have not demonstrated gender differences in the exercise of leadership (Eagly and Johnson 1990) or have found them to vary depending on the context, popular wisdom, and women's self-reports, they continue to identify distinct leadership styles and characteristics between women and men.

Why is it then that the strength of these perceptions persists? It is an issue of identity, both in the perception others hold of diverse leaders and that diverse leaders themselves embrace. Being a leader is not divorced from gender and racial/ethnic identity, but rather one dimension of self-identity. Second, it is often not the differences in what diverse leaders do as much as the different experience they face when they lead. Furthermore, because they do not make up the dominant group in leadership positions, the tendency is to view traits women and racial/ethnic minority groups hold as negative or deficient rather than to examine how these differences are strengths that diverse leaders bring to their leadership roles, that is, our anxiety about difference.

In Chin et al. (2007), African American women, for example, described their assertive styles often being misinterpreted as hostile and aggressive while Asian American women described their quiet communication styles being misinterpreted as passive. Hall, Garrett-Akinsanya, and Hucles (2007, p. 283) define black feminist leaders as: "Black activists who, from the intersections of race and gender, develop paths, provide a direction, and give voice to black women." Kawahara, Esnil, and Hsu (2007, p. 310), in their interviews of Asian American women leaders, found they held a collectivist view of their leadership styles and used bicultural values to achieve their leadership goals. Native American women described their leadership as: "In the 21st century, American Indian women will stand beside, rather than behind, [their] men in their effort to preserve their tribes and treaty rights" (Kidwell, Willis, Jones-Saumty, and Bigfoot 2007, p. 327) and because of the inherent threat posed by broader society against their men if they were to distance themselves. Differences do make a difference.

Scapegoating and Marginalizing Outsiders

A group builds its cohesion by seeking out the commonalities among its members. It is the differences that must be transcended. In forming leader and group identity, we often find the phenomenon of scapegoating subgroups who are viewed as different and, therefore, as less than. Racial/ethnic minority groups and women have often been marginalized in such a process and kept from achieving leadership positions or scapegoated in unfair and biased appraisals of their strengths. As a nation, we have scape-goated and accorded outsider status to those in the minority. For example, Latino Americans have been labeled "welfare maggots," Native Americans have been labeled as "savages," African Americans have been viewed as aggressive. Asian Americans, once considered "the yellow peril," later became the "model minority." These negative attributions of status and identity were based on stereotypic portrayals in response to the nation's struggle to coalesce and address economic and social problems. Chinese became the "yellow peril" when they threatened the jobs of laborers, as did Mexican migrant workers now labeled "illegal aliens." The enslavement of African Americans was viewed as necessary to the Southern farm economy while the internment of second- and third-generation Japanese Americans was declared necessary to national security during World War II.

Bolstering a group's identity by scapegoating a subgroup plays into the insecurities and anxieties of the group. Leaders can and have exploited these issues to negotiate and build their power and status within groups by holding themselves as the embodiment of the group's ideal identity. The enlightened leader can transcend the will of the group, whose identity and behavior have been derailed from more humanistic goals, or realign the power structure of warring subgroups to strive for equality and equity of all.

HISTORICAL CONTEXTS AND DYNAMICS OF LEADERSHIP   •

To understand how diversity intersects with leadership in a changing world, we need to understand the contexts of leadership more broadly and within history. Leadership is not divorced from the cultural, social, political, and economic contexts of which it is a part. How did leadership emerge during the twentieth century? What did leaders embody and how did they reflect the group's identity? What leadership styles were effective in providing what followers needed and wanted? Similarly, leadership dimensions studied in the literature often reflected the zeitgeist of the times and the ongoing concerns of the nation and its people. The totalitarianism of Hitler and Mussolini is contrasted with the optimism and hope of John F. Kennedy by their leadership styles and how they catered to the concerns of the people.

During the early part of the twentieth century, we saw the United States shift from an agrarian to industrialized society; developments in technology focused on the mechanization and production of goods and training a production-line workforce. We saw the phenomenal growth of companies with strong and directive leadership viewed as conducive to high productivity and national leadership. Franklin Delano Roosevelt, the thirty-second president, displayed that strong leadership following the Great Depression of 1929 and the need for the nation to gain hope from the New Deal that he promoted. Dwight D. Eisenhower, the thirty-fourth president, brought his prestige as commanding general of the victorious forces in Europe during World War II and obtained a truce in Korea. As he pointed out as he left office, "America is today the strongest, most influential, and most productive nation in the world."

Adolf Hitler became the Chancellor of Germany in 1933 and declared himself Führer, combining the offices of President and Chancellor into one. His charismatic oratory skill won him the popularity to gain power with the Nazi Party and establish the Third Reich after World War I. He emphasized nationalism and anti-Semitism to promote the Aryan race in Germany, that is, a pure white bloodline of blond-haired and blue-eyed Germans, and promulgated the genocide of six million European Jews during World War II. Hitler was racist in his belief that Jews, Slavs, Blacks, Asians, Arabs, and all nonwhite races were inferior to white people and were tainting his bloodline, which he perceived as a personal threat. While he exercised a fanatical egotistical and dictatorial leadership, the will of the German people supported him.

Post–World War II, the United States and the world grappled with the aftermath of the dictatorships of Hitler in Germany and Mussolini in Italy, resulting in leadership studies on the authoritarian personality seeking to identify the effectiveness of autocratic vs. democratic vs. laissez-fare types of leadership. In wrestling with the political differences of communism vs. democracy, which included the emergence of Russia and China as world powers following World War II with communism as their political ideology, the United States struggled to define democracy and democratic styles of leadership as part of its national identity. This was instrumental to identify Chinese immigrants as "the yellow peril," to eradicate communism in the McCarthy era, and to justify the forced removal and internment of 120,000 Japanese Americans (of whom 62 percent were U.S. citizens) from the Pacific Coast by President Roosevelt as a national security need. In all cases, the identification of racial/ethnic difference and scapegoating minority groups was used to define national loyalty, to promote national and group identity, and promulgate the insider status of white Americans at the cost of curtailing the civil rights of nonwhite Americans. These were not simply the acts of a leader but were in collusion with the dominant group. On a contrasting note, women in China have been making progress toward attaining equality since the 1950s. Women came of age during the age of Chairman Mao Tse Tung who taught that "women hold up half the sky"; he used his leadership and this phrase to be liberating and intended his teaching to promote a reaction against the predominant Confucian thinking of a patriarchal and hierarchical society.

It might be interesting to note that these concerns—authoritarian vs. democratic leadership—were mirrored in the educational systems post WWII. The values, organizational structure, and patterns of leadership embodied by the educational system "sets the table" for the enculturation of the next generation. After World War II, the demand for services grew exponentially with the growth of technology. Production and technology spread globally as production was outsourced from U.S. companies with growing labor costs and as other countries entered the market to produce goods and services that were less expensive and in many cases of higher quality (e.g., automobiles, electronic equipment, watches, cameras, and the like). U.S. companies faced an increasingly competitive and difficult economic environment laced with dramatically changing industry boundaries, increasingly rapid technology advancements, government interventions, and many international dynamics (Ferris, Schellenberg, and Zammuto 1984).

Changes in the social and cultural contexts in the United States paralleled these economic changes. The popular literature identifies Baby Boomers, Generation Xers, and the New Millennials as "types" that characterize individuals born during certain periods in the twentieth century and reflects on the shifting social zeitgeist whereby social norms and values that predominate within society evolve over time. These types reflect a social construction of reality and define social problems and the dominant intellectual and cultural climate, that is, "the spirit of the age."

During the 1960s, the United States rallied around issues of equity, equality, and social justice in the era of the Peace Movement, Civil Rights Movement, Women's Movement, all fighting for some form of human rights; all came together to define a period in the nation's psyche and identity, fueled by the passion of Baby Boomers, born after World War II, who came of age during the height of the Vietnam War and the protest over the draft, which ended in 1973. In his book *Boomer Nation*, Steve Gillon (2004) defined this generational cohort as the first group to be raised with televisions in the home, identified as "the institution that solidified the sense of generational identity more than any other." Starting in the 1940s, people in diverse geographic locations could watch the same shows, listen to the same news, and laugh at the same jokes. The music of rock and roll was another expression of their generational identity with transistor radios as the personal devices used. Gloria Steinem challenged the inequities to women, Martin Luther King led protests and the Civil Rights movement, and John F. Kennedy inspired the nation to reach the moon; these leader exemplars reflected the demands and need for inspirational and visionary leaders. It was an age seeking the validation and inclusion of all groups in the nation.

The economic, social, and political contexts of the 1960s influenced the studies on leadership that began to examine transformational vs.

transactional styles of leadership, which emphasized visionary leadership, empowerment, and interpersonal relatedness. These styles focused on the interaction between the leader and the group being led and also how leaders embody and are empathic with the needs and hopes of their followers. These leadership types rely on the charisma and vision of leaders who can unite and inspire the group; their leadership reflects the zeitgeist of the 1960s. We might define these as the interaction of leadership with culture—organizational, cultural, or national. As disenchantment followed, the United States began to look at different forms of leadership and was less egotistical in trying to affirm or demonstrate how democracy was better. Kao, Sinha, and Wilpert (1999) discuss indigenization in management as an integrative process and illustrate how cultural values, norms, and expectations are interwoven into managerial styles and organizational functioning; this approach reflects a recognition that management and leadership theories fashioned from perspectives rooted in cultural contexts of Western societies have limited application in Asian countries. Comparison of U.S. management styles with Japanese management styles of leadership reflected a growing awareness of difference. For example, in Japan, it has been noted that the work ethic requires a twenty-four-hour commitment to the corporation and that business practices are influenced by Confucian values in defining who become leaders; organizations situate the importance of family as the defining unit of leadership, orderly succession by a defined hierarchy of relationships, and loyalty to the group. The influence of the Japanese management style was being felt throughout the American corporate landscape. The successful application of the Theory Z concept recognized that employees represented a vital resource just as important as capital and should be managed to promote their loyalty and facilitate competitive advantages (Dulebohn et al. 1995; Carnevale, Gainer, and Meltzer 1990). The emergence of the "Me Generation" in the 1970s was a reaction to and disenchantment from the earlier era of the Baby Boomers; it was a generation not known for putting duty before self and believing that the needs of the individual should come first. This is viewed not as being selfish, but as: "Being yourself," and "Believing in yourself."

The 1980s presented a change in philosophy and organizations found that it was important to foster a sense of mutuality and trust in the relations between management and workers, to develop employees as assets with the view of increasing competitiveness, and to assist the organizations' compliance with the increased government regulations in trade (Kochan, Katz, and McKersie 1986; Walton 1985). Generation X, described by Douglas Coupland in his book *Generation X: Tales for an Accelerated Culture* (1991) as those born in late 1980s and early 1990s had the reputation as apathetic, cynical, disaffected, streetwise loners and slackers, reactionary to the Baby Boomers and disenchanted with its ideals. At the same time, Generation X is noted as an entrepreneurial and tech-friendly generation driven by the Internet's growth—for example, Google, Yahoo. The rise and fall of Dot.com companies starting the early 1990s through 2000 was all hype. Too many companies rushed in to develop computer games and interactive media without a clear business plan or understanding enough about the Internet. Many investors and stockholders put their money into the computer and Internet industries in the United States in hopes of riding the Internet wave and of reaping high profits until the 2000 stock market crash.

The 1990s also saw the impeachment of President Bill Clinton by the House of Representatives on December 19, 1998, and his acquittal by the Senate on February 12, 1999, on the charges of perjury and obstruction of justice as he lied about the Monica Lewinsky scandal and Paula Jones lawsuit. The Enron scandal, revealed in late 2001, followed a series of revelations involving irregular accounting procedures bordering on fraud, perpetrated throughout the 1990s, involving Enron and its accounting firm Arthur Andersen and its subsequent bankruptcy. These and other events led to the call for ethical leadership—that is, responsibility of leaders to be ethical and have integrity, to call for transparency, and practice a values-based model of leadership to enable followers to regain trust in their leaders.

Leadership for a Changing World

In the twenty-first century, rage over the Iraq war, fear of terrorism, the war on terrorism, and recent natural disasters affecting the United States appear to call for different leadership and a global focus in the New Millennium. Social problems are now different with concerns over global warming, terrorism, world peace, and weapons of mass destruction compared with the Great Depression, the Cold War, nuclear threat, and the arms race of the previous century. It is now different from early periods in history where dichotomies between United States and China focused on individualism vs. collectivism, democracy vs. communism, and capitalism vs. socialism. We find the distinctions less clear as China becomes more driven by capitalism and the United States emphasizes more collectivism.

Most women today are employed outside the home. Nancy Pelosi is Speaker of the House and Hillary Rodham Clinton, former first lady, is U.S. Senator from New York and ran for president in 2008. By the year 2010, the Millennial generation (born between 1982 and 2000) will outnumber both Baby Boomers and Gen-Xers. Millennials have been characterized as those raised in an era of technology, using the Internet, and who will be the most significant consumer sector for the media and entertainment industries. It is said that Millennials will want order, direction, and structure as they enter the workplace, and leaders/managers will need to learn how to give it (Howe and Strauss 2000). The attention to generational diversity will be important as they work alongside Generation-Xers and Baby Boomers. The complexity and interaction of these groups characterize the culture or zeitgeist of the twenty-first century.

Multinational corporations continue to flourish. By virtue of this organizational structure and the growing diversity within many countries throughout the world, leadership and business practices of necessity need to be informed by the diverse mix characterizing both its leaders and followers. A new generation of leaders, expatriates (i.e., those assigned to work for these multinational companies outside the U.S.) are provided financial incentives that both elevate and isolate them from the cultural and socioeconomic communities in which they live—in effect, creating a new elitist class.

The dawn of the twenty-first century found the United States facing more economic uncertainty and increased government regulation. The Sarbanes-Oxley Act of 2002 (Pub. L. No. 107–204, 116 Stat. 745) was enacted in response to a number of major corporate and accounting scandals including those affecting Enron that cost investors billions of dollars when the share prices of the affected companies collapsed and shook public confidence in the nation's securities markets. It is considered the most far-reaching set of reforms of American business practices in establishing new or enhanced standards for all U.S. public company boards, management, and public accounting firms. Kiechel and Sacha (1999) listed the following as trends that will reshape the workplace throughout the next decade:

- The average company will become smaller, employing fewer people.
- The traditional hierarchical organization will give way to a variety of organizational forms, the network of specialists foremost among these.
- Technicians, ranging from computer repairmen to radiation therapists, will replace manufacturing operatives as the worker elite.
- A horizontal division of labor will replace the vertical division.
- The paradigm of doing business will [continue] to shift from making a product to providing a service.
- Work itself will be redefined: constant learning, more high-order thinking, less nine-to-five.

Research on leadership suggests that transformational styles of leadership and authenticity are desirable for today's leader in a global and diverse society. This includes leadership vision, embracing the values and concerns of diversity, and promoting social justice goals. The growing interdependence, cultures of collaboration, and shared accountabilities among different groups highlight the importance of team approaches over individual solutions to leadership. With a growing emphasis on multiculturalism, global citizenry, diversity, and multiple perspectives, effective leadership is increasingly viewed as inclusive, empowering, collaborative, and authentic. The multinational, multicultural dimensionality of today's organizations requires leaders to be global in focus and sensitive to respecting people from around the world and from very diverse backgrounds, beliefs, and mores. This means becoming culturally literate and transculturally competent in a global world, with a growing focus on complexity and multidimensionality in today's world.

If leadership is co-created in vivo with the group, and if it is to meet the needs of a changing world, it must be interactive, dynamic, and contextual. Leader and group identities need to be aligned, and an understanding of group dynamics and the psychology of differences must inform the exercise of leadership. One might consider the following dimensions toward more inclusive models of leadership:

- Use collaboration as a process that draws on the relational aspects of women and collective characteristics of non-Western cultures.
- Understand the importance of contexts in weighing how the zeitgeist of historical and contemporary contexts drives what followers or a group wants from its leader. The fear of violence and rise in terrorism has meant that people want a leader who can make them feel safe. During economic downtime, that is, depression, fear of job loss, people want a leader who will guarantee prosperity or identify a suitable enemy, that is, scapegoat.
- Align leader and group identity toward multidimensionality and difference. During times of crisis, people are insecure and seek leaders who will build their identity and self-worth. The ideal leader will value differences, and avoid building this identity and self-worth of many at the expense of few, that is, marginalizing groups, creating out-groups, dehumanizing those who are different.
- Promote inclusion to empower all members, to ensure that all voices are heard, and to address the needs of all groups.
- Exercise transformational leadership, that is, have a vision for change, be values based to promulgate social justice goals, and subscribe to ethical principles and integrity in the conduct of leadership.

Though the experience for diverse leaders might be different, how they lead might also be different to incorporate and consider the complexities and needs of diverse followers. It will be increasingly difficult for leaders to capture the hearts and minds of diverse groups and followers unless they recognize, appreciate, and respond thoughtfully to the differences in these constituencies.

REFERENCES

Avolio, B. J., W. L. Gardner, F. O. Walumbwa, F. Luthans, and D. R. May. "Unlocking the Mask: A Look at the Process by Which Authentic Leaders Impact Follower Attitudes and Behavior." *The Leadership Quarterly* 15 (2004): 801–23.

Carnevale, A., L. J. Gainer, and A. S. Meltzer. *Workplace Basics: The Essential Skills Employers Want*. San Francisco, Calif.: Jossey-Bass, 1990.

Chin, J. L., and J. Sanchez-Hucles. "Comment: Diversity and Leadership." *American Psychologist* 62(6) (2007): 608–9.

Chin, J. L., B. Lott, J. K. Rice, and J. Sanchez-Hucles. *Women and Leadership: Transforming Visions and Diverse Voices*. Malden, Mass: Blackwell Publishing, 2007.

Coupland, D. *Generation X: Tales for an Accelerated Culture*. New York: St. Martin's Press, 1991.

Dovidio, J. F., and S. L. Gaertner. "Affirmative Action, Unintentional Racial Biases, and Intergroup Relations." *Journal of Social Issues* 52 (1996): 51–76.

Dulebohn J. H., G. R. Ferris, and J. T. Stodd. "The History and Evolution of Human Resource Management." In *Handbook of Human Resource Management*, edited by G. R. Ferris, S. D. Rosen, and D. T. Barnum, 18–41. Cambridge, Mass.: Blackwell Publishing, 1995.

Eagly, A. "Foreword." In *Women and Leadership: Transforming Visions and Diverse Voices*, edited by J. L. Chin, B. Lott, J. K. Rice, and J. Sanchez-Hucles, xvi-xix. Malden, Mass.: Blackwell Publishing, 2007.

———. *Sex Differences in Social Behavior*. Hillsdale, N.J.: Lawrence Erlbaum, 1987.

Eagly, A., and L. L. Carli. *Through the Labyrinth: The Truth about How Women Become Leaders*. Boston, Mass.: Harvard Business School Press Book, 2007.

Eagly, A., and B. Johnson. "Gender and Leadership Style: A Meta-Analysis." *Psychology Bulletin* 108 (1990): 233–56.

Eagly, A., and S. J. Karau. "Role Congruity Theory of Prejudice Toward Female Leaders." *Psychological Review* 109(3) (2002): 573–98.

Eagly, A., M. Makhijani, and B. Konsky. "Gender and the Evaluation of Leaders: A Meta-analysis." *Psychological Bulletin* 117 (1992): 125–45.

Ferris, G. R., D. A. Schellenberg, and R. F. Zammuto. "Human Resource Management Strategies in Declining Industries." *Human Resource Management* 23 (1984): 381–94.

George, William W. *True North: Discover Your Authentic Leadership*. San Francisco: Jossey-Bass, 2007.

Gillon, S. *Boomer Nation: The Largest and Richest Generation Ever, and How It Changed America*. New York: Free Press, 2004.

Hall, R. L., B. Garrett-Akinsanya, and M. Hucles. "Voices of Black Feminist Leaders: Making Spaces for Ourselves." In *Women and Leadership: Transforming Visions and Diverse Voices*, edited by J. L. Chin, B. Lott, J. K. Rice, and J. Sanchez-Hucles, 281–96. Malden, Mass.: Blackwell Publishing, 2007.

House, R. J. *Culture, Leadership, and Organizations: The GLOBE Study of 62 Societies*. Thousand Oaks, Calif.: Sage Publications, 2004.

Howe, N., and W. Strauss. *Millennials Rising: The Next Great Generation*. New York: Vintage Books, 2000.

Kao, H. S. R., D. Sinha, and B. Wilpert. *Management and Cultural Values: The In-digenization of Organizations in Asia.* Thousand Oaks, Calif.: Sage Publications, 1999.

Kawahara, D., E. M. Esnil, and J. Hsu. "Asian American Women Leaders: The Inter-section of Race, Gender, and Leadership." In *Women and Leadership: Transforming Visions and Diverse Voices,* edited by J. L. Chin, B. Lott, J. K. Rice, and J. Sanchez-Hucles, 297–313. Malden, Mass.: Blackwell Publishing, 2007.

Kidwell, C. S., D. J. Willis, D. Jones-Saumty, and D. S. Bigfoot "Feminist Leadership among American Indian Women." In *Women and Leadership: Transforming Visions and Diverse Voices,* edited by J. L. Chin, B. Lott, J. K. Rice, and J. Sanchez-Hucles, 314–29. Malden, Mass.: Blackwell Publishing, 2007.

Kochan, T., H. Katz, and B. McKersie. *The Transformation of American Industrial Rela-tions.* New York: Basic Books, 1986.

McGrory, M. "Pelosi's a Salve for a Wounded Party." *The Boston Globe,* November 16, 2002, A12.

Kiechel, W., and B. Sacha. "How Will We Work in the Year 2000?" *Fortune* 127 (1999): 21–44.

Klein, R., H., C. Rice, and V. Schermer, V. *Leadership in a Changing World: Dynamic Perspectives on Groups and Their Leaders.* Lanham, Md.: Lexington Books, 2009.

Northouse, P. G. *Leadership: Theory and Practice.* Thousand Oaks, Calif.: Sage Publi-cations, Inc, 2004.

Porter, N., and J. H. Daniel. "Developing Transformational Leaders: Theory to Practice." In *Women and Leadership: Transforming Visions and Diverse Voices,* edited by J. L. Chin, B. Lott, J. K. Rice, and J. Sanchez-Hucles, 245–63. Malden, Mass.: Blackwell Publishing, 2007.

Ragins, B., B. Townsend, and M. Mattis. "Gender Gap in the Executive Suite: CEOs and Female Executives Report on Breaking the Glass Ceiling." *Academy of Manage-ment Executive* 12 (1) 1998: 28–42.

Steele, C. M. "A Threat in the Air: How Stereotypes Shape Intellectual Identity and Performance." *American Psychologist* 52 (1997): 613–29.

Terry, G. *The Principles of Management.* Homewood, Ill.: Richard Irwin Inc., 1960.

Walton, R. E. "The Future of Human Resource Management: An Overview." In *HRM Trends and Challenges,* edited by R. E. Walton and P. R. Lawrences. Boston, Mass.: Harvard Business School Press, 1985.

Wikipedia. "Cleopatra VII." Http://En.Wikipedia.Org/Wiki/Cleopatra (accessed December 10, 2007).

Wikipedia. "Empress Dowager Cixi." Http://En.Wikipedia.Org/Wiki/Empress_ Dowager_Cixi (accessed December 10, 2007).

Wikipedia. "Joan of Arc." Http://En.Wikipedia.Org/Wiki/Joan_Of_Arc (accessed December 10, 2007).

Vroom, V. H., and A. G. Jago. "The Role of the Situation in Leadership." *American Psychologist* 6(1) (2007): 17–24.

Yalom, I. D., with M. Leszcz. *The Theory and Practice of Group Psychotherapy.* 5th ed. New York: Basic Books, 2005.

4

Some Psychoanalytic Views on Leaders with Narcissistic Personality Organization and Their Roles in Large-group Processes

Vamik D. Volkan

On June 1, 2002, about nine months after the terrorist attacks of September 11, 2001, President George W. Bush unveiled new policy guidelines for the United States that included military preemption, showing "strength beyond challenge," taking unilateral action, and extending "democracy, liberty, and security *to all* regions" (Bush 2002; italics added). From a psychological point of view, it is easy to see that these policy guidelines reflect omnipotence and entitlement as well as a link between an acute massive shared trauma (the September 11 attacks on American soil) and an ideological response to it (Volkan 2006). We can also wonder if the president's personality organization and motivations coming from his internal world influenced these guidelines. In any case, in just a few years time, we would witness the limits of omnipotence and entitlement.

People are usually interested in their political leaders' personality characteristics that *can be observed*—their thinking and feeling patterns, habitual behavior, modes of speech, and physical gestures. If a social crisis occurs or a catastrophic event takes place, the population's interest in the political leader's personality, among and outside the leader's followers, increases. In times of crises and terror, followers' shared expectations, conscious or unconscious, distort their perception of the leader's personality characteristics. For example, under such circumstances, as they search for a savior to ease their anxiety, the followers may see omnipotent characteristics in the leader. However, if the leader cannot help the followers differentiate where the real dangers end and where the fantasized dangers begin, a split takes place between those who continue to contaminate the leader's personality characteristics with omnipotence and those who now may see the leader as weak or arrogant, as someone who cannot ease shared anxiety. Proper separation between the two types of dangers, even when realistic danger exists and even increases, does not cause as much anxiety as when the public trust in the leader's ability to evaluate and communicate what is real and what is fantasized is eroded (Volkan 2004). The population on both sides of the split now focuses even more on an examination of the leader as a person and his or her personality characteristics. This situation existed in the United States in early 2008 when this chapter was written.

As deadly events continue in Iraq, there is more and more interest in President George Bush's personality organization, not only in the United States but also in many areas of the world. I suspect that many books will be written about President Bush's personal motivations for going to Iraq and about his handling the "war on terrorism." Such a book written by a psychoanalyst, Justin Frank (2004), a controversial one, already exists. Despite the interest in this topic, historians, political scientists, and scholars *in general* minimize the role of leaders' personalities when they investigate major world events and the rationale for political leaders' decision making in relation to such events. This is especially true concerning unconscious aspects.

Often political leaders themselves deny the possibility that their habitual way of behaving, thinking, feeling or their more hidden internal psychological motivations may give direction to events that begin major historical processes. One example comes from a dialogue between David Ben Gurion, considered the "father" of the state of Israel, and the Israeli historian Yehoshua Arieli. Apparently, Ben Gurion asked Arieli whether the personalities of political leaders were important in history. Arieli responded that the answer depended on many factors such as the times, historical conditions, the social and political system, and, of course, the individual's stature in government; his answer was a qualified "yes." Ben Gurion, however, interrupted Arieli by stating that history is made by the nation, not by leaders (Malkin and Zhahor 1992). I would have taken Arieli's side in his dramatic encounter with the legendary Israeli leader.

One reason for minimizing the role of a leader's personality in scholarly essays on historical or political processes—in spite of the general interest in this topic by people in the street, especially during times of crises or of lingering shared anxiety about societal welfare—may be due to the dominant role of the so-called rational actor models in international and domestic affairs, which support the assumption that a political leader's decision-making is logical and unaffected by psychological factors, especially within countries where democratic principles prevail. (For a review of such models see: Barner-Barry and Rosenwein 1985; Volkan et al. 1998.) President Bush and those around him have already maintained that decades from now when historians, political scientists, and other scholars look back at the war in Iraq, they will appreciate why the United States was involved in it and why it was carried out as it was. This implies that future historians, political scientists, and other scholars will examine the war in Iraq from the point of view of a "rational actor" model. I think that this assumption is true, even though I also believe that some books will be written that illustrate how Bush's personal psychological motivations influenced him to pursue "omnipotent" goals. Be that as it may, the examination of this historical event—at this time we do not yet know how it will end—by focusing on logical evaluations of rationalized assumptions will remain the routine method of understanding the incredible human tragedies associated with the war in Iraq.

The origin of rational actor models goes back to August L. von Rochau's (1853) description of *Realpolitik*. Such models, under different names, dominated thinking about political decision-making throughout the twentieth century, especially during the height of the Cold War, and still dominate how we analyze ethnic, national, religious, and ideological large groups' interactions with their leaders. These models focus on a rational calculation of cost and benefits; even theoretically, such models are based on a number of working assumptions. Rational calculations are also often used in political propaganda, which influences the public—even the scholars—to turn their attention toward logically explained data and avoid disturbing psychological considerations.

Political leaders do rationally process a great deal of data and information in the process of making decisions about policy and propaganda in international and domestic affairs, including what they perceive to be in the national interests, personal interest to maintain their power or keep their approval rating high, the "will of the people," the designs of foreign enemies, or domestic opposition. In fact, on many occasions, when the leader has few alternatives and the available information is concise and accurate, the issues at hand may be handled without the interference of psychological factors; when the decision maker's internal world is calm, rational actor models can be sufficient to explain his or her choices, and there is little need to probe into hidden psychological influences. However, when political decisions are made under especially complex or stressful conditions for the leader or for the large group he or she leads (i.e., national, ethnic, religious, ideological), rational actor models of political decision making often fall short as satisfactory explanations. At such times, leaders, according to their personality and especially their own internal psychological *organization* behind their personality characteristics, may tame or inflame various political or diplomatic processes.

Furthermore, when leaders' internal worlds are agitated due to their own personal perceptions, their macro political decisions may become "personalized"—that is, leaders may unconsciously equate the political or diplomatic circumstances at hand with an unresolved personal conflict or may otherwise be influenced by personal desires and inhibitions, strong emotions, and unconscious fantasies. Indeed, during certain critical moments, a single person's internal psychological organization can definitely shape historic decisions and with long-ranging consequences—even in countries such as the United States where governmental systems of checks and balances substantially protect political processes from individual leaders' personality organizations. It is in such moments that a leader's personality proves to be what the distinguished political theoretician Robert Tucker has called "a decisive trifle" (1973, p. xi).

Generally when an ethnic, national, religious, or ideological large group is *regressed* (Volkan 2001, 2004, 2006) the "fit" between a large group and a political leader with exaggerated self-love (narcissism) is likely to be strongest: the narcissistic leader's belief in his or her own superior power, intelligence, and omnipotence creates comfort for the regressed large group and an illusion of safety. Thus, the followers use the narcissistic leader's personality as an "antidote" for shared anxiety. In turn, leaders with narcissistic personality organization use the dependency and adoration of their regressed followers as one way to protect and maintain their grandiosity and hide their own dependency needs. Leaders are then inclined to manipulate, in an exaggerated manner, the societal and political signs of large-group regression (Volkan 2001) consciously, but more importantly, unconsciously. The shared psychological processes of members of a large group dovetail with the internal psychological processes of leaders with narcissistic personality organization. They, in turn, tame or inflame large-group regression along with its signs or symptoms. However, there may also be occasions when such leaders bypass the "wishes" of the large group and make decisions that can lead to the initiation of some historical process, even drastic ones. In this case what counts primarily is not the "fit" between leader and followers but the leaders' own attempts to find solutions for their inner demands by using the historical arena.

The relationship between political leaders and their followers is rather like a busy street. In normal times, the traffic—information and political decision-making as well as other means of influence—flows smoothly in both directions between the leaders' influence and the public's awareness. Naturally, the flow is sometimes greater in one direction and sometimes in the other, as at rush hour on a busy highway. At other times, however, for one reason or another, the street is officially declared "one-way" from leader to public, as seen in the political propaganda of totalitarian regimes. Even in democratic countries, during times of crisis and terror as witnessed following September 11, 2001, in the U.S.A., there was more focus on the "traffic" traveling from the leader/government to the public, since the public was seeking a "savior" to protect them.

In this chapter, I first define what I mean by the term "large group" and its regression and then illustrate the "fit" between a leader with narcissistic personality organization and the leader's regressed followers and how such a leader manipulates the signs and symptoms of large-group regression and becomes "reparative" or "destructive." If communication is a two-way street, the leader with a narcissistic personality organization often sends more traffic from the leader/government to the public than the other way around. Because we still need the test of time to evaluate President George W. Bush's personal motivations—when or if substantial data about them becomes available—in this chapter, my examples come from those political leaders who are long gone and about whom we do possess enough material to make psychological formulations without too many "countertransference" reactions.

WHAT IS A "LARGE GROUP"?

Beginning with Sigmund Freud (1921), many psychoanalysts wrote about mass psychology and examined political propaganda, wars, and post-war conditions. This vast topic will not be reviewed in detail here (for a review, see Volkan 2004). Because of their clinical interests, psychoanalysts in general focused more on examining small groups and the psychodynamics involved when seven to fifteen individuals got together for a series of meetings. Wilfred Bion's work (1959) is among the best known of such studies. A "small group" with a definite leader, a structured task, and an awareness of time evolves as a "work group" and performs the task with an adaptation to reality. When such a group's security is threatened or when it is not given a realistic and structured task, it begins to function according to certain "basic assumptions," which Bion described in detail.

In psychoanalytic literature the term "large group" sometimes refers to 30 to 150 members who meet regularly in order to deal with a given task. When the task given to such "large groups" is unstructured and vague by design, the "large group" regresses. At this time, observers notice increased anxiety, chaos, and panic among its members (Rice 1965, 1969; Turquet 1975). Otto Kernberg (2003a, b) noted that to escape its panicky atmosphere, regressed "large groups" exhibit narcissistic or paranoid characteristics and reorganize themselves by sharing and using primitive mental mechanisms. Kernberg states that whether a panic-stricken "large group" will evolve narcissistic or paranoid reorganization depends on the existing sociocultural environment, realistic external pressures, and constraints affecting the members' economic, social, or political well-being. Kernberg's description of narcissistic reorganization of chaotic regressed "large groups" corresponds to Bion's (1961) observations of "dependent basic assumption" small groups. "Large groups" in their attempts at narcissistic reorganization seek an omnipotent narcissistic leader, idealizing this leader while acting out a "parasitic dependency" (Kernberg 2003a, p. 685). Kernberg's description of paranoid reorganization of chaotic regressed "large groups," on the other hand, corresponds to Bion's (1961) "fight-flight basic assumption" small groups. If the group's reorganization is in the paranoid direction, the "large group" seeks a leader who is hypersuspicious and ready to fight against enemies as they are defined by the leader or the followers.

Kernberg uses the term "large group" when he refers to groups composed of 30 to 150 individuals. He uses the term "crowds" when he refers to spectators at a big sports event or large theatrical performance. He reminds us that there are no "empirical studies" on regression in "unstructured crowds" (Kernberg 2003a, p. 687). But, he describes how during some festive occasions unstructured crowds can disintegrate and become panic-stricken. He also mentions disorganization in crowds after natural disasters and then speaks of mass movements, societal and cultural processes. Kernberg primarily illustrates the emergence of aggression in small groups, "large groups," crowds, and societies when regression and disorganization sets in. "The dread of the consequences of such aggression mobilizes defenses of a narcissistic or paranoid kind" (p. 687).

In this chapter, my focus is on ethnic, national, or religious groups and I use the term *large group* only to refer to tens, hundreds of thousands, or even millions of individuals. Paraphrasing Erik Erikson's (1956) statement about personal identity, I use the phrase *large-group identity* to refer to a group that shares a permanent sense of sameness while also sharing certain similar characteristics with other large groups. Ethnic, national, or religious large-group psychodynamics are different from the psychodynamics of small groups, "large groups" (composed of 30 to 150 people), or crowds. For example, a crowd in a football stadium becomes a group and remains so just before, during, and perhaps soon after the sports event. On the other hand, let us consider an ethnic large group. The membership in such a group begins in childhood. For practical purposes, the identity of such a large group functions as a "second skin" for every member, most of whom will never see each other or even be at the same location during their lifetimes. Furthermore, each individual's *core* personal identity is intertwined with the large-group identity, and mental images of the group's history, myths, songs, food, dance, heroes, or martyrs connect them at all times. Members also, in general, share certain projections whereby they label "others" enemies or allies. (For details see Volkan 1988, 1999, 2004.)

Under certain external conditions, large ethnic, national, or religious groups also regress. When large-group regression sets in, the ethnic, religious, or national large groups become involved in certain processes that serve to maintain, protect, and repair their identities. What Kernberg wrote about the mobilization of narcissistic or paranoid defenses and the search for narcissistic or paranoid leaders in all kinds of groups, crowds, and masses, is also applicable to the regression of ethnic, national, or religious groups. Since such large groups have their own specific characteristics, often built upon a centuries-old continuum, the examination of the signs and symptoms of their regression should also include psychological processes that are *specific* to such large groups. Political leaders will consciously or unconsciously manipulate such specific signs and symptoms, to secure the large-group identity in peaceful or destructive ways.

Large-group Regression

Temporary or lasting *individual regressions* after a traumatic external event are often clearly observable. For many weeks following September 11, 2001, a woman who lived outside New York City, for example, found herself eating only macaroni and cheese. The woman's eating behavior represented a personal regression—macaroni and cheese is a dish commonly eaten by American children, and in fact, when the woman was a child, her mother used to give her some whenever she felt anxious. After September 11, the daughter knew intellectually that her mother, who lived in New York City, had survived the World Trade Center attack, but unconsciously she feared that she had died or had come close to death. By eating only macaroni and cheese, the daughter was exhibiting a regression that kept her mother "alive." Some weeks later, her mother came to visit, and after actually seeing her, the daughter gave up obsessively eating macaroni and cheese. She now "knew" that her mother was alive. Less drastic regressions and progressions are also part of normal daily life for most of us. It is only when regression becomes stubborn and long lasting that we speak of psychological difficulties.

For the focus of this chapter, I now turn my attention to *regression in large groups* when a majority of group members are exposed to a massive trauma that produces shared anxieties, expectations, and thought and action patterns. Some signs of large-group regression have been known since Freud (1921). Robert Waelder (1971) wrote that Freud's theories are mostly applicable to regressed groups where group members lose their individuality and rally blindly around their leader. We also know that within regressed groups, *severe* splits occur between those who follow the leader and those who oppose (usually secretly) the leader. For example, during the large-group regression under the dictator Enver Hoxha, Albanians were divided into "good" families and families with "black spots" (Volkan 2004). The regressed followers also sharply separate themselves from other (enemy) groups, experience magical thinking, and focus on minor differences that separate the group from "others" (Volkan 2001).

Some signs of regressed groups lead to the creation of societal processes that are very *specific* to the group in question. Here, I refer only to key specific signs and symptoms: the exaggerated reactivations of groups' "chosen glories," "chosen traumas," and "purification."

Chosen glories are the shared mental representations of events and heroes which, when activated, increase self-esteem among group members. Such events and the persons associated with them are heavily mythologized over time and these mental representations become large-group markers. Chosen glories are passed on to succeeding generations through transgenerational transmissions made in parent/teacher–child interactions and through participation in ritualistic ceremonies recalling past successful events. They link children of a large group with each other and with their group, and the children experience increased self-esteem by being associated with such glories.

In times of stress, war or war-like situations when the large group is regressed, political leaders may exaggerate chosen glories and use them to mobilize the masses. During the Gulf War, Saddam Hussein depended heavily on chosen glories and even associated himself with Sultan Saladin who had defeated the Christian crusaders in the twelfth century. Through the reactivation of a past event and a past hero, Saddam aimed to create the illusion that a similar triumphal destiny was awaiting his people and that, like Saladin, he was a hero. It did not matter to Saddam that Saladin was not an Arab, but a Kurd, and ruled from Egypt rather than Iraq. However, both Saladin and Saddam were born in Tikrit. This was enough for Saddam to associate himself with the glory of Saladin. All that mattered was that the foreign invaders had been defeated in the past and would be defeated again.

Chosen trauma refers to the mental representation of an event that has caused a large group to face drastic losses, feel helpless and victimized by another group, and share a humiliating injury (Volkan 1991; Volkan and Itzkowitz 1994). Although each individual in a traumatized large group has his or her own unique core identity and personal reaction to trauma, all members share the mental representations of the tragedies that have befallen the group. Their injured self-images associated with their mental representation of the shared traumatic event are "deposited" into the developing self-representation of children, as if these children will mourn the loss associated with the previous generation's massive trauma, reverse the humiliation or turn passivity into activity. If the children cannot deal with what is deposited in them and its associated tasks, these children, as adults, will in turn pass the mental representation of the event and tasks to the next generation. The chosen trauma emerges as a crucial large-group marker, as the shared representations of the event and tasks create an invisible link between its community members, passed down generation to generation.

Because they involve attempted resolutions of unconsciously given tasks, chosen traumas influence the large-group identity more pervasively than chosen glories. Chosen traumas bring with them powerful experiences of loss and feelings of humiliation, vengeance, and hatred that trigger within the group's members a variety of shared defense mechanisms that attempt to reverse these experiences and feelings. They therefore differ significantly from chosen glories, in which facts may become embellished or mythologized, but there is no need to reverse the images of experiences and feelings handed down by ancestors.

During times of stress, when the ethnic, national, or religious group's identity is threatened, chosen traumas are reactivated and can be used by leaders to inflame the group's shared feelings about themselves and their enemy. A *time collapse* occurs and the chosen trauma is then experienced as if it happened only yesterday: feelings, perceptions, and expectations associated with a past event and past enemy heavily contaminate those related to current events and current enemies, leading to maladaptive group behavior, irrational decision-making, and resistances to change. Earlier I (Volkan 1997) described in detail how Slobodan Milošević and those who assisted him created a propaganda machine in which the Serbian chosen trauma (the 1389 Battle of Kosovo) was exaggerated and reactivated, resulting in a time collapse. Atrocities that took place against Bosniaks and Kosovar Albanians built an emotional foundation made possible with such a time collapse.

The regressed group, such as Milošević's followers, became involved in a ritual, which I call *"purification"* (Volkan 2001, 2004). In "purification" the regressed large group becomes like a snake that sheds its skin: unwanted elements within the group or elements that may contaminate the group are discarded to allow the group to deal with shared anxiety stemming from threats against the large-group identity. How a large group "purifies" itself is a specific process unique to that group alone. The process of purification may be benign, as when a group discards an outmoded shared symbol, or malignant, as in ethnic cleansing. It is an activity characteristic of a large group in transition, seeking to crystallize a "new" or modified identity when its existing identity is threatened by regression, and also when it attempts to move out of regression.

An example of benign purification appeared when, after the Greek war of independence in the 1830s, Greeks expelled from their language Turkish words that had been in use for centuries while they were part of the Ottoman Empire. An example of malignant purification, on the other hand, took place in the former Yugoslavia in the 1990s with cultural cleansing (such as the destruction of mosques and centuries-old libraries) and ethnic cleansing of Bosniaks from certain areas.

Leaders with narcissistic personality organization utilize the demands of their personality organization to manipulate regressed large groups' signs

and symptoms, especially specific ones pertaining to their regressed followers, by reactivating the group's chosen glory or chosen trauma, and directing
the purification rituals in harmless or most destructive ways. Since leaders
with narcissistic personality organization are prone to respond to feelings of
humiliation, shame, inferiority, or envy with anxiety and often with aggression, their decision-making at times cannot be simply explained by calling
it rational actor model decision-making and/or simple initiation of political,
diplomatic, or even military actions. Leaders with narcissistic personality
organization, especially under conditions stressful for their groups and/or
for themselves, utilize large group's chosen glories and chosen traumas as a
response to their own internal make-up. For example, the chosen glories are
personalized to support such a leader's grandiosity. Chosen traumas may
actually represent images of their humiliated and helpless selves. The leader
may attempt to reverse such personal feelings by initiating or supporting the
"reversal" of chosen traumas on the historical arena. "Purification" can also
be personalized and the leader may modify or destroy people or things in
the outside world to remove perceived threats against his grandiosity.

"REPARATIVE" OR "DESTRUCTIVE" LEADERS WITH
NARCISSISTIC PERSONALITY ORGANIZATION

"Narcissism," of course, is not a "bad word" and is as normal in human psychology as are sexual or aggressive desires and natural anxiety about internal
conflicts. Indeed, healthy narcissism is necessary for anyone to survive, work,
and maintain a solid identity. But narcissism is also subject to frustrations,
which may lead to unhealthy weakened or inflated self-love (Weigert 1967).
It is when people have *exaggerated* love of self that they exhibit the repeated
thought, behavior, and feeling patterns that in combination are called *narcissistic personality*. Such individuals think that they are unique and grand,
which causes them to feel omnipotent and to act as though they are better
than anyone else. But people with narcissistic personalities live in a paradox:
while they love themselves too much and feel grandiose and omnipotent,
they also, in the shadows so to speak, possess an aspect that is devalued and
"hungry" for love. Periodically, this hunger asserts itself into awareness and
creates anxiety, shame, or humiliation in the person. Accordingly, such individuals' personality organization splits between a *grandiose self* and a *hungry
self*. The splitting in the personality organization reflects a lack of cohesive
identity. The personality characteristics reflecting the grandiose self are *overt*,
while those characteristics reflecting the hungry self are *covert* (Akhtar 1992;
Kernberg 1975; Volkan and Ast 1994).

Volkan and Ast (1994) referred to political leaders with narcissistic
personality organization as "successful narcissists": they are successful in

manipulating their external environment and finding a "fit" between their internal demands and external realities. Thus, by manipulating their external world, including their followers and enemies, they attempt to secure the protection and maintenance of their grandiose selves. Some political leaders, under historical circumstances, in fact may remain "successful" for decades or even for their lifetimes after becoming leaders. Others may remain "successful" for shorter periods of time. This manipulation of the external environment results in leaders with exaggerated narcissism becoming either "reparative" or "destructive."

By the term *reparative,* I refer to leaders with narcissistic personality organization who dedicate themselves to taking their followers out of their regressed state and changing their internal and external worlds to lift up the followers' individual self-esteem and modify their large-group identity. Reparative narcissistic leaders achieve these tasks, or try to achieve them, without mass killings of any group of people. By the term *destructive,* I refer to leaders with narcissistic personality organization who resort to mass destruction of an "outside" group, while influencing their followers who go along with supporting such destructive acts, to remain in a regressed state. These leaders, too, attempt to lift up their followers' self-esteem and modify their large-group identity, but only by comparing themselves with the group targeted for destruction.

Both types of leaders choose "chosen glories," "chosen traumas," or both to stimulate large-group identity, depending on their desire to inflame shared mental images of recent traumas. Both make extensive use of "purification" rituals to modify the existing large-group identity. Both may destroy some of the group's old symbols or "protosymbols" (Werner and Kaplan 1963) and change cultural values and customs. But in the long run, what makes one type of leader with narcissistic personality organization reparative or the other type destructive depends on how they target a selected "outside" group (even one within the same legal boundary) for destruction. At times, it may be difficult to differentiate between the two types of leaders with narcissistic personality organization. Indeed, a reparative leader may later become a destructive one.

For leaders with narcissistic personality organization to become "successful"—whether they are reparative, destructive, or both does not matter—they have to not only have the necessary intelligence but also the necessary ego functions to test existing realities in the environment and manipulate them. Some narcissistic individuals become leaders because their grandiose selves push them to excel and be "number one." Others may not have typical narcissistic personality organization initially, but historical circumstances (the external world) change them. Narcissistic characteristics may evolve, become internalized and assimilated, as they learn to "love" power and being "number one." For example, leaders who remain in power for decades, such as Cuba's Fidel Castro or Libya's Muammer Khadafi—whether originally they had *typical* narcissistic personality organizations or not—ended up behaving to one degree or another as "successful narcissists." Their cases should be included in any study of political leaders with narcissistic personality organization.

In the next section, I provide the metaphor of a baked apple pie (Volkan 2004) to illustrate the internal map of narcissistic leaders' personality organization and the psychodynamics of processes that make them reparative, destructive, or both.

INFLUENCING LARGE-GROUP PROCESS
WHILE LIVING UNDER A "GLASS BUBBLE"

Let us create a model of the mind of a person with narcissistic personality organization. Imagine serving a freshly baked apple pie. While placing the pie on the dinner table, a bottle of salty salad dressing spills and soaks a small section of the pie. To protect the edible and larger section of the pie, we cut off the spoiled section and push it to the periphery of the serving plate. The large, edible piece symbolizes the portion of the narcissistic leader's self-image that is invested with exaggerated self-love (grandiose self); the smaller, spoiled piece stands for the individual's devalued aspects (hungry self). Because people with narcissistic personality organization are unable to integrate the inflated, grandiose part of themselves with the devalued, humiliated aspects, it becomes essential that the "good" piece not touch the "spoiled" piece (splitting).

The large, good part of the pie must be protected at all times. Individuals with narcissistic personality characteristics often have conscious or unconscious fantasies of living gloriously alone under what I call a "glass bubble" (Volkan 1979), pushing the spoiled slice even further away and covering the large piece with a transparent protective dome. One such person literally referred to herself as a beautiful flower under glass, but the "glass bubble" often appears in symbolic ways, such as in the case of an individual who repeatedly fantasized himself as being Robinson Crusoe *without* his Man Friday. There was no need to have Friday around because the patient believed himself omnipotent; the sea surrounding the Island of Juan Fernandez functioned as a "glass bubble."

Political leaders with narcissistic personality organization often need "cronies" or special people who are given unspoken tasks to become a "glass bubble" around the leader. Such "cronies" or special people see that the leader's grandiose self is safe and impenetrable. With Norman Itzkowitz, Andrew Dod and I wrote a psychobiography of the thirty-seventh president of the United States, Richard Nixon (Volkan, Itzkowitz, and Dod 1997), and, I believe, we clearly illustrated that Nixon had a narcissistic personality organization. What became known as the "Nixon Method" of presidency reflected a "glass bubble" syndrome. Some individuals in Nixon's entourage such as H. Robert Haldeman and John Ehrlichman developed functions above and beyond their actual political duties in response to Nixon's need for splendid isolation. It is no wonder they were nicknamed the "Berlin Wall" surrounding the leader's lonely internal kingdom. In *The Making of the President,* Theodore White writes that he saw Nixon stroll down New York City's Fifth Avenue one day, "smiling as if amused by some inner conversation. His habit of great concentration lent itself to inner colloquy" (White 1969, p. 53).

But, pushing the spoiled piece of pie to the edge of the plate and covering the good piece of pie with a "glass bubble" is not enough. A person with a narcissistic personality organization is constantly aware of the "hungry self," which needs to be controlled to avoid anxiety, shame, humiliation, and/or helplessness. The main defensive task of such a person's ego is to control the internal relationship between the grandiose and hungry selves. A political leader with a narcissistic personality organization applies various ego tasks to deal with the spoiled piece of pie, as it reflects in the leader's political decision-making, leader-followers or leader-"enemy" interactions and historical processes. Dealing with the spoiled piece of pie in one way makes the leader with a narcissistic personality organization "reparative." Returning to our apple pie metaphor, the reparative leader tries to wipe the salad dressing from the spoiled piece or attempts to sweeten it and improve it enough to allow it to remain on the same plate as the unspoiled piece and perhaps even to touch it. Such a leader wishes for his or her followers to achieve an imagined and hoped for high level of functioning to reflect the leader's shining self-image and be extensions of his or her superiority. One of the best examples of reparative leaders with narcissistic personality organization is Kemal Atatürk, the founder of modern Turkey.

Norman Itzkowitz and I wrote an extensive psychobiography of this Turkish leader (Volkan and Itzkowitz 1984). A brief summary of Atatürk's life as it appears in conventional history is as follows: Mustafa was born in 1881 in Selanik (now Thessaloniki, Greece), a port city of the Ottoman Empire. His father, a customs clerk and small businessman, died when the boy was seven years old. Mustafa left home as a young teenager to enter military school where a teacher gave him a second name, Kemal (meaning "perfection"). He graduated near the top of his class. Although he became an officer in the Ottoman military, he was critical of the Sultan and became active in antigovernment organizations. After distinguished service in World War I, highlighted by his heroic leadership against Allied forces at Gallipoli, he was promoted to the rank of general at the age of thirty-five. As Allied forces threatened to overrun what remained of the Ottoman Empire after World War I and the Sultan proved powerless to fend off Italian, French, British, and Greek incursions, Kemal sought to salvage Turkish independence. He left Istanbul for Anatolia, the "heartland" of the Turkish people, and organized an army to resist invading Greek forces. Fearing Kemal's growing power, the Sultan, under pressure from the Allies, ordered his dismissal, prompting Kemal to establish a provisional nationalist government in Ankara, to which he was elected leader. While in Ankara, then only a provincial town, Kemal planned campaigns against the Greeks, who had invaded Anatolia, and ultimately defeated them in 1922, leading to a peace agreement with the Allies. The Sultan went into exile, and modern Turkey was established in 1923 with Kemal as its leader. After coming to power, Kemal adopted the surname "Atatürk," meaning "Father Turk." As the first president of the Turkish Republic, he instituted drastic political and cultural changes to modernize and secularize Turkey: abolishing the Caliphate, dismantling Islamic law and curtailing religious influences over the state, instituting a legal system based on European models, emancipating women, replacing Arabic script with the Latin alphabet, and instituting modern economic procedures. According to a generally held Turkish belief, Atatürk almost single-handedly inspired his war-weary country to reestablish its independence and create a new Turkish identity through cultural revolution. Though he died in 1938, he was venerated in an extraordinary way in Turkey as though he still lives until recent years when a religious party won elections in Turkey and attempts were made to diminish the influence of Atatürk's image on Turkish political life. Even now, many secular Turks simply refer to him as Ata (father) or Atam (my father), and he is immortalized as "The Eternal Leader."

Without providing any further history here, I wish to highlight how Atatürk in his own words described how he developed a narcissistic personality organization during his childhood and how he sensed his wish to be "reparative." He was born into a house of death (i.e., his three siblings before him had died), and he had a grieving mother. After he was born, his mother gave birth to two more siblings, and one of them also died in early childhood, this in addition to the death of his father. The following statement, made when he was an adult, reflects his premature maturation, or the defensive inflation of his grandiose self:

> Since my childhood, in my home, I have not liked being together with either my mother or sister, or a friend. I have always preferred to be alone and independent, and have lived this way always. . . . Because when one is given advice one has either to accept and obey it—or disregard it altogether. Neither response seems right to me. Wouldn't it be a regressive retreat to the past to heed a warning given to me by my mother who is more than 20 or 25 years older than I? Yet were I to rebel against it I would break the heart of my mother, in whose virtue and lofty womanhood I have the firmest belief. (Quoted in Aydemir 1969, vol. 3, p. 482)

Atatürk saw himself as above others—and his followers perceived him as such. He did not, however, seek fantasized enemies or subgroups to devalue or destroy in order to remain superior. His narcissism expressed itself quite differently:

> Why, after my years of education, after studying civilizations and the socializing processes, should I descend to the level of common people? I will make them rise to my level. *Let me not resemble them; they should resemble me!* (Quoted in Aydemir 1969, vol. 3, p. 482; italics added)

Modern Turkey was born in 1923 upon the ashes of the Ottoman Empire, which, during its last century, continually lost ground to its enemies, mostly Westerners. When Atatürk came to power he, unlike Slobodan Milošević of more recent times, did not focus on reactivating a chosen trauma, initiating time collapse as entitlement for revenge. The "chosen trauma" that he focused on was the regression of his own society under the Ottoman Empire. Thus, instead of preaching revenge, he pushed the enemies' (the Westerners') ideals as a solution for his own people's progression. It is beyond the point here to discuss how well Atatürk succeeded in modernizing Turkey. My focus is on his attempt to raise the self-esteem of his followers, whom he perceived as "hungry" for a better life. He sweetened the spoiled piece of pie.

Some may object to my characterization of Atatürk's actions as reparative: some may see Atatürk as a micromanager of his followers' behavior, perhaps even a Westernizer for Westernization's sake. He also initiated "purification": getting rid of many existing societal, cultural, and religious traditions or customs. Atatürk's secularization program could be said to have interrupted existing family and child-rearing practices, causing another type of societal regression. The Islamic law used in matters of marriage, divorce, and inheritance during the Ottoman period, however, had been very unfavorable to women, and Atatürk believed that "[a] bad family life inevitably leads to social, economic, and political enfeeblement. The male and female elements constituting the family must be in full possession of their natural rights and must be in a position to discharge their family obligations" (Atatürk 1952, vol. 2, p. 183). Atatürk sought to remove existing burdens from his followers' minds so they could function more creatively and productively. Though his innovations sometimes required legal enforcement, their intent and effects were always to enhance his followers' personal autonomy, to turn the existing societal regression into progression. Although Atatürk was indeed a lonely man internally, he did not have paranoid characteristics; he willingly exposed himself and his "glass bubble" to the public.

The opposite of a reparative narcissistic leader is one who is determined to destroy the spoiled piece of pie. For this leader, a destructive one, it is not enough to push the spoiled piece of pie further away from the good piece on the same plate or even "externalize" it onto another plate. The spoiled piece of pie has to be destroyed. Such a leader has "malignant narcissism" (Kernberg 1975; Volkan and Ast 1994). Here the observable characteristics of the grandiose self are accompanied by paranoid expectations and psychopathic elements.

There have been many attempts to understand the mind of the man who presided over the Holocaust, and scholars have reviewed the various possible psychological influences on the formation of Hitler's personality. Because so much is known about Hitler and the Third Reich, I will not attempt to present a psychobiography of Hitler. I will simply refer to the personality patterns that are reflected in his writings, such as *Mein Kampf* [*My Struggle*] (Hitler 1925, 1927). What we do know is that his ideology, propaganda, and activities aimed to create two collectives: the first, the Nazis, who were supposed to be tough, grandiose, superior, and powerful; the second, Jews, "Gypsies," homosexuals, and others deemed sub- or even nonhuman. The idea that the latter group—the small piece of the pie—"had" to be destroyed, alone leads to the conclusion that Hitler's personality fits well with our understanding of the internal organization of malignant narcissism. Whichever "diagnosis" of Hitler's personality is the correct one does not matter for the purpose of this chapter. What I want to illustrate here is the reflection of a malignant narcissistic personality organization on a historical arena.

Hitler had an especially talented confederate in Joseph Goebbels, whom he appointed head of Nazi propaganda in 1928 and who is credited with creating the "Fuhrer myth" while he was Minister of Propaganda and Public Enlightenment (Propaganda und Volkssaufklarung) under the Third Reich (Bramsted 1965). Austrian historian Victor Reimann—who was arrested by the Nazis in 1940 and spent the next five years in Nazi prisons—observes, "The Hitler/Goebbels combination is perhaps unique in world history" (1976, p. 2). Goebbels was the architect of the "glass bubble" in which Hitler could maintain and hide his grandiose self where it could remain uncontaminated and unconnected with Nazi cruelties so that any atrocities that came to light could be blamed on others; "If only the Fuhrer knew became a byword in the Third Reich" (p. 6). Goebbels forbade jokes about the Fuhrer and sought to conceal Hitler's personal weaknesses: a god does not have weaknesses. Hitler's drawings and watercolors from his days as a struggling artist were collected so that no one could critique Hitler as an artist. Goebbels banned even the use of quotations from Hitler's *Mein Kampf* without the permission of his Propaganda Ministry.

It was Goebbels who was ultimately responsible for crafting Hitler's image and many of his signature gestures, Goebbels who made compulsory the use of the title "Fuhrer" and introduced the greeting "Heil Hitler." Goebbels saw to it that Hitler was presented as a "god" to the post-1919 Treaty of Versailles Germans, who had been humiliated, both materially and emotionally. Hitler's image in his "glass bubble" was that of a beneficent god, a friend of children and animals, a lover of nature, and a spotlessly clean person.

There were yet more explicit efforts to associate Hitler with God's image in German minds. Walter C. Langer reports German press notices "to the effect that, 'As [Hitler] spoke, one heard God's mantle rustle through the room'"; one German church group even passed a resolution stating that "Hitler's word is God's law, the decrees and laws which represent it possess divine authority" (1972, p. 64). The party adopted a creed that clearly echoed Christian professions of faith: "We all believe, on this earth, in Adolf Hitler, our Fuhrer, and we acknowledge that National Socialism is the only faith that brings salvation to our country" (p. 64). At the Nuremberg rally of September 1937, the inscription below a giant photograph of Hitler read, "In the beginning was the Word . . ." the opening line of the Gospel of John. On another occasion, a photographic portrait of Hitler surrounded by a halo appeared in the front window of each of the large art shops on the Unter den Linden in Berlin (p. 64).

It is clear, then, that even leaders with malignant narcissistic personality characteristics need special persons who become the "glass bubble" around the leader and maintain their own self-esteem by becoming extensions of the powerful leader. In turn, they help the leader protect the illusion that his or her grandiose self is safe and impenetrable. Followers carry out the demands of malignant destructive narcissism, as in Hitler's case, which "spares" the leader from feeling responsible for those acts of destruction. The malignant leader combines exaggerated narcissism with pathological paranoid and psychopathic characteristics. He is afraid that the bubble will become penetrable, allowing devalued or "dangerous" others to enter the leader's lonely kingdom. But this statement itself needs further scrutiny. Even Hitler showed "reparative" qualities. Nazis themselves, in Judith Stern's terms, were made into "small gods" by their imitation of Hitler (Stern 2001). In a sense, Hitler attempted to enhance the self-esteem of his followers. But, as a malignant narcissist, this reparative activity could only take place at the expense of other groups that were dehumanized and destroyed. Those followers that were made "little gods" were not actually given their personal "freedoms" but were used to enforce the leader's glass bubble.

Shame, Humiliation, and the Leader with Narcissistic Personality Organization

Volkan et al. (1999) suggested that a political leader's established personality organization tells us a great deal about how this person will respond to an external event that, in the leader's mind, becomes contaminated with an anxiety producing internal danger signal. Freud's (1926) series of situations dangerous to the ego of a growing child is well known. The first is fear of an actual loss of "mother." The second involves the loss of mother's love. The third, during the oedipal phase of life, is the loss of penis (castration anxiety). The fourth danger Freud proposes involves fear of not living up to the internalized expectations of the superego, thus loss of self-esteem. We can add a fifth fear for people with unintegrated self-representation: losing the "good" or idealized part of the self-representation by mixing it with the "bad" or devalued part—or, in the case of a narcissistic personality organization, losing the omnipotence of the grandiose self by synthesizing it with the devalued self and object images that comprise the "hungry self."

When political leaders "personalize" an external event and experience it as a *derivative* of one of these danger signals or various combinations of them, they may add a factor to political decision-making or action that emanates from their personality organizations. For example, for leaders with exaggerated obsessional personalities, the threat of a loss of control, such as over emotions or over balancing opposite elements, induces anxiety. They direct their energy toward achieving orderliness and predictability. When faced with a decision, especially under stressful conditions, obsessional people typically will try to find a solution by searching for some rule, principle, "morality," or external requirement to supply the "right answer" and reestablish "control" over frustrating external factors.

For leaders with narcissistic personality organizations, the danger signal is the threat against or the loss of the grandiose self, which includes derivatives of loss of mother, mother's love, body parts, and self-esteem. Such a danger signal for narcissistic leaders is accompanied by feelings of shame, humiliation, envy, and helplessness. These feelings cause the greatest threat to these leaders' mental equilibrium, so they avoid these feelings at all costs or, once they feel them, they may strike back at people or elements that directly or symbolically threaten their superiority. They defensively retreat into their glass bubbles even further to insure that no threatening people or images penetrate the protective dome.

A political scientist as well as a psychoanalyst, Blema Steinberg, has provided one of the best examples of how a narcissistic political leader's decision-making and actions relate to feelings of shame and humiliation. Steinberg (1996) meticulously documented various external events (not summarized in this chapter) that induced humiliation in President Richard Nixon, leading to his decision to bomb North Vietnamese sanctuaries in Cambodia in mid-March 1969 and the subsequent invasion of Cambodia in 1970. There is strong evidence that Nixon reached the decision to bomb Cambodia while he was in his "lonely kingdom" under a "glass bubble." We learn, for example, from Henry Kissinger that Nixon decided to bomb the Cambodian sanctuaries while in an airplane flying from Washington, D.C., to Brussels and that his decision was made without consulting the relevant advisors "in the absence of a detailed plan" (1979, p. 242).

The plane ride was the beginning of Nixon's ten-day ceremonial visit to Europe, which of course had been planned much earlier. The day before this flight, on February 22, 1969, the North Vietnamese had renewed their offensive actions. One can easily image, from a *Realpolitik* point of view, that Nixon's decision to bomb was a response to the renewed North Vietnamese offensive. At the time, Cambodia, a monarchy with seven million subjects, was trying to stay neutral, but the North Vietnamese had established sanctuaries in the border area between the two countries. Earlier, Nixon had examined research and intelligence which indicated that bombing these sanctuaries would drive the North Vietnamese further west, and deeper into Cambodia, perhaps eventually causing Cambodia to fall to the communist regime, and therefore he had decided not to attack the bases (Hersh 1983). So why did he change his mind suddenly without any consultations? There were factors emanating from his narcissistic personality organization (Volkan, Itzkowitz, and Dod 1997). To him, the North Vietnamese move "was a deliberate test, clearly designed to take the measure of me and my administration at the outset. My immediate instinct was to retaliate" (Nixon 1978, p. 380). Upon Kissinger's request, Nixon agreed to postpone his decision for forty-eight hours, and then later cancelled the original bombing plan. He ordered another strike on March 9, only to rescind it a second time. The first B-52 raid on North Vietnamese bases in Cambodia finally commenced on the morning of March 18. He kept the bombing secret from the American public and told Kissinger: "[The Department of] State is to be notified only after the point of no return" (Ambrose 1989, p. 258). Only after ordering the retaliation on North Vietnamese bases in Cambodia did Nixon meet with some of his advisors, giving them the impression that their input would be considered, even though the attack was a *fait accompli*.

For the focus of this chapter, what should interest us are the code names of the Cambodia bombings. The first one was code-named "Breakfast." The second attack in mid-April was code-named "Lunch." "Lunch," according to Kissinger, is based in part on another humiliating situation. This time, the desire was to retaliate against North Korea, which had recently shot down a U.S. spy plane: "But as always when suppressing his instinct for a jugular response, Nixon looked for some other place to demonstrate his mettle. There was nothing he feared more than to be thought weak" (1979, p. 247). I have no idea who came up with the code names pertaining to food. What comes to mind is that "Breakfast" and "Lunch" might be for Nixon's "hungry self." If his "hungry self" is fed, then his "grandiose self" will not be threatened. We also know that "Lunch" was succeeded by the code name "Dinner" and eventually expanded into an entire "Menu." It is beyond the purpose of this chapter to examine in detail the history after the attacks that were treated symbolically as "food," but Steinberg reminds us that Nixon's actions would have a powerful ripple effect: the U.S. invasion of Cambodia on May 1, 1970, marked the beginning of a full-fledged civil war that devastated Cambodia and killed more than a million people (1996, p. 206).

CONCLUDING REMARKS

The intensity of the thought, feeling, and behavior patterns in people with narcissistic personality organization changes according to the degree of their grandiosity. Some have chronic difficulty relating to others and at times have a blurred vision of reality. Those who also possess areas of integrated identity and have clearer perceptions of external realities—those who, alongside their belief in their superiority, know where to stop and what to pursue and how to separate where the realistic dangers end and fantasized dangers begin—are better adjusted to life and may become quite successful in the world's eyes. Indeed, for some individuals with narcissistic personality organization who actually are very smart, handsome, powerful, and effectively manipulative, their inner craving for achievement and applause often will direct them to leadership positions in education, business, social organizations, or politics. Such a person, as stated earlier, is a "successful narcissist." He or she values becoming "number one" in a group. For example, Richard Nixon's "need" to be "number one" remained constant throughout his adult life. He was elected president of the Whittier Alumni Association, the Duke University Alumni Association of California, the Orange County Association of Cities, and the 20-30 Club, all while still in his twenties. At the age of thirty-three, he was elected to Congress; at thirty-seven he became a U.S. Senator, and in 1952, at the age of thirty-nine, he became the second-youngest man to be elected vice president of the United States. He also collected "firsts," whether significant or *trivial*, from becoming the first U.S. president to visit the People's Republic of China to being the first candidate to visit a particular small rural town on the campaign trail. According to his aide, John Ehrlichman, "There was a running gag on a Nixon campaign; everything that happened was a "historic first" (Volkan, Itzkowitz, and Dod 1997, p. 94). Accumulating such "firsts" was a sign of his need to collect emotional nutrition for his grandiose self so that no one, not even himself, would know that his anxiety concerned the spoiled, unwanted part of the apple pie in his mind.

By "successful" political leader, I am *not* referring to the moral worth of their individual deeds but to the fact that they each were able to find an echo of their personalities in the external world by which they achieved primacy in the eyes of others. For successful leaders with narcissistic personality organization, a "fit" occurs between their internal demands and their followers' responses to them, especially when the followers are in a regressed state. Some such leaders are able to maintain that "fit" over an extended period of time, and some are not. Furthermore, it is difficult to judge if a political leader's decision, made while the leader is under a "glass bubble," is going to be reparative or destructive. For example, Egypt's Anwar Sadat—another leader with a narcissistic personality organization—used the "Nixon method" for making decisions: He would not depend on his advisors; he thought he knew better than anyone else and hence, he was a lonely decision maker. Sadat would go to his village about forty miles from Cairo and create his own "glass bubble": He would wear a *galibia*, smoke a pipe, and make major decisions all by himself, such as the one that initiated the visit to Israel when he spoke at the Knesset in 1979. Thus, making decisions while in a "glass bubble" does not mean that such a decision will be destructive. It can also be a decision that may lead to a kind of healing between enemies.

Sufficient narcissism, even exaggerated narcissism, I think, is necessary for a political leader to be an efficient leader. Narcissism makes a leader comfortable as "number one." Thus, I repeat: narcissism is not a bad word. But, it can also be used for the initiation of horrible events, especially if the large group to which the leader belongs is experiencing regression and perceives an entitlement for revenge for recent traumas and/or chosen traumas. If a leader with narcissistic personality organization reactivates and inflames a chosen trauma and helps create an atmosphere of time collapse and victimization, the possibility that a destructive event could evolve should be anticipated. When a generalized feeling of victimization settles in a large group, a sense of entitlement for striking out can follow. It is obviously doubtful that any future political leader will go through psychoanalysis before assuming power. On the other hand, psychoanalysts who seriously observe and study political processes and leader-followers interactions should speak out about danger signals coming from destructive leaders with narcissistic personality organization.

REFERENCES

Akhtar, S. *Broken Structures: Severe Personality Disorders and Their Treatment*. Northvale, N.J.: Jason Aronson, 1992.

Ambrose, S. E. *Nixon: The Triumph of a Politician, 1962–1972*. New York: Simon and Schuster, 1989.

Atatürk, K. *Atatürk' ün Söylev ve Demeçleri* [Speeches and Statements of Atatürk] (vols. 1–2). Istanbul: Türk Inkilâp Tarihi Enstitüsü, 1952.

Aydemir, S. *Tek Adam* [The Singular Man], vols. 1–3. Istanbul: Remzi Kitabevi, 1969.

Barner-Barry, C., and R. Rosenwein. *Psychological Perspectives on Politics*. Englewood Cliffs, N.J.: Prentice-Hall, 1985.

Bion, W. R. *Experiences in Groups*. London: Tavistock Publications, 1961.

Bramsted, E. K. *Goebbels and National Socialist Propaganda*. East Lansing, Mich.: Michigan State University Press, 1965.

Bush, G. W. Commencement Speech to the Graduating Class of West Point, June 1, 2002.

Erikson, E. H. "The Problem of Ego Identity." *Journal of the American Psychoanalytic Association* 4 (1956): 56–121.

Frank, J. *Bush on the Couch: Inside the Mind of the President*. New York: Regan Books, 2004.

Freud, S. "Group Psychology and the Analysis of the Ego." In *The Standard Edition of the Complete Psychological Works of Sigmund Freud*. Translated by J. Strachey, 18:63–143. London: The Hogarth Press, 1921/1955.

———. "Inhibitions, Symptoms and Anxiety." In *The Standard Edition of the Complete Psychological Works of Sigmund Freud*. Translated by J. Strachey, 20: 77–175. London: Hogarth Press, 1926/1959.

Hersh, S. M. *The Price of Power: Kissinger in the Nixon White House*. New York: Summit Books, 1983.

Hitler, A. *Mein Kampf* [My Struggle]. Boston: Houghton Mifflin Company, 1933.

Kernberg, O. F. *Borderline Conditions and Pathological Narcissism*. New York: Jason Aronson, 1975.

———. "Sanctioned Social Violence: A Psychoanalytic View—Part I." *The International Journal of Psycho-Analysis* 84 (2003a): 683–98.

———. "Sanctioned Social Violence: A Psychoanalytic View—Part II." *The International Journal of Psycho-Analysis* 84 (2003b): 953–68.

Kissinger, H. A. *The White House Years*. Boston: Little, Brown, 1979.

Langer, W. C. *The Mind of Adolf Hitler*. New York: Basic Books, 1972.

Malkin, E., and Z. Zhahor. *Leaders and Leadership: Collected Essays* (in Hebrew). Jerusalem: Zlaman Shezar Center and Israeli Historical Society, 1992.

Nixon, R. M. *RN: The Memoirs of Richard Nixon*. New York: Grosset and Dunlap, 1978.

Reimann, V. *Goebbels: The Man Who Created Hitler*. Translated by S. Wendt. New York: Doubleday, 1976.

Rice, A. K. "Individual, Group, and Intergroup Processes." *Human Relations* 22 (1969): 565–84.

———. *Learning for Leadership*. London: Tavistock, 1965.

Steinberg, B. *Shame and Humiliation: Presidential Decision-making on Vietnam, a Psychoanalytic Interpretation*. Montreal: McGill-Queen's University Press, 1996.

Stern, J. "Deviance in the Nazi Society." *Mind and Human Interaction* 12 (2001): 218–37.

Tucker, R. C. *Stalin as a Revolutionary, 1879–1929: A Study in History and Personality*. New York: Norton, 1973.

Turquet, P. "Threats to Identity in the Large Group." In *The Large Group: Dynamics and Therapy*, edited by L. Kreeger, 87–144. London: Constable, 1975.

Volkan, V. D. "The Glass Bubble of a Narcissistic Patient." In *Advances in Psychotherapy of the Borderline Patient*, edited by J. Le Boit and A. Capponi, 405-31. New York: Jason Aronson, 1979.

———. *The Need to Have Enemies and Allies: From Clinical Practice to International Relationships*. Northvale, N.J.: Jason Aronson, 1988.

———. "On 'Chosen Trauma.'" *Mind and Human Interaction* 3 (1991): 13.

———. *Bloodlines: From Ethnic Pride to Ethnic Terrorism*. New York: Farrar, Straus, and Giroux, 1997.

———. *Das Versagen der Diplomatie: zur Psychoanalyse nationaler, etnischer und religiöser Konflikte* [The Failure of Diplomacy: The psychoanalysis of National, Ethnic and Religious Conflicts]. Giessen, Germany: Psychosozial-Verlag, 1999.

———. "September 11 and Societal Regression." *Mind and Human Interaction* 12 (2001): 196-216.

———. *Blind Trust: Large Groups and Their Leaders in Times of Crises and Terror*. Charlottesville, Va.: Pitchstone Publishing, 2004.

———. *Killing in the Name of Identity: Stories of Bloody Conflicts*. Charlottesville, Va.: Pitchstone Publishing, 2006.

Volkan, V. D., and G. Ast. *Spektrum des Narcissmus* [Spectrum of Narcissism]. Göttingen: Vandenhoeck & Ruprecht, 1994.

Volkan, V. D., and N. Itzkowitz. *The Immortal Atatürk: A Psychobiography*. Chicago: University of Chicago Press, 1984.

Volkan, V. D., and N. Itzkowitz. *Turks and Greeks: Neighbours in Conflict*. Cambridgeshire, England: Eothen Press, 1994.

Volkan, V. D., N. Itzkowitz, and A. Dod. *Richard Nixon: A Psychobiography*. New York: Columbia University Press, 1997.

Volkan, V. D., A. Salman, R. M. Dorn, J. S. Kafka, O. F. Kernberg, P. A. Olsson, R. R. Rogers, and S. B. Shanfield. "The Psychodynamics of Leaders and Decision-making." *Mind and Human Interaction* 9 (1999): 129-81.

von Rochau, A. L. *Grundsätze der Realpolitik* [Basis of Realpolitik]. Frankfurt: Ullstein, 1853/1972.

Waelder, R. "Psychoanalysis and History." In *The Psychoanalytic Interpretation of History*, edited by B. B. Wolman, 3-22. New York: Basic Books, 1971.

Weigert, E. "Narcissism: Benign and Malignant Forms." In *Crosscurrents in Psychiatry and Psychoanalysis*, edited by R. W. Gibson, 222-38. Philadelphia: Lippincott, 1967.

Werner, H., and B. Kaplan. *Symbol Formation*. New York: Wiley, 1963.

White, T. H. *The Making of the President, 1968*. New York: Pocket Books, 1969.

II

CASE STUDIES

5

The Co-creation of Current and Prospective Political Leadership in America: 9/11, the Bush Years, and the 2008 Race for the Presidency

Harold S. Bernard and Robert H. Klein

Our purpose in this chapter is to consider the issue of leadership in the United States at this point in our history. We consider the current leadership of the U.S. as well as the prospective leadership of the country going forward, from a group dynamics (Bion 1959; Durkin 1981) and social systems (Klein, Bernard, and Singer 2002; von Bertalanffy 1968) point of view. Thus, our intention is to discuss the current leadership, and those who are offering themselves up to lead the country going forward, in relation to those they are seeking to lead: namely, the American populace.

We believe our framework is consistent with that of most of the authors who are contributing to this volume. We start from the assumption that leadership is co-created: that is, the leadership that emerges in a given place at a given time is a function of the interaction between the individuals who are leading, or are seeking to lead, a particular body politic, and the wishes and needs of that body politic, which exert a powerful influence on the nature of the leadership that is proposed and ultimately exerted. Implicit in this point of view is a developmental perspective: that is, there is an ongoing mutual regulatory system that is established, and that system is dynamic and unfolding, not static over time. Each response serves as a stimulus that influences every other response made by all participants in the system. Of course, it is never possible to completely tease out which comes first, the "chicken" or the "egg," nor is it always crucial to do so once a system is in operation. Nevertheless, to recognize the mutual influence that leaders and those they are leading have upon one another is invaluable.

When we talk about the American body politic, we will be talking about a large and in many ways disparate entity. Nevertheless, we believe it is legitimate to conceptualize American society as a large group. That is, there are dispositions, or inclinations, within American society that are predominant so that they can be said to characterize the group as a whole. An example would be the strong need to respond to the humiliation of the attacks of 9/11/01 (hereafter called 9/11) in ways that expressed our collective outrage and sought to recapture our collective pride. There were of course people within the body politic who did not feel this way, but the sentiment was widespread enough that we believe it characterized American society as a whole.

We have decided to limit our observations to the time frame between 9/11 and today. We hope that the reason for this is obvious. Clearly, the attacks on the United States on that day were an unprecedented event in our history. They were the first attacks on our soil by a foreign entity since the beginning of our republic more than 200 years ago. As such, they had a profound effect on our collective psyche, an effect we are still in the midst of dealing with. Thus, we see this event and its aftermath as a natural line of demarcation and will address the issue of leadership from this day forward. To a significant extent, the events of 9/11 constitute our "chosen trauma" (Volkan 1988, 1991, 2001, 2004) as a nation. Volkan uses this phrase to refer to the shared mental representation of an event by a large group that allows it to face drastic losses, feel helpless and victimized, and share a humiliating injury, all of which creates an invisible bond between and among community members. Whatever sense of impregnability we carried as a nation was lost on that day. We were caught unaware, whatever defensive systems we had in place proved completely inadequate, and almost 3,000 of our citizens were arbitrarily and brutally murdered. We were shocked, to be sure, and we had the necessity of trying to make sense of what had occurred and how to respond. As with any trauma, one of the most important aspects of recovery is that the victim (in this case our country) has to develop an account of what has occurred. It is not always possible to be certain about our account; when certainty is not achievable, victims need to arrive at the best account they can as part of the working-through process. Thus, there was a crying need for leadership: to help us develop an account of what had occurred, and to take the lead in formulating a response, or set of responses, that would help the populace express its collective outrage and regain its sense of pride as well as security.

When the possibility of further attacks and humiliation (i.e., when the trauma is not necessarily a one-time event) exists, the need for leadership is all the greater. In the case of the attacks of 9/11, the trauma was every bit as much about what might happen again in the future as it was about what had occurred on that day. One anecdotal piece of evidence will illustrate what we mean. Recently a colleague of ours had occasion to go to the top floor of a famous high-rise building in Manhattan and was struck by the anxiety this generated within him, noting that the attacks had occurred six and a half years earlier. Of course this particular individual spends some of his time in New York City, which is where the majority of the damage was done, and the majority of lives were lost, on that fateful day. However, there is substantial evidence that the fear that Americans still experience in the aftermath of 9/11 is not confined to people in any particular geographical location. The experience of travel has changed, as has the experience of entering into office buildings and other places where there are elaborate security systems in place that never existed before.

TRAUMA AND THE RESPONSES IT ELICITS

Traumatic events such as the attacks of 9/11 stimulate overwhelming fear, which in turn generates enormous anxiety (e.g., Herman 1997; Klein and Phillips 2008; Klein and Schermer 2000). Collectively, we are a nation that is much more fearful and anxious than we were prior to the attacks. As we know from both individual and group psychology, fear can induce regression. When this occurs, the tendency is to think in more primitive, black-and-white ways. There is less tolerance for nuance and ambiguity. Careful analytic thinking and well-tempered judgment diminishes. Raw, unfiltered emotions tend to hold sway.

One of the manifestations of this regression to a more primitive emotional state is the felt need to retaliate. Psychologically, retaliation (if it is successful) holds out the possibility of accomplishing numerous tasks:

1. Alleviating anxiety—all of the pent-up concerns about being victimized again get channeled into mounting a counterattack. Even though most members of society do not participate directly in this effort, the response is on behalf of the populace at large, and everyone within the populace has the opportunity to feel like a forceful response is being mounted on their behalf and that they are participating in it.
2. Expressing rage—those who were presumably responsible for the humiliation become the hated enemy, and the need to strike back at them becomes intense. Evidence for this in the aftermath of 9/11 is all the reports of bias and scapegoating against Muslims, regardless of their conduct and records of citizenship (Jacques 2007).
3. Overcoming feelings of helplessness—trauma victims invariably experience feelings of helplessness; the urge to escape from the passive position and to take action of any kind is enormously powerful.
4. Reducing shame about exposed vulnerability—one of the most difficult challenges for an individual or society whose vulnerability has been revealed is to find a way to overcome the loss of pride and

feeling of humiliation that is typically felt. The events of 9/11 made this a particularly daunting challenge. In essence, a relatively small group of very well-organized enemies of our country and everything it stands for brought us to our knees. We were obviously ill prepared, and the fact that the attackers killed themselves in the process of humiliating us, thereby making it impossible to take it out on them, and that their presumed leaders were elusive (and taunting as well), contributed to an enormous frustration. There was a strong need to retaliate to regain our pride in ourselves.

All this was prelude to what occurred in early 2003. While there were interim responses, the eighteen months or so between the attacks of 9/11 and the offensive that the U.S. launched against Saddam Hussein and the government of Iraq were largely spent preparing for that effort (Woodward 2002, 2004). There was the need to make demands that the Iraqi government would not meet to provide a justification for an offensive thrust. There was the need to develop a military plan, as well as to attempt to mobilize whatever international support could be garnered. But it was clear following the attacks of 9/11 that a powerful military response would be launched as soon as possible to respond to the strong need that the American public had to retaliate against those who had humiliated us. That the target chosen was not in fact those who had perpetrated the attacks was beside the point, given the frenzied need that existed to strike out against someone.

LEADERSHIP

Leading vs. Reflecting

Leadership is a much more complex matter than it might at first appear. At one level, it involves leading the way: setting out on a course and effectively influencing others to bring them along. However, if leaders attempt to do this and are too far out of touch with those they are leading, they will fail. "Buy in" occurs when people feel their leaders are representing their conscious and unconscious wishes and aspirations. Hence, effective leaders need to be aware of the sentiments of their constituents and embody those sentiments in the positions they take. Thus, a dynamic tension exists between two components of the responsibility of leaders: to set the course for those they are leading, while at the same time to represent the wishes and sentiments of their constituents. Of course, the leader's efforts to set a course partly shape these wishes and sentiments. However, if leaders or prospective leaders suggest approaches that are too far afield from the sentiments of their constituencies, they lose credibility and appeal. Thus, effective leadership involves successfully walking the tightrope of defining direction and at the same time responding to peoples' sense of what they need. From our perspective, we would say there has been an empathic failure, or a failure of proper attunement, demonstrated by the current leaders of our country.

This age-old tension is currently being debated in relation to the "superdelegates" who will be casting votes at the upcoming Democratic convention (Democratic National Committee 2007). By definition, they are not bound by the votes that have been cast in the states they will be representing at the convention. The rules allow them to consider whatever factors they choose in determining whom to support for their party's presidential nomination. However, there is substantial pressure on them to reflect the will of those who participated in their state's caucuses and primaries. If they do not reflect the voters' choice, they will be attacked for thwarting the wishes of the electorate and being "undemocratic." This is the case despite the fact that the vote in their states will have occurred months before they are voting, they may view the circumstances as having changed, and they are explicitly charged with using their best judgment at the time they are voting. It is not hard to understand why many superdelegates are struggling with how to discharge their responsibility. (Authors' note: This chapter was written in April 2008, well in advance of the selection of a Democratic presidential nominee.)

Attunement

An accurate empathic connection, or a healthy attunement, between leader and led is crucial. The importance of this was clearly illustrated by the dust-up that occurred during Senator Obama's quest for the Democratic nomination in relation to his former pastor, the Reverend Jeremiah A. Wright, Jr. The pastor had married Obama and baptized his children. The title of Obama's campaign book, *The Audacity of Hope* (2006), came from the title of a speech the Reverend delivered, and he had clearly played an important role in Obama's spiritual life for many years. Moreover, he was widely credited with many good works during his thirty plus years as head of his church. Thus, the Senator was resistant to disowning the Reverend or saying anything that would offend him.

At the same time, the Reverend's incendiary comments from the pulpit and then at a national press conference (April 28, 2008) raised deep fears within much of the American electorate (Sullivan 2008). Senator Obama's unwillingness to clearly break with the Reverend was threatening to undermine his painstaking work to convince Americans that he was indeed attuned with their wishes, needs, and perspectives. It contributed to a perception of the Senator as weak of will and perhaps also as a closet radical who, in his heart of hearts, hated America. There were other contributors to this concern within the electorate: the Senator's refusal to wear an American flag lapel pin, his wife's statement implying she had never felt proud of her country, and the (baseless) rumor that he was in fact a Muslim as opposed to a Christian. The apparent high regard in which Rev. Wright holds Rev. Louis Farrakhan raised still further concerns about Obama's beliefs in relation to race and U.S. policies. These associations might well lead many Americans to conclude that he, Obama, was a potentially dangerous leader as well whose position on a variety of important issues was misattuned and not reflective of theirs. Clearly, the Senator was called upon to take a stand to reassure people about who he really was.

This was especially true because of the Senator's vulnerability on a number of fronts. As a result of his association with Reverend Wright, he was no longer viewed as "above" or impervious to racial and religious considerations. It gave his opponents the opportunity to mobilize deeply held racial and religious fears and stereotypes, to his detriment. Through the operation of projective identification, various undesirable and frightening characteristics could be projectively located in him. In addition, because of his relative lack of political and leadership experience, plus the fact that he has authored two successful books (Obama 1995, 2006), he could be labeled an "egghead," or even "an effete intellectual snob," the term Spiro Agnew coined more than thirty years ago. Again through the operation of projective identification, latent fears and distrust along with an anti-intellectual backlash were triggered. There is evidence that the Senator recognizes this danger and is working to counteract it (Powell and Zeleny 2008). Recently, one of us spotted the following bumper sticker: "My bulldog is smarter than your honor roll student." Whether intended or not, this could serve as a political metaphor comparing Mrs. Clinton with Mr. Obama.

Embedded in the presentation of Mrs. Clinton as a "just plain (beer drinking)" lady, we would suggest, is a covert accusation that Mr. Obama is elitist. This appears to be a concealed attempt to stimulate fears that Obama is an intellectual classist who lacks attunement with the needs and wishes of most of the electorate. What it means to try to portray a black man as elitist, intellectual, and classist is in itself an interesting twist on conventional reality and politics. Just how successful these efforts will be, of course, remains to be seen. Worthy of note, however, is the cover of a recent edition of *Newsweek* magazine (May 5, 2008) with a picture of a bunch of arugula on the left (an apparent reference to Mr. Obama's comment: "Anyone gone to Whole Foods lately and seen what they charge for arugula?") and an overflowing stein of beer on the right (a reference to Mrs. Clinton hoisting a pint with ironworkers), with a caption that reads: "Obama's Bubba Gap."

The Senator did distance himself from the Reverend, and in no uncertain terms (Powell and Kantor 2008). However, some lasting damage may very well have been done to his image as a result of this episode. To the extent that he continues to be identified with Reverend Wright in the minds of some, his effort to be a candidate who can transcend race, bridge differences in a postpartisan fashion, and bring renewed hope to the American populace is severely compromised. Ultimately, the results at the polls will offer at least suggestive evidence for how greatly his association with the Reverend has harmed the Senator.

Creating Sentiments

It is important to appreciate that leaders play a role in *creating* the sentiments of those they are leading. Thus, leaders both create and cultivate sentiments, and follow and express sentiments, in exerting leadership. This can best be illustrated by examining the current political climate in the United States, specifically the prominence of fear in the current political landscape. While the terrorist attacks of 9/11 are incontrovertible, what has happened since is anything but inevitable. Our country and our leadership were confronted with an unprecedented challenge: how to respond to the first attack on our soil in our nation's history.

A certain amount of fear in response to what occurred was (and perhaps still is) inevitable. Nevertheless, the extent of the fear that still permeates our body politic was not inevitable.

Of course, realities fuel this fear with which any leader would have to deal. First there is the threat of further terrorist acts. While there are some questions about the credibility of what our leaders have said and implied about the ongoing threat, it seems clear that there have been subsequent efforts, however inept, to wreak havoc here in the United States. But have these been relatively minor perturbations or indications of a major and ongoing threat to our well-being? The way our leadership has described them and the media have reported them has a great deal to do with how the American populace has construed these incidents.

There is also the reality of the economic conditions in the country at present. While addressing something as complex and multidimensional as the U.S. economy is daunting at best, because different indicators suggest different and sometimes diametrically opposed conclusions, it is fair to say that many people are feeling concerns on the economic front as this is being written. The reports of unethical corporate practices, tax breaks for the wealthy, the mortgage debacle, the rising cost of oil, the declining value of the dollar, and the loss of jobs have left the public reeling. Concerns about economic security are steadily rising. Our place in the world and specifically the global economy is uncertain. This complex reality also feeds the fear, anxiety, and gloom that remain prominent in our country (Zakaria 2008).

However, it is our view that the current leadership of our government has done a great deal to fan rather than to quell this collective anxiety. When there is a sense of fear within any constituency, one can ask to what degree the leadership of that constituency "contains" vs. "inflames" that fear. It is our contention that the current leadership in the United States has done much more of the latter than the former.

Disseminating Slanted Information

One way it has done so is to feed the populace inaccurate, incomplete, and/or slanted information. As an example, consider the information the Bush administration provided about the supposed links between the terrorist acts of 9/11, Al Qaeda, and Saddam Hussein and his alleged weapons of mass destruction. Not only was this impression mistakenly disseminated in the United States, it was unfortunately conveyed on the world stage. Only after the fact did full and accurate data emerge (Woodward 2002, 2004). Because all but a select few had access to the raw data to permit informed reasoning, the public's ability to reach conclusions about these connections (or lack thereof) was necessarily inferential. It is by definition impossible to disprove an assertion when you are not privy to all the data that the disseminator of that assertion has available. The absence of access to full and accurate information leads inevitably to flawed reasoning and to inaccurate conclusions. Just what part the media play in this process is the subject of another discussion. Our leadership continues to create the impression that the ongoing risk of a terrorist attack is substantial if not imminent, despite the fact that there has been no successful attack in the more than six and a half years that have elapsed since 9/11. Some might argue, of course, that only our continued vigilance has prevented such further attacks; this can never be definitively proven or disproven. But it is this combination of increased anxiety and limited access to full and accurate information that renders the public more susceptible to being led and misled. Their role in the reciprocal mutual influence process becomes compromised. As primitive fears and anxieties hold sway, the public becomes less able to provide corrective feedback. Primitive emotional responses dominate more rational thinking, and the capacity to question and challenge what the leadership is disseminating is diminished at best. As in any group large or small, members must feel a sufficient degree of safety and security to be able to remain open to new information, to thoughtfully investigate alternatives, and to risk seeking the truth.

Since 9/11, however, a series of foreign and domestic failures have been accompanied by the damaging, corrosive impact of leaks and disclosures of information held secret from both the U.S. and international communities. With regard to foreign affairs, our country has experienced an embarrassing failure to find weapons of mass destruction, to tie Iraq to the 9/11 attacks, and to convincingly connect Iraq and Al Qaeda despite our contentions to the contrary on the world stage. The reputation of Colin Powell, our Secretary of State at the time, was apparently sacrificed to promote the administration's political agenda. Furthermore, evidence has recently emerged to indicate that extensive secret planning had been initiated in anticipation of the invasion of Iraq, characterized by *Frontline* as "Mr. Bush's War" (2008), well before Iraq's possession of weapons of mass destruction could be confirmed or disconfirmed. The President's go-it-alone, provocative "cowboy" mentality, epitomized in his statement "Bring it on!," has largely served to alienate even our staunchest allies. It has resulted in the United States acting independently as the "world's policeman," as if we believe we are without fault or blemish and that it is our (self-appointed) messianic duty to behave in this fashion.

Following the disturbing discovery that much of the information used to justify our invasion of Iraq was faulty and incomplete came news about the extent of the behind-the-scenes power wielded by the Cheney/Rumsfeld alliance (Woodward 2002, 2004), the questionable behavior and lack of accountability of Blackwater, Inc. and Halliburton in Iraq and their apparent ties with the Bush administration (Broder and Risen 2007; Glanz and Rubin 2007). Shortly thereafter came revelations about Abu Ghraib (*Wikipedia* 2008), other secret detention centers, the use of torture, the abridgement of human rights, the violations of the Geneva convention guidelines, and the denial of due process for suspected enemy combatants (Hersh 2004). To justify our policies and actions or to maintain a view of us as a nation that is honorable and trustworthy, became increasingly difficult. Just what was our national identity? Were we no longer "The Good," "The Moral," "The Righteous," "The Defender of the Oppressed," "The Protector of Human Rights"? Worse yet, could we be capable of committing the kinds of atrocities of which we were accused? U.S. prestige at both the domestic and international levels plunged. Those who supported the United States likewise suffered: witness the political plight of Tony Blair, our primary supporter on the international scene. Those who attacked us were afforded a strong platform from which to do so.

Unfortunately, these failures and the accompanying losses in our collective sense of safety, security, trust, and self-esteem have been experienced at the domestic level as well. When the events of 9/11 occurred, for example, the president's inability to formulate a strong and effective set of responses in their immediate aftermath was obvious to all. Subsequently, the country witnessed his inability to quickly and effectively respond to the devastation of Hurricane Katrina. The dreadfully inept responses of FEMA were only highlighted by the President's incongruous congratulatory remarks to the then director of FEMA, Michael Brown: "Heckuva job, Brownie" (http://www.cnn.com 2005). What was then labeled as apparent indifference to the plight of the poor, largely black population of New Orleans and the surrounding region became one more source of national concern and embarrassment.

Continuing reminders from the administration that we are engaged in a war on terror have also led to other widely questioned decisions based on the presumed need for "national security" (http://www.whitehouse.gov .infocus/national security). Some have maintained, for example, that civil rights have been violated in the administration's use of unauthorized domestic surveillance techniques in dealing with suspected terrorists. On the economic front, Mr. Bush's dogged insistence that we are not facing a recession (Fox 2008) has led to further erosion of credibility and trust in U.S. leadership and a feeling that our leaders are out of touch with the reality that affects the lives of all but the most privileged Americans. Mr. Bush's seeming lack of awareness of economic conditions has led his critics to question his relationship to reality: Does he really believe some of the things he says? Is he really that out of touch? From our point of view, this is another example of misattunement between leader and led.

But without access to full and accurate information, how can those being led exert a corrective influence upon those who are leading? We would argue that the skillful management of information by any administration can effectively mitigate and even eliminate the existence of a corrective feedback loop between leaders and constituents.

However, one additional question needs to be raised here: to what extent do people who are being led actually want access to full and accurate information? Would we/they even choose to pursue acquisition of such information? People in government are now regarded by many as difficult to believe. Although journalists are obliged to cover the news, their more important mission may be to uncover the news that powerful people wish to keep hidden. This is no small task. As Bill Moyers (2008) said in his recent acceptance speech when awarded the Ridenour Courage Award in the field of journalism, "The job of trying to tell the truth about people whose job it is to hide the truth is almost as complicated and difficult as trying to hide it in the first place." If the process of gaining access to such information is so difficult even for experienced professionals, how much more difficult is it for the general public? Furthermore, being in possession of such information, assuming that were possible, would not necessarily lead to greater enlightenment. It would, after all, require the populace to sift through enormous amounts of information and then exercise thoughtful reasoning and responsible judgment. We would argue that, as Bion (1959) suggested in his discussion of Basic Assumption Dependency, a significant part of us wishes to be relieved of such complexity and responsibility. We believe there is a widely experienced regressive wish among the populace to uncritically believe what we are told, to fully trust our leaders, and to remain in a dependent psychological position, protected and cared for by an omnipotent, omniscient, benign leader. Thus, we believe the populace plays an important role in the process of being insufficiently informed, and at times misinformed, about what is occurring in the world, and is by no means simply a passive victim of their political leaders. We do not construe this as a "crisis in authority," as David Brooks (2008) stated in *The New York Times*. Rather, it is a crisis in leadership. The authority of the office of the president, and the role and responsibilities of the president, are not what is being questioned. It is the leadership of the current incumbent: how he takes up his role and responsibilities and exercises his authority. In the view of many, his leadership has rested on the politics of social and religious intolerance, the stimulation of fear and the revival of trauma, and the identification of a suitable enemy as a rallying point. In the process, confidence in his leadership, his capacity to deal with complexity, and his decision-making ability have been eroded. Furthermore, as his secret use of unethical practices that violate human rights has leaked out, his trustworthiness has been profoundly undermined.

Mr. Bush has come to personify the parent who says, "Do what I say, not what I do." Polls taken as this chapter is being written indicate that U.S. citizens no longer feel led by a competent, trustworthy, and visionary leader, nor, at a deeper level, by a protective, knowledgeable, and loving parent. On the international level, our adversaries say this disparity between what we say and what we actually do is evidence of dishonesty, corruption, and hypocrisy. Our supporters are shaken and uneasy, and their number is dwindling. As a result, the image of the United Sates as a protector and defender of freedom and the oppressed has become increasingly implausible and difficult to sustain. Our moral image and international prestige have sunk to a new low. This tarnished view of the United States, mirrored back to us by the rest of the world, further erodes our trust and confidence in our current leadership. CNN and Gallup polls conducted in the spring of 2008 reported that Mr. Bush received the highest disapproval rating of any modern American president (aol.com, May 2, 2008).

Thus, we would argue that cumulative losses of trust and confidence in our leaders, repeated blows to our national pride and self-esteem, troubling questions about our national identity, and mounting concerns about our economic security and our place in the world have been coupled with ongoing arousal of intense rage as well as fear about our safety and security and limited public access to full and accurate information. Together these conditions have set the stage for the upcoming national election in the United States. The election, and the leaders who emerge, must be viewed in this context. Not only will this context continue to be shaped and determined by the candidates themselves, but it needs to be understood as the result of the terrorist attacks of 9/11, and the powerful, disturbing, and embarrassing events and disclosures that have emerged since then.

LANGUAGE AND "FRAMING"

One of the best ways to understand the nature of the leadership that has been provided to the American public in the aftermath of the terrorist attacks is to consider not just the accuracy of information provided, but the language that has been employed to frame our understanding of what occurred, as well as what the current state of affairs is. George Lakoff, a professor of linguistics at the University of California at Berkeley, has done pioneering work in describing the enormous power that words, images, and metaphors have in shaping how people view things. He calls it "contextual framing," by which he means that the language that is chosen has great influence over how the phenomenon in question is perceived. Once a conceptual framework is established, it defines the terms of the debate (2002).

A case in point is to frame our ongoing effort against terrorism as a "war" on terror. The use of the word "war" loads the deck in a number of ways. War implies an all-out unified commitment to fight to the death an external enemy. There is little room for dissent when a country is at war: if one is not behind the war foursquare, then one is presumably a traitor. As Bion (1959) described, when Basic Assumption Fight/Flight has been mobilized, there is no tolerance for the nuances of careful thinking; rather, participants are told "You are either with us or against us." A war typically requires that every possible resource needs to be mobilized to fight that war and that every other priority is secondary to winning the battle. This is played out whenever legislators oppose or even question an appropriation to fight the "war": they are accused of not supporting our brave military men and women and of being "soft" on issues of national security. The extent to which this language has succeeded in framing the debate is evidenced by the felt need of such legislators to defend their patriotism and prove that they are just as supportive of our military as are those who rubberstamp whatever is asked for.

Are we really in a "war" against terrorism? The Congress has not declared war as our Constitution requires when our country officially goes to war, but of course that was true of the Vietnam "war" of the 1960s and 1970s as well. We have not subsumed every other priority to winning this "war," though some who are opposed to our policies point to the many problems that have been more or less neglected because of the resources we have invested, and continue to invest, in the war in Iraq and the "war" against terrorism more generally. We have created a new cabinet-level position and infrastructure that focuses on matters of security within our borders: the Department of Homeland Security. The threat to our homeland has become a concern of our government, and rightfully so, but this does not mean we are fighting an all-out war. The appropriateness of particular measures is a legitimate matter for political debate, as is the need to balance the incremental gains likely from particular measures against the costs involved: the loss of life and limb not only of Americans but of Iraqis as well; a very substantial economic cost, which involves the diversion of resources that would otherwise be available to address other needs; and significant incursions against our civil liberties, to name just a few. Thoughtful consideration of these matters is not possible when dissent is construed as being unpatriotic.

Thus the use of the phrase "war on terrorism" frames the debate in a way in which dissenters inevitably lose. They are thrown on the defensive and feel the need to "prove" they are as patriotic as those who support the administration's policies. The focus on the desirability of particular actions gets lost as the discussion becomes more and more ad hominem. The body politic loses out because arguments about motives and so-called patriotism drown out substantive discussion.

Another example that is currently in the news, not unrelated to the framing of the discussion about our struggle against terrorism as a "war," revolves around the use of the word "loyalty." As this is being written, some Democratic superdelegates are switching their allegiance from Senator Clinton to Senator Obama (http://demconwatch.blogspot.com; Democratic National Committee 2007). Many of them are being accused of being "disloyal," either because of their previously expressed preference or because of their personal history with Senator Clinton and/or her husband. It is obvious that loyalty in relationships is seen as a virtue, and disloyalty is seen as heinous. But the question needs to be asked: "loyalty" to what? What if one has become convinced that Senator Obama is the superior candidate, either because his principles seem more closely aligned with one's own or because he seems more electable? Is it not legitimate to be loyal to one's principles or loyal to the role definition of a superdelegate, which is to cast one's vote for the person whom you believe will best represent the party in the election? Again, the use of the term "loyalty" loads the debate and turns it into something about the personal virtue of the superdelegate rather than the relative virtues of the candidates who are being considered.

Thus the choice of language has an enormous influence on how issues are construed and considered. They "frame" the debate and in this way profoundly influence how it unfolds. It behooves observers and participants alike to pay careful attention to the profound influence that the choice of language has on the political dialogue.

THE CANDIDATES AND WHAT THEY REPRESENT

As a political campaign unfolds, candidates come to represent different things to the electorate that is considering them. Candidates work to create a persona that is appealing to enough of the populace to be elected. In part, they attempt to lead the populace in a direction they believe is desirable, and in part they attempt to be responsive to what they believe the populace is looking for. Thus their personas are co-created by them and the people they are seeking to lead. Both conscious and unconscious factors contribute to this co-creative process. We would like to consider what each of the prospective leaders of our country (John McCain, Hillary Clinton, and Barack Obama) has come to represent to the American public at this juncture in the contest.

John McCain is a genuine American hero. Though he mostly plays down his personal story, his campaign has made sure it has become known. Not only was he a prisoner of war of the North Vietnamese for five and a half years, but when he was offered the possibility of release during that period, he apparently refused to accept it unless the men under his command were also released. Because they were not, he remained in captivity. He literally wears his heroism on his sleeve: he is unable to raise one of his arms above his shoulders. To be understated about a personal story such as his makes him all the more admirable in the eyes of many.

As his public persona conveys strength and steadfastness, so, too, are his policies crafted to create a sense of America's fortitude in the world. Senator McCain's view is that the only "mistake" that was made in relation to the prosecution of the Iraq war is that we did not have more troops on the ground from the beginning (Presidential Candidates on the Issues, Election Guide 2008, http://politics.nytimes.com). He has been a primary supporter of the recent "surge" of additional American troops. He believes that America can, and must, "win" the war. He represents the notion that we have everything we need to bring about such an outcome and thus maintain and enhance America's stature in the world as the preeminent global power. He represents the point of view that our strength allows us to accomplish virtually anything, rather than that the limits of our power have been highlighted by our efforts against the new kind of enemy we are facing in our "war" on terrorism.

At the same time, Senator McCain has cultivated an image as a maverick (http://mediamatters.org). He has repeatedly bucked traditional Republican doctrine, much to the chagrin of the conservatives whose support he desperately needs and whom he is now working very hard to reassure. On issue after issue, from campaign finance reform to global warming, Senator McCain has taken moderate positions and has forged alliances with moderate Democrats in proposing legislative solutions. He seems to be a "straight shooter," and to be nondoctrinaire in his approach to problems. Though this has caused him some difficulties with the traditional Republican base, and he is now engaged in attempting to assuage that base as much as possible before focusing exclusively on whomever will be his Democratic opponent, this image will undoubtedly serve him well in the general election. It is commonly accepted lore that the candidate who is most successful in appealing to the middle group of independents and undecideds is likely to win a general election, and McCain is well positioned to attempt to be that candidate. He wants people to consider him conservative, but a problem-solver rather than an ideologue. On a deeper, unconscious level, we would argue that McCain is seeking to capitalize on the electorate's wish/need at this time to have as a leader someone who is a strong father figure ready to protect us from external threat.

Hillary Clinton has cultivated a very different political persona. She portrays herself as an experienced public servant who has a long track record of solving problems and getting things done. She believes that bipartisanship can be achieved by moving toward the middle of the political spectrum, which is the same tack her husband took during his eight years in the presidency. She has succeeded in forging alliances with, and winning the respect of, many of her Republican colleagues in the Senate. Again like her husband, she has the reputation of being someone intimately involved in the details of policy. She represents intelligence, competence, and managerial expertise.

At the same time, Senator Clinton portrays herself as a caring and empathic person and, despite her worldly success, a fighter who has not lost touch with what it is like to be struggling in today's world (Alexovich 2008; Dowd 2008). Both she and McCain are trauma survivors, he having survived the horrors of captivity and she having survived public disclosure of her husband's infidelity. She takes every opportunity to remind people of her humble roots, in an effort to legitimize her claim that she understands and can represent well the middle class as well as the poor in our country. It was obviously uncomfortable and embarrassing for her when she needed to respond to the recent disclosure from their publicly released tax returns (April 4, 2008) that she and her husband had earned more than $109 million from 2000 to 2006 (http://blogs.suntimes.com).

Another important aspect of Senator Clinton's appeal is her gender. Though she usually does not discuss it directly, she is obviously the first female to seriously contend for the presidential nomination of one of the two major political parties. This is a source of great pride to many women and a source of admiration among some men as well. While Mrs. Clinton's gender is an asset in some ways, it presents her with an enormous challenge as well. There is tremendous pressure on her to be adequately "feminine," while at the same time adequately strong to be the chief executive of our country and the commander in chief of our armed forces. Senator Clinton's challenge is to traverse this tightrope as best she can. She of course wants the support of as many women as possible, but she does not want to ask for support *because* she is a woman. She is aware that some people will not ultimately vote for her just because she is a woman, but there is nothing she can do about that. On an emotional level, she is a "breakthrough" candidate, and her nomination and election would be historic milestones in the evolution of women's empowerment in our society. It would also speak volumes in our effort to restore our image in the rest of the world as a fair and just democratic society.

Barack Obama represents something quite different in relation to the partisanship that has increasingly come to characterize our body politic. He portrays himself as the candidate who can move our government *beyond* partisanship (Weisman 2008). Unlike those who believe that partisanship is inevitable and that the best candidate is the one who can advocate forcefully and "win" the majority of the political battles, Senator Obama says that what is necessary at this point, and what is possible with his leadership, is to transcend partisan politics and to come together in postpartisan consensus. At first blush this seems naïve in that Senator Obama presents with only limited experience in elected positions and the voting record of a politician who is an unrequited liberal. This may be why Senator Obama does not talk as much about concrete policy positions as he does about underlying values. He contends that there is a deeper level of consensus beneath the policy differences between liberals and conservatives and that he has the capability of finding that common ground and unifying the nation behind him.

A related aspect of Senator Obama's appeal is his constant invocation of hope as a theme of his campaign. He juxtaposes the negativity and partisanship that characterize the current political scene with the hopefulness that he believes he can inject into the body politic. He represents the new leader, a man outside the old political system, the voice of change, and the hope for a better future. Bion (1959) talked about hopefulness as the primary underlying affect in Basic Assumption Pairing. His notion is that one of the tendencies of groups is to look to others within the group to create something new on its behalf. The optimism this generates is intoxicating, and there is evidence of this in some of the support that Senator Obama has generated for his candidacy.

Of course a crucial aspect of Senator Obama's candidacy is his color. While he is in fact of mixed ethnic origin, having had a white Midwestern mother and a black African father, he identifies himself and is clearly seen as a black candidate. Like Mrs. Clinton, he is the first person with his demographic profile to be a possible candidate of one of the two major political parties in this country. At one level his candidacy and his possible election represents the possibility that the country has finally transcended the big-otry and racism that has been so endemic in its history. At the same time, this may not be the case at all. One of the great unknowns in this election is how many people, in the privacy of the election booth, will be unwilling to vote for a black man, despite what they might indicate to pollsters. That said, Senator Obama (like Senator Clinton) is a breakthrough candidate, and his nomination and election would also be a historic milestone in the movement toward equality of people of color in our society. (Of course, one can only imagine what would happen if Obama were to capture the popular vote within the Democratic party, only to have the superdelegates overturn this result by supporting Mrs. Clinton in sufficient numbers to give her the nomination. Issues of trust, betrayal, and racism would imme-diately emerge center stage.)

NEEDS OF THE POPULACE

What are the needs of the populace to which these candidates are appeal-ing? Certainly citizens need to feel safe and secure in their daily lives. The attacks of 9/11 both highlighted this need and made it much more salient in the minds and hearts of the American public. During the years of Soviet hegemony, Americans felt the need to keep up with the Soviet Union so as not to be overtaken by Communism. When the Soviet Union broke up and Eastern Europe became much more independent from its eastern neigh-bor, there were no longer two superpowers; America presumably reigned supreme. In this context, 9/11 was particularly shocking. Americans lost their sense of invulnerability. Despite our geographic distance from those interested in hurting us, we could no longer feel impregnable. As we have indicated, the consistent drumbeat from our government about the ongo-ing threat of terrorism, and the dangerousness of the world we are living in, have made us a much more fearful nation. As a natural consequence, there is nothing more important to the American public than that its leadership provide it with a sense of safety and security.

Related to this need is the importance attached to feeling confident that the information that our government disseminates is accurate. If the public does not feel that it is being given honest appraisals and accurate informa-tion, then its feeling of safety is compromised. This is what was so destruc-tive about the rationale that was proffered for the incursion into Iraq. The current administration's bold assertion that there was confirmation that Iraq possessed weapons of mass destruction that were a grave threat to its neighbors, and to the world more generally, made our unilateral decision to initiate military action seem justified to many, if not most, Americans. When it was subsequently shown that the information the government claimed it had did not in fact exist, the loss of respect that our country suffered around the world was not the only cost that was incurred. In addition, it made our own populace less trusting of the credibility of our government and, as a result, less safe.

Among the three candidates vying for the presidency as this is being written, there are significant differences on this front. Senator McCain has a long and impressive military history. He has been on the public scene a long time, and even his age and white hair work in his favor. He has been a strong supporter of the incursion into Iraq and still talks confidently about "winning" the war. He represents the strong commander in chief that many Americans are looking for: a trustworthy, tried and true protector.

Senator Clinton has also staked a claim to the support of those who are looking for a strong leader of our military and our country. She has served for a number of years on the Senate Armed Services Committee. While she has pledged to pull our country out of Iraq, she takes pains to make it clear that she would not be reluctant to use our military might. As an example, she has talked about "obliterating" Iran if it attacks Israel (April 22, 2008). She has worked to counter any suggestion that as a woman she would not be a strong and formidable leader of our country.

Like Senator Clinton, Senator Obama has committed to ending our involvement in Iraq. He too has tried to assure Americans that he would be a strong commander in chief, but he does not have as much that he can point to as he tries to make his case. As a result, he is probably the least attractive candidate to people who are looking for a strong and confident commander in chief.

The other thing that Americans look for from their prospective political leaders is hopefulness about the future. Though this is always the case, some aspects of our current situation make this particularly so. On the international scene, we have been humbled by our inability to clearly and decisively prevail in Iraq, as well as by our inability to capture Osama bin Laden, who continues to thumb his nose at America whenever he chooses. On the domestic front, there is a great deal of anxiety about our economic circumstances. There is a prevailing anxiety that heightens the need that always exists for a reassuring leader who will bring about a more secure and prosperous future. Linked with this wish, too, is the need to restore our tarnished self-image as a nation. There is a felt need to effectively counteract the deep sense of humiliation, the underlying loss of self-esteem, and the disturbing impact on our collective sense of national identity that we have suffered as a result of 9/11 and its aftermath (Zakaria 2008).

Of course all three of the current candidates seek to appeal to this need, but their approaches are quite different. Senator McCain's appeal rests largely on his reputation as an independent and pragmatic thinker who is not tied too rigidly to ideology. Despite his recent efforts to reassure his conservative base, he has a long history of going his own way on various issues, often to the consternation of the members of his own party. He promises Americans that he will transcend orthodoxy and be responsive to what people really need.

Senator Clinton represents the position that by mastering the details of policy and then effectively "reaching across the aisle" to forge alliances with enough people on the other side, she will be able to effectuate changes that meet the needs of the voting public. Her argument is that the best hope for the future is to accept that the political system is not going to change, but that one can improve the lives of people by engaging in the system in a competent and effective fashion.

By way of contrast, Senator Obama is offering a vision of the future that is "post partisan" (Weisman 2008). He represents the view that traditional partisan politics can be transcended by a leader committed to doing so. He talks of bringing people together in a way that his opponents will not, and cannot. There are obviously many people who find this a very appealing idea, so much so that as of this writing he is the leading candidate for the Democratic nomination. Others see his vision as naïve and empty. His voting record is solidly liberal, and it certainly is not clear just how he is going to forge alliances with the many political leaders whose beliefs are very different from his. Only sworn into the Senate in 2005, he has, nevertheless, tapped into a desire to transcend the ugly partisanship of recent years that might carry him all the way to the White House.

CONCLUSION

We believe that the current American political landscape, and especially the 2008 presidential race, illustrates the way in which leadership is co-created by those who are attempting to exert it and those they are seeking to lead. Each of the prospective presidential candidates is attempting to represent a virtue or set of virtues that are partly a reflection of what they believe they bring to the table and partly a reflection of their best understanding of what the American public wants and needs at this point in our history. Why is it that Americans feel the need to feel secure and powerful again? Partly it is because of what occurred on 9/11 and what has occurred since (fighting a war in which we have been more humbled than triumphant), and partly it is because we are being told that they need to and deserve to feel this way again. Why do Americans feel that they need a competent and effective manager of our government? Partly it is because of the problems that have accumulated in recent times, and partly it is because we are being told that this is what we need for our lives to be better. And finally, why do Americans feel the need to be hopeful about a better future? Partly it is because things have gone poorly for our country in recent years, and partly it is because we are being told that it is possible to transcend the ugly partisanship that has characterized American politics in recent years and come together in post-partisan consensus.

Thus, leaders do not simply lead, and constituents do not simply follow. Each influences the other in a mutual and reciprocal process that is ongoing. It does not end when a new leader is finally chosen; rather, it continues on and ends only when a particular leader leaves the scene, to be followed of course by someone new. It is crucial to understand this co-creative process if we are to really comprehend the nature of the relationship between leaders and those they are attempting to lead.

REFERENCES

Alexovich, A. "Clinton's Closing Pitches in North Carolina and Indiana." *New York Times*, May 5, 2008.

Bion, W. *Experiences in Groups*. London: Tavistock, 1959.

Broder, J. M., and J. Risen "Blackwater Logs Most Shootings of Firms in Iraq." *New York Times*, September 26, 2007.

Brooks, D. Op-ed. *New York Times*, January 4, 2008.

Democratic National Committee. "Call for the Democratic National Convention 2008," 2007.

Dowd, M. "Butterflies Aren't Free." *New York Times*, May 7, 2008.

Durkin, H. The Group Therapies and General System Theory as an Integrative Structure. In *Living Groups: Group Psychotherapy and General Systems Theory*, edited by J. Durkin. New York: Brunner/Mazel, 1981.

Frontline. "Mr. Bush's War," 2008.

Fox, J. Double-talking the Dollar. *Time*, May 5, 2008.

Glanz, J., and A. J. Rubin. "From Errand to Fatal Shot to Hail of Fire to 17 Deaths." *New York Times*, October 3, 2007.

Herman, J. *Trauma and Recovery*. Rev. ed. New York: Basic Books, 1997.

Hersh, S. M. "Torture at Abu Ghraib." *New Yorker*, May 10, 2004.

Jacques, M. "This Scapegoating Is Rolling Back the Gains of Anti-racism." *The Guardian*, February 15, 2007.

Klein, R. H., H. S. Bernard, and D. L. Singer, eds. *Handbook of Contemporary Group Psychotherapy*. Madison, Conn.: International Universities Press, 2002.

Klein, R. H., and S. Phillips, eds. *Public Mental Health Service Delivery Protocols: Group Interventions for Disaster Preparedness and Response*. New York: American Group Psychotherapy Association, 2008.

Klein, R. H., and V. L. Schermer, eds. *Group Psychotherapy for Psychological Trauma*. New York: Guilford Press, 2000.

Lakoff, G. *Moral Politics: How Liberals and Conservatives Think*. 2nd ed. Chicago: University of Chicago Press, 2002.

Moyers. B. Acceptance Speech for the Ridenour Courage Award. http://www.alternet.org/story/ (accessed April 8, 2008)

Obama, B. *The Audacity of Hope*. New York: Crown Publishers, 2006.

——. *Dreams from My Father*. New York: Times Books, 1995.

Powell, M., and J. A. Kantor. "A Strained Wright-Obama Bond Finally Snaps." *New York Times*, May 1, 2008.

Powell, M., and J. Zeleny. "Tagged as Elitist, Obama Shifts Campaign from High-flown to Folksy." *New York Times*, May 6, 2008.

Sullivan, A. "Jeremiah Wright Goes to War." *Time*, April 27, 2008.

Volkan, V. D. *The Need to Have Enemies and Allies: From Clinical Practice to International Relationships*. Northvale, N.J.: Jason Aronson, 1988.

——. "On 'Chosen Trauma.'" *Mind and Human Interaction* 3 (1991): 13.

——. "September 11 and Societal Regression." *Mind and Human Interaction* 12 (2001): 196–216.

——. *Blind Trust: Large Groups and Their Leaders in Times of Crises and Terror*. Charlottesville, Va.: Pitchstone Publishing, 2004.

von Bertalanffy, L. "General Systems Theory and Psychiatry." In *American Handbook of Psychiatry*, edited by S. Arieti. New York: Basic Books, 1968.

Weisman, J. "GOP Doubts, Fears "Post-partisan'" Obama. *Washington Post*, January 7, 2008.

Woodward, B. *Bush at War*. New York: Simon & Schuster, 2002.

——. *Plan of Attack*. New York: Simon & Schuster, 2004.

Zakaria, F. "The Post-American World." *Newsweek*, May 12, 2008.

6

Managing Systemic and Leadership Problems in a Corporate Setting: A Case Study

Peter Gumpert[1]

Recently, two opposing views of leadership are evident in the rapidly changing corporate world. One of these views is that collaborative work environments lead to both employee satisfaction and sustained high performance. We sometimes refer to this as the participative leadership or "servant leader" approach (e.g., Greenleaf, Spears, and Covey 2002). It asserts that leadership that strengthens employees and promotes teamwork and collaboration is highly desirable, particularly in environments that require innovation and adaptation. The approach is based both on accumulating evidence about the usefulness of collaborative work environments and on the recognition that organizations are complex systems that must function successfully over time in even more complex environments (e.g., Gharajedaghi 1999).

The other, opposing view sees people in senior leadership positions as heroes (or sometimes villains) held personally responsible and accountable for corporate financial performance. This approach identifies the organization with its topmost leaders. It is partially a response to powerful pressures from the financial community to achieve results quickly (e.g., maximizing this quarter's profit picture or growth) and is partially based on many people's wish to have simple, unitary explanations for extraordinarily complex phenomena and events.

This second view of leadership—the leader as a heroic figure—is particularly seductive for the senior leaders themselves. The leaders are tempted to see themselves rather than workers below them in the hierarchy as personally responsible for good outcomes. When things are going well, they are highly rewarded and greatly admired and have a great deal of influence inside and outside the organization. When things are not going well, they are blamed, feel shamed, and are sometimes replaced. They therefore tend to be willing to sacrifice long-term organizational performance and the people in their organizations to show strong current-period results. The subordinates they choose will, when required, exchange long-term strength and the capacity to be innovative for cost cutting to achieve favorable short-term numbers in adverse conditions. Heroic leaders have learned to protect themselves financially against inevitable corporate difficulties and downturns. As has been pointed out by de Geus (1997/2002), remarkably few corporations in the world survive as long as forty years. In 1996, the New York Stock Exchange celebrated its 100th birthday. It is interesting to note that only one of its listed companies (General Electric) had survived the period.

To see leadership style as a stable dispositional characteristic of the persons selected to be leaders is tempting. Though some heroic-style or servant-style leaders have chosen that style because it fits their personality, the culture of the organization also plays a strong role in the selection, training, and retention of certain leaders. A less obvious factor is that not only the organization itself but also the systems that the organization is typically exposed to also exert strong influence on the way it—and its leaders—function.

The company described in the pages that follow does *not* fit the model of the corporation that is oriented strongly to short-term performance and good financial results. Indeed, the company strongly values high product and service quality, long-term relationships with employees and customers, and an enduringly collaborative and innovative employee culture. It is therefore an ideal case to illustrate how "hero-like" leadership can be created and maintained, and how it can present a danger to the organization and its members. This is especially true because the two sets of leaders described in the case do not fit the stereotypes of participative or heroic leaders. The case also serves to illustrate the powerful effects on both leaders and members of the systems in which they must function.

This chapter, then, presents the story of a leadership and organizational failure. It illustrates the effect of the failure on both people and organizational performance and considers the steps taken to address the failure. Following the case narrative, the broader implications of what happened are examined. The chapter has three goals: (1) to present briefly some principles regarding a range of factors, including leadership, that affect work group and organizational functioning; (2) to examine a detailed case that illustrates the operation of the principles; and (3) to discuss some of the implications of the principles. I assume that the principles are applicable to work groups of all sorts and sizes.[2]

Five principles are illustrated and discussed in the context of the case. Most of them have been articulated by others, notably in the literature of group process and group psychotherapy; a useful summary is available in

Klein, Bernard, and Singer (1992). The interaction of these principles in a complex organizational context, however, has not been addressed.

FIVE PRINCIPLES

1. Both system factors and leader characteristics—and their interaction—strongly influence the way an organization functions and performs. These factors and characteristics frequently operate out of conscious awareness, even when some aspects of them are recognized and voiced. If the target group is part of or closely involved with one or more larger systems, salient themes and characteristics of the larger systems often have powerful effects on the functioning of the local group and its leaders.
2. The characteristics of the system often have a subtle but powerful influence both on which leaders are chosen and on their leadership behavior.
3. The personal characteristics of top leaders, middle managers, and informal leaders influence the way the organization functions and can have substantial effects on its performance. Furthermore, senior leaders, middle managers, and informal leaders with certain personality disorders or traits[3] have an especially strong and often negative influence on the way the organization functions and performs.
4. Both systems and leaders can exert forces on the group or organization that are cohesive (tending to bring people together) or alienating/isolating (tending to move members apart or into opposition). For example, if a large system tends to engender destructive processes of intergroup conflict resolution, members of its subgroups are more likely to be destructively competitive (e.g., mistrustful, deceitful, withholding) with one another.
5. If a group or organization wishes to work collaboratively and the systems within which it functions are alienating in their effects, it must put in place processes and structures that consistently protect against the alienating forces and that support collaborative relationships.

INTRODUCTION TO THE CASE

The parent corporation (and a new division referred to here as ND) delivers certain technical services to large organizations; the parent organization has been in existence for more than four decades. Though this organization is not well known to the public, the technical work it produces is highly respected by people who are familiar with it. ND provides services to a category of customers that was relatively unfamiliar to the corporation and that has great growth potential. The parent corporation's major interest, however, is not growth, but technical excellence, innovation, stability, and the durability of its relationships with its customers and workers.

During the ninth year of ND's existence, the parent corporation's CEO reluctantly decided to replace its leaders because he was concerned about and dissatisfied with important aspects of ND's functioning and performance. The case presentation tells this story in some detail.

The Parent Organization and Its Contribution to the Problems That Developed

The ethos of the parent corporation, particularly at the individual contributor level, is generally collaborative. It values open exchange of information and cross-divisional cooperation in solving difficult problems. Its infrastructure emphasizes communication and collaboration among members in the service of understanding customer problems and contributing to ideas about technical and related matters. The *top-level* culture of the parent corporation, however, has been in some ways an exception to the corporation's generally espoused values about collaboration. Each of the major divisions has acted for many years as if it were an autonomous fiefdom. There has been, among senior leaders, a good deal of subsurface competitiveness, mutual under-the-table criticism, and hiding of information. Polite isolation has persisted at these very senior levels, despite frequently expressed values about the importance of collaboration in general and the importance of using the entire range of the company's knowledge and skills to solve important problems. On the whole, corporate officers were careful to insulate their subordinates from the competition at the top level. This top-level system was nevertheless a factor subtly affecting ND because its founding general manager had long been a member of the top corporate group. Thus, the way the parent organization functioned at the top partially shaped and maintained the stance of ND toward other divisions of the corporation.

In the beginning months of ND, managers in other divisions expressed skepticism about whether the new venture could—or indeed should—survive beyond its first year or two. As ND did grow and prosper, those same managers often criticized it as not being fully a part of the larger company. The founding general manager was, of course, protective of his young organization and sought to differentiate it from other divisions in a positive way—partially to protect its members, and partially to motivate them. He emphasized growth and diversification as important to ND's survival, both in terms of its stature in the parent corporation and in terms of bringing in sufficient revenue to be safe from reverses. A small but very painful layoff during the third year solidified and strengthened this view.

History and Characteritics of the New Division

The corporation formally created ND when it authorized it to seek and negotiate a large contract with a new customer, which ND did successfully. This customer, which had many organizational as well as technical problems, decided to hire the corporation (through ND) to help with a major long-term project; the initial five-year contract was renewable.

.

The External Organizational Consultant's Role

The consultant to ND had worked earlier as a consultant and personal coach to the general manager of the new entity, while the general manager was serving in another capacity. Later the corporation's president brought the external consultant in to assist ND (then about twenty people). He hoped the consultant could help understand and ameliorate a seriously escalated conflict that had developed between ND's general manager and his deputy and between factions that that conflict had created. Mediation in the conflict was ultimately unsuccessful, and it was resolved by transferring the deputy and a few of his close coworkers to other divisions in the corporation. The consultant was asked to help heal the damage that had been done by the conflict and ended up remaining as principal organizational consultant to ND for several additional years, as it grew to employ more than 500 staff members. In that context, he worked closely with all the senior managers, including those who succeeded the original top leader. Several months after the founding general manager retired and new leaders were chosen, the consultant ended his work with ND. However, he did continue to work with the corporation, its various officers, and the Board of Directors.

The Early Period

The founding general manager, his direct subordinates, and the external organizational consultant had worked hard together to create a strong, durable culture of participative leadership, teamwork, and collaboration in the organization. They created and supported a team-based structure at all organizational levels and provided extensive training in participative/collaborative leadership. They created a periodic check on important aspects of ND's organizational culture in the form of a survey whose results they formally reported to the whole ND organization and supplemented this by periodic interviewing across the organization. They also made significant attempts to collaborate with other divisions that could provide temporary staff to work on technical problems that ND encountered. The latter effort proved to be somewhat more difficult than ND's internal collaboration, particularly where there was skepticism about the quality of ND's technical work with its customers.

ND grew and prospered and did effective work. Its first major contract was renewed for a ten-year period, and other customers—some major and some minor—were added. ND's entrepreneurial stance continued to be valued.

ND's Clients Complicated the Picture

The ND's principal work, helping client organizations improve and integrate critical technical systems, turned out to be extraordinarily complex and difficult to carry off—much more so than anyone had anticipated. The improvement programs repeatedly failed to meet both temporal and performance goals, failed to keep promises, and had serious cost overruns. Contractors were endemically late in delivery, corporate heads felt under scrutiny and pressure, senior managers were criticized and sometimes replaced by their superiors, and suspicion and blame were in evidence everywhere. This created a sense of uncertainty and concern among ND workers, who tried to distinguish ND from other participating contractors while trying also to help them succeed. The other contractors, furthermore, sometimes blamed ND for their own difficulties and urged the hiring corporation to reduce or eliminate ND's role. ND people in the field, in turn, blamed the other contractors. ND's first major client, then, was characterized by periodic internal turmoil; at one point it asked that ND's founding GM be replaced as the formal leader of the project. Later it demanded that another ND manager be removed from the leadership position as well. This was not easy for ND's staff members, who devoted long hours and much thought to the work and felt that customers on whose behalf they worked frequently devalued them. Thus, the state and behavior of certain major customers had powerful effects on the ND staff members who worked on these contracts. Fortunately, the ND organization provided support to staff members, who were therefore better able to manage the work.

Given the difficulty and the scale of the work ND was doing, settling on objective criteria for evaluating the quality of the work done was difficult. In the absence of such objective criteria, ND's leaders relied on pleasing and satisfying people in their customer organizations as a primary indicator of the quality of their subordinates' technical and other work. Because customer satisfaction can be highly capricious, this led some ND members to feel unjustly criticized and unsupported; at times they spoke of feeling compromised and betrayed by their own leaders. Because the leaders wanted to maintain a good relationship with these customers, they sometimes yielded to the temptation to blame their staff.

The Original Leadership

Some members of ND saw the founding general manager as difficult to deal with. They described him as passionate, talented, and insightful—but also as temperamental and volatile. People in the organization who knew him reasonably well were fully aware that despite his occasional outbursts of anger, he could be counted on to be fair and knew that his actions were never destructive to his people. Some saw him as overresponsive to customer demands and as wanting to micro-manage quality and service to customers. In contrast, they viewed the deputy he had selected as a calm, particularly thoughtful, and even-tempered manager. A small subset of middle managers vocally emphasized the difficulties of the founding GM and, from time to time, expressed to each other the wish that he would retire early. He, not surprisingly, sensed this and felt that people he had taught and helped were abandoning him and were contemptuous of him. His perception was not unrealistic. During this period, he repeatedly expressed concern to his external consultant about the broader organizational implications of what he was experiencing. So, the early factional struggle in ND seemed to have continuing ripples in the organization.

The Consultant as Informal Leader

From the beginning, the consultant had served a containing function in the organization. He was a consistent, calming presence (on site two to three days a week), a vocal advocate of teamwork and collaboration, and a chronicler of the organization's progress toward its vision. Thus, he served, at times, as the "conscience" of the organization. He gradually became involved in some of the organization's work with its customers and was instrumental in developing an engagement model that helped to guide the relationship between ND staff members and their customer organizations. He was involved in the interviewing of senior managers in customer organizations to guage how ND was doing. Staff knew he was able to maintain the confidentiality of people's conversations with him and saw him as someone they could count on to help the founding general manager. They called on him from time to time to help with the resolution of conflicts. He helped design major meetings and facilitated both offsite meetings and regular leadership meetings. They asked him to assist with the writing of major documents, including some contract renewal applications.

As the consultant became increasingly involved with the content as well as the process of ND's operations—and as the organization grew—he was in less direct touch with the members of ND who were not senior leaders or who worked in customer sites. Because he was closer to the concerns and struggles of senior leaders of the organization than other staff members were, they began to see him as a *de facto* member of the senior leadership team and as less closely involved with the larger ND organization. He was also less aware than would have been optimal of the continuing difficulties between ND and the broader corporate organization. Both factors limited his effectiveness in important respects. Thus, the consultant was gradually seduced by the system and its urgencies and by his own wish to play a consistently useful part in the developing ND organization.

When the founding general manager did retire (on schedule), his deputy GM was promoted to the role of GM; this person, in turn, chose a deputy who was passionate about the work and very active. The new deputy had been one of the *sub-rosa* opponents of the founding GM. The corporation's Board promoted the new deputy to the vice-presidential level, and all parties handled the leadership transition well.

The Newer Leadership

The new general manager had been more confident being a deputy to the founding GM than being the ultimately accountable GM himself. He had great respect for and relied heavily on his own deputy, whose leadership style was confident and enthusiastic. By deferring to the judgment of the deputy, the new GM seemed to manage whatever insecurities he had. Thus, the deputy and the GM were widely viewed as "joined at the hip." ND people regarded the management style of the new leaders as more secretive and less inclusive than had been the case during the tenure of the founding GM. The organization came to be viewed internally as being run by a small, closed circle of people. Isolation of subgroups within the ND, and the "paranoid subculture" that usually accompanies isolation, were developing.

ND staff viewed the new deputy GM as bright and talented, but some also characterized him as unpredictable, particularly in the sense that he seemed to entertain short-term enthusiasms and to lose interest in the people and tasks that had earlier been high on the priority list. The deputy was given to splitting (identifying "good guys" and "bad guys" and generating unproductive conflict between them) and to inviting continuing admiration and unwavering support from subordinates. The deputy also chose to place himself at the head of an important new project, appearing to seek credit for the project's progress.

The new leaders had continued some of the founding GM's approach. They trained their subordinates well in the "we're different and better than the old parent corporation" perspective, and continued to emphasize entrepreneurship. But, they also behaved very differently than the founding GM. They expressed dissatisfaction with the performance of a number of middle managers and senior individual contributors, and removed them from their positions. They encouraged and helped some of the more seasoned staff members leave the organization, partially because some of these senior people were not fully comfortable with the increasingly entrepreneurial and isolated direction ND seemed to be taking. At the same time, the leaders added senior people who did not have ties to or experience with the broader parent organization, and who could be counted on to remain loyal to the new leaders' strategic view. This pattern continued despite the fact that the original reasons to adopt an isolated stance (to protect a fragile start-up while it developed) had all but disappeared. It is interesting to note in this context that the new GM on more than one occasion expressed to the other corporate officers that he was "running a small business" and that he therefore had to consider whether he should use and pay for parts of the broader infrastructure that were not immediately applicable to ND. As might be anticipated, this rather bald statement of isolation disturbed the other corporate officers. The new GM seemed to be avoiding rather than actively managing the important boundary between ND and the other corporate divisions.

Internal Effects of ND's New Leaders

Some senior people in ND felt unjustly blamed for difficulties they encountered in their work programs. The tendency to blame ND program directors for failures and difficulties "rolled downhill," and directors' subordinates also began to feel uneasy. Thus, people grew increasingly protective of their personal reputations. A tendency to hide mistakes inevitably followed; this was accompanied by an increasing tendency to identify "good guy" (on my side) vs. "bad guy" (not on my side) categories of staff members at various levels. Political factions were forming.

At the same time, people talked about a growing emphasis on personal loyalty in ND and an increasing tendency for its high-level managers to plan and act in secrecy. The deputy GM became widely viewed as the real power in ND, and people expressed disappointment in the more passive GM. The leaders promoted new middle managers from within or recruited people from other companies, and personal loyalty to the new GM and his deputy seemed to be a selection factor. Employees saw dissent as not invited, and it became muted and secretive.

Some ND staff members saw the loyalty and support they gave to top management as not fully reciprocated. Some people complained that their relationship with the deputy had been temporary and capricious. Others felt that top management had made false promises to them and that it had abandoned them and their projects in favor of a new direction or enthusiasm. More broadly, people began to be seriously concerned about favoritism in ND. Some felt uneasy about their role in the organization going forward and worried that their futures were contingent on factors other than their job performance. This loss of trust in leadership led also to a subtle undermining of the commitment to teamwork that the organization had carefully built and maintained in the earlier period.

The importance of continued growth and a diverse portfolio remained a strong emphasis, and ND's entrepreneurial strategy was even more clearly encouraged. This emphasis diluted the organization's attention to maturing existing customer relationships; people felt that developing exciting new programs (and having to recruit new people to staff them) would be more visible and more strongly rewarded than strengthening relationships with older customers or doing technical work of durable excellence.

ND made quick hires to meet immediate staffing requirements, without careful attention to integration and enculturation into the culture of the parent corporation. ND gave lip service to some of the central values of the larger corporate organization, but without serious commitment. The hurried hiring was itself an important factor, making ND subject to the usual pathologies of rapid growth, such as neglecting collaboration between work programs.

The recruitment of new customers and new ND staff members who had little experiential understanding of ND's central tasks perpetuated the startup ethos in the organization. The kind of careful examination of work programs and work products that was completely natural in other corporate divisions was infrequent at best.

Both internal solidarity and morale in ND appeared to be deteriorating in the two years after the leadership change. There was increasing employee turnover in the ND organization, which was unusual in the corporation, and this worried corporate-level human resources people. ND's growth was not accompanied by consistent attention to internal solidarity and teamwork—particularly teamwork between work programs. ND staff members became increasingly isolated from each other and developed a tendency to hide their mistakes and problems.

In summary, ND's top leadership did not serve some of its most important functions, such as developing and maintaining a consistent vision and strategy; managing the boundaries between the local organization and others in its environment; adhering to well-understood performance criteria; helping staff members contain anxiety and distress through difficult periods; and creating a sense of consistency, steadiness, and safety.

At the same time, the organizational consultant had become somewhat less active as a process consultant to the organization than he had been in the earlier period. Though his various contributions continued to be of value, the new leaders increasingly viewed him as part of the "old guard," and his relationship with ND gradually ended.

External Effects of ND's New Leadership

People in other parts of the corporation viewed ND as isolated—not sharing knowledge, experience, and special skills with people in other divisions, and not valuing the perspective and experience that other divisions and the corporate infrastructure could bring to ND's work. While ND saw itself as entrepreneurial, the view from the outside was more negative: "ND will go after any contracts that might come along"; or "ND is oriented to growth for growth's sake." ND was rumored to be acting like "an ordinary consultancy" rather than as a provider of valuable, enduring technical expertise.

At the same time, the corporation viewed ND as failing to engage in enough regular and thorough reviews of the value and potential of its technical work. Indeed, ND took customer satisfaction and work program growth as the most important indicators of success, and gave less weight to transferable technical innovation than other divisions of the corporation.

People in the parent corporation continued to raise questions about the quality, importance, and durability of some of the work ND had undertaken. They considered the work being done by ND staff members as different from and less valuable than would be most desirable to the broader corporation. For the most part, ND's critics did not find in ND's work the creativity that was the basis of the parent corporation's reputation.

External Attempts to Induce Changes Were Not Successful

Several times, two successive corporate presidents discussed with the GM and his deputy many of ND's problems. Little or no change followed these discussions. ND's top leaders, instead, spoke and acted as if they felt misunderstood and inappropriately devalued. They appeared to see ND's strategy as one that the broader corporation should adopt and that should shape its future.

Within the first year of his appointment, the most recent president had embarked on a course leading to greater integration among the corporate divisions; in one case, he ordered a full-scale merger between two of the largest divisions. He and other senior managers viewed ND's isolation with great concern. After much worry, thought, and counsel, the president decided to replace the leadership of ND with someone who had spent much of his career in one of the older divisions in the corporation.

A Summary of Important Contributing Factors

In about two years, ND had gone from a highly cohesive organization with mostly satisfied members to one that was fragmented and factionalized, with substantial membership uneasiness and dissatisfaction. The general manager, the external consultant, and other members of the leadership team, through consistent attention and effort, had maintained the earlier cohesiveness of the organization. The organizational consultant did survey and interview sensing of the organization at least twice a year. The consultant and the leaders paid careful attention to establishing frequent and carefully honest two-way communication with staff members at all levels and to encouraging and supporting small work teams in all programs and at all organizational levels. The ND organization retained a coach to help staff members, managers, and teams that felt they needed assistance. The executive group of vice presidents and program directors met twice weekly, once in a formal business meeting and once in a 90-minute early-morning meeting that was deliberately agendaless and conducted by the organizational consultant. Members of this group were encouraged to bring up anything that might be on their minds, including anything that pleased them or was disturbing them, anything that they wanted help with, and any interpersonal difficulties that might be emerging. The GM's door was open to all staff; he interacted warmly and in a supportive as well as truthful way with everyone who came to him.

The organizational consultant met weekly with the founding GM (at times including one or another subgroup) to help the GM contain his anxiety, impulses, and concerns. The GM was unusually bright, perceptive, and capable but continued to have some difficulty managing his anxiety. He had substantial insight into his personal difficulties and was mature enough to manage them. His anxiety was, not surprisingly, particularly high in the year before his retirement.

This consistent (and largely successful) effort to maintain a participative, collaborative work culture was much needed, in part because there had been an early history of factions within ND. Furthermore, senior managers in the broader corporate system were politely distant and from time to time engaged in _sub-rosa_ conflict with one another; the influence of this on ND was subtle and indirect, but real. People in the other divisions, highly skilled in criticism, were critical of the work and choices of ND; the GM could not always buffer this. Finally, the major tasks ND undertook and the difficulties induced by ND's customer organizations were a constant source of stress. People who worked in the field needed support and a containing "home" environment.

After the top leadership succession took place, the organization gradually began to fragment. An analysis of the reasons follows:

1. *Certain influences, partially imported from the top levels of the corporate culture, remained:* These included isolation, splitting and factional disintegration, criticism of others, and placing blame for failures and difficulties. While the top-level organizational culture was not a particularly strong factor, it did have subtle, pervasive influence.
2. *The new ND leaders did not establish and maintain a containing environment:* Their apparent lack of openness, steadiness, and consistency gradually undermined trust in ND's senior leadership.
3. *Presence of "cluster B" personality traits in ND's senior management amplified the mix of divisive forces:* The new GM was rather passive, giving free rein to the much more charismatic deputy GM, who engaged in splitting and stimulated feelings of abandonment in staff members. The deputy also subtly communicated his need for consistently renewed admiration and was often critical of other people (including the GM) when in one-on-one conversations with staff members.
4. *Customer systems had their own difficulties, and affected ND staff members:* People in some prominent customer organizations often experienced and communicated a fear of being criticized and blamed, and some actively contributed to destructive intergroup conflict. The extraordinary

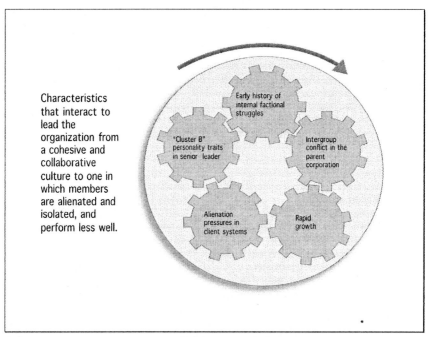

Figure 6.1.   ND's movement toward alienation/isolation.

difficulty of the tasks the customers' employees struggled with—and sometimes tried to undermine—exacerbated this.

5. *Unmet personal needs*: ND staff members needed but did not receive consistent support, reliable, truthful, and open leadership and positive identification with a broader whole.

Corrective Action

From the organizational consultant's perspective, the early work culture of ND had been seriously damaged. Forces from ND's customers, leaders, and members had aligned themselves to produce fragmentation, isolation, and unproductive conflict resolution processes. In a meeting with the president of the corporation, the vice president of human resources, and the incoming general manager of ND, the consultant communicated the following desirable characteristics of a future ND:

- An organization that brings good work and stimulating ideas to the corporation as a whole—work that the corporation can be proud of and that is likely to be helpful or informative to people in other divisions.
- An organization that evaluates the value, importance, and future contribution of any major piece of work from several perspectives and that invites others in the corporation to be part of the evaluation process. The organization should be capable of being assiduously honest about missteps and difficulties as well as pleased with its solid work.
- An organization that is consistently supportive of its members as they do their work.
- An organization that is internally strong, with good cooperation and a reliably collaborative stance among its own work programs and practices, and an organization whose members are able to work closely and fruitfully with people in other corporate divisions.

The consultant suggested that a change in top leadership would be far from enough to bring these conditions about. He discussed with the president and the incoming GM various steps that they might take. The president and the GM agreed to the following:

They agreed that a thoughtful realignment of ND's values, goals, and work culture would be necessary to ensure that ND would be and remain connected broadly to the rest of the corporation and that ND's strategies and the corporation's strategies and goals would remain aligned. They harbored no illusions that they could accomplish this quickly or easily.

They agreed that ND and its work programs should emphasize the development and strengthening of relationships with its client organizations rather than focusing so strongly on growth; indeed, they felt that ND's future growth had to be managed and guided carefully to bring it into full consistency with the corporation's growth strategy.

They agreed that it was necessary to rebuild trust and confidence in ND's management team and throughout the ND organization. This would certainly be required to protect the ND organization from whatever fragmenting forces might continue to be significant, both inside ND and in major customer systems. It would also help facilitate collaborative activity inside ND and between ND and other divisions in the corporation.

Anticipated Pitfalls for the New GM

At this writing, the new GM approaches his position and tasks. He is likely to be viewed in ND both with great curiosity and with concern. Trust in the new leader will build gradually, beginning with a lot of open-minded, serious listening on his part. The group is likely to try to pull the new person subtly into the ND's current inner circle and into the current ND culture. The new GM must avoid these pitfalls. He should remain, therefore, in close and regular contact with the corporation's president and its other divisional leaders and with the broad goal of contributing to integration in the corporation.

THE PRINCIPLES REVISITED

Now that I have presented the illustrative case study, we can assess and perhaps refine the initial principles.

1. Both system factors and leader characteristics—and their interaction— strongly influence the way an organization functions and performs. These factors and characteristics most often operate on an unconscious level, even when some aspects of them are recognized and voiced. If the target group is part of or closely involved with one or more larger systems, salient themes and characteristics of the larger systems often have powerful effects on the functioning of the local group.

The characteristics of the top-level corporate system in which the ND was embedded, and some of the customer systems ND worked with, clearly influenced the organization and its leaders. This systems-theory idea has been articulated many times, beginning with the General System Theory articulated by von Bertalanffy (1968) and in the work of A. K. Rice (1963). ND people who worked in the problematic customer systems were aware of the organizational and interpersonal difficulties involved, but this awareness did not fully mitigate the extent to which they "brought the problems home with them" and were influenced by them. The consistently supportive systems that ND leaders initially created and maintained were enormously important in preventing the customer system problems from more strongly infecting the ND organization.

When ND's leadership changed, the supporting systems that had been functioning well were rendered less and less effective, and the ND work culture gradually devolved to one in which isolation, splitting, factions, mistrust, and so on were much in evidence. Group psychotherapists, including Agazarian (2001), Nitsun (1996), and others, have written extensively about the conditions that give rise to subgrouping and other potentially destructive phenomena in psychotherapy groups. In ND, the founding GM had had some of his own stylistic difficulties, but he was aware of them and took steps to keep them from becoming seriously problematic. The new ND leaders, in contrast, had less insight; their "pathologies" were well aligned with the alienating/isolating historic and larger-system themes that affected ND, and the effects of these were therefore amplified.

2. The characteristics of the system often have a subtle but powerful influence both on which leaders are chosen, and on their leadership behavior.
3. The personal characteristics of top leaders, middle managers, and informal leaders influence the way the system functions and can have strong effects on its performance. Furthermore, senior leaders, middle managers, and informal leaders with certain personality disorders or traits have an especially strong and often negative influence on the way the organization functions and performs.

It is tempting to speculate that the ND's new leaders were chosen in part because their personal characteristics were consistent with some of the more problematic aspects of the broader corporate system. No evidence for this is available, however, and the speculation is probably without merit in this case. What is much clearer is that in some instances the top leaders of ND chose some direct subordinates who were manipulative, critical of others, or otherwise interpersonally difficult—or were sufficiently compliant or passive to allow serious problems to develop in the ND work culture.

4. Systems and leaders can exert forces on the group or organization that are cohesive (tending to bring people together) or alienating/isolating (tending to move members apart or into opposition). For example, if a large system tends to engender destructive processes of intergroup conflict resolution, members of its subgroups are more likely to be competitive (e.g., mistrustful, deceitful, withholding) with one another.

5. If a group or organization wishes to work collaboratively and the systems within which it functions are alienating in their effects, it must put in place processes and structures that protect against the alienating forces and that support collaborative relationships.

In retrospect, the original effort by the founding GM and his staff to establish a collaborative work culture was of great importance to the initial success of the ND organization. It is interesting to note, however, that these protective processes were rendered relatively ineffective within a short time after the founding GM was replaced. It is, of course, much easier to undermine cooperation and trust than to build it (Deutsch 1973). It seems likely that the new leaders' behavior aligned itself with the alienating-isolating forces that came from the surrounding systems, including the top-level corporate culture. This suggests that systemic and leader forces, when aligned, can be additive or potentiating in their effects.

Some Potentially Testable Implications for Small Groups and Larger Systems

The system characteristic and leadership trait perspective presented above has various implications for other groups; I suggest a few examples:

Small Groups

- Prominent organizational characteristics of a psychotherapy clinic setting often influence group therapists. This influence is likely, in turn, to have effects on the groups they lead. Longings for interpersonal intimacy in a psychotherapy group may be more difficult to confront, for example, if the clinic that sponsors the group has characteristics that lead its clinicians and other members to be isolated and alienated from one another. In discussing inpatient group psychotherapy, Rice and Rutan (1987, pp. 64–65) have articulated a similar perspective.
- Significant, memorable events in a group tend to influence the group for a long time, even after the group's direct memory of the event has faded. For example, a serious quarrel between a member and the leader that results in the precipitous loss of the member can make other members feel apprehensive and unsafe in the group.
- In an organizational setting, the internal characteristics and success of small work teams will depend in part on the nature of the system that surrounds them. If the broader system has a history of interpersonal destructiveness or abandonment, for example, teams and teamwork will tend to be fragile and not resilient (Gewirtz and Gumpert 2003; Porath, Gewirtz, and Gumpert 1999).

- If the larger system has one or more significantly personality-disordered leaders, the smaller groups within it will tend to have difficulty; the particulars of the difficulty will depend on the characteristics of the influential leaders (Kernberg 1983). A narcissistic leader, for example, may generate a strong tendency toward compliance with and submission to the leader and a tendency to mute or hide individual initiative and disagreement.

Larger Systems

- An organization that has difficulty resolving internal conflicts productively will also have difficulty collaborating or even cooperating successfully with organizations outside its boundaries.
- An organization or nation in which leaders and members have difficulty trusting the good will of others is likely to approach other organizations or nations with suspicion and will tend to act in an untrusting and untrustworthy (self-protective) fashion (Deutsch 1962).
- An organization or nation that is strongly oriented toward the powerful-powerless dimension of relationships between people and groups will emphasize power in its internal relationships as well as its relationships with other entities.

Some Broader Implications

Leaders and the Corrupting Influence of Power

Positions of formal leadership, especially those that involve power and influence, are remarkably seductive to their occupants. Though they are especially attractive to people with certain personality disorders, they can have a "corrupting" influence on virtually anyone, and especially on those who lack insight into their own psychological processes. They tempt people, for example, to overvalue their own importance and contributions, to disregard or undervalue the contributions of others, and to view subordinates as interchangeable and easily replaced. The corporation described in the case study above has literally thousands of highly educated, skilled, and innovative staff members whose work *and relationships with one another* are crucial to the company's continuing success (Gumpert 2005). Corporate and national leaders who undervalue their staff members or citizens are badly distorting the reality they must deal with. They also stand in danger of failing to nurture the environments that lead all members to do their best work, to develop helpful relationships, and to develop their abilities and skills.

A second issue we should note is the remarkable ease with which a corporation (and probably a nation) can be moved from supporting cohesion and collaboration to engendering isolation and alienation among members. Recovering from such a change is far more difficult than creating it.

The Powerful Effects of Social Systems

Traditional mental health professionals who treat individual patients have had a tendency to downplay the effects of work settings and other social systems on their patients' thoughts, feelings, and actions. In a similar way, many organizational professionals have tended to disregard the important and sometimes insidious role that leader characteristics play in work systems, large and small. Group therapists are more aware of the complex interplay of system, leader, and member characteristics, but they too can be blind to the effects on their groups of the various systems beyond their group's formal boundaries. Most professionals see what they are trained to look for, and it is easy for them to miss broader or deeper issues that are also significant in the functioning of the people and groups they work with. Thus developing a more complete perspective is important despite the greater complexity it introduces. The case above illustrates the co-creation of leaders and systems and also shows that the systems people are in close contact with have a great deal of influence on the states and behavior of leaders and members of organizations. Corporate cultures strongly affect their members, as do the cultures of important customer systems. The question of how such systems have their effects is far from clear and deserves careful study.

CONCLUSION: PROTECTING THE ORGANIZATION

The principles illustrated in the case study presented here strongly suggest that organizations, especially organizations that value innovation and collaborative work environments would do well to:

1. Do a careful, periodic analysis of the alienating and otherwise interpersonally destructive forces their employees are exposed to, both from the organization itself and from other systems with which the employees are in close, repeated contact.
2. Create durable, well-maintained protective mechanisms that shield employees from the effects of such forces, or that mitigate their destructive effects—such as consistent, truthful two-way communication and a supportive team-based environment.
3. Select leaders with enough maturity, self-insight, and emotional competence to prevent them from adding destructive elements to the work

environments they help lead. Leaders do not have to be perfect—but they do have to recognize their own limitations, be willing to monitor them consistently, and have enough insight to avoid being seduced by the puffery that all too often infects people in leadership positions.

NOTES

1. The author is most grateful to Robert Klein, Victor Schermer, and Cecil Rice (editors of this volume) for their illuminating and enriching comments on earlier versions of this chapter. Their comments and suggestions have led to important improvements in the content.

2. A long-term psychotherapy patient of mine, a very senior engineer, once reminded me that in organizations, "scale really matters." By this, he meant that very large organizations usually involve a level of complexity not usually found in smaller groups. Their sheer size and complexity makes such large-scale groups far more difficult to work with and to influence than smaller ones. The organization described in the case presented herein has several thousand members; by my patient's definition, this organization is still small. The W. L. Gore manufacturing organization has a different view of when organizations are too large. They have suggested that an organization exceeding 125 members can no longer act like a "family" whose members know one another well and work together in full comfort. In any event, the corporation described in this chapter delivers service to very large organizations, often larger than it is by a factor of ten or more. So, the *customers'* size, complexity, and resistance to change can strongly affect the organization delivering services.

3. This is particularly true of the so-called Cluster B personality disorders, including histrionic, narcissistic, and borderline disorders. High-functioning people with these characteristics are frequently found in leadership positions in organizations (see Kernberg 1994, chapters 12 and 13; see also http://en.wikipedia.org/wiki/Personality_disorder#List_of_personality_disorders_defined_in_the_DSM).

REFERENCES

Agazarian, Y. *A System-centered Approach to Inpatient Group Psychotherapy*. London and Philadelphia, Pa.: Jessica Kingsley Publishers, 2001.

de Geus, A. *The Living Company: Habits for Survival in a Turbulent Business Environment*. Boston, Mass.: Longview Publishing Limited, 1997/2002.

Deutsch, M. "Cooperation and Trust: Some Theoretical Notes." In *Nebraska Symposium on Motivation*, edited by M. R. Jones, 275–318. Lincoln: University of Nebraska Press, 1962.

———. *The Resolution of Conflict: Constructive and Destructive Processes*. New Haven, Conn.: Yale University Press, 1973.

Gewirtz, M., and P. Gumpert. "Sustaining Leadership Teams at the Top: The Promise and the Pitfalls." In *The Collaborative Work Systems Fieldbook: Strategies, Tools, and*

Techniques, edited by M. Beyerlin, 149–73. San Francisco: John Wiley & Sons, 2003.

Gharajedaghi, J. *Systems Thinking: Managing Chaos and Complexity*. Boston: Butterworth Heinemann, 1999.

Greenleaf, R. K., L. C. Spears, and S. R. Covey. *Servant Leadership: A Journey into the Nature of Legitimate Power and Greatness, 25th Anniversary Edition*. Mahwah, N.J.: Paulist Press, 2002.

Gumpert, P. "The Connected Company." *Reflections: The Sol Journal* 6, 6/7 (2005): 40–52.

Kernberg, O. *Internal World and External Reality: Object Relations Theory Applied*. New York: Jason Aronson, 1983/1994 [paperback].

Klein, R. H., H. S. Bernard, and D. L. Singer, eds. *Handbook of Contemporary Groups Psychotherapy: Contributions from Object Relations, Self Psychology, and Social Systems Theories*. Madison, Conn.: International Universities Press, 1992.

Nitsun M. *The Anti-Group: Destructive Forces in the Group and Their Creative Potential*. London: Routledge, 1996.

Porath, M., M. Gewirtz, and P. Gumpert. "Theory, Implementation, and the Measurement of Critical Success Factors at Malden Mills Industries." In *Developing High Performance Work Teams, Volume 2*, edited by S. D. Jones and M. Beyerlein, 129–61. Alexandria, Va.: American Society for Training and Development Press, 1999.

Rice, A. K. *The Enterprise and Its Environment*. London: Tavistock Publications, 1963.

Rice, C. A., and J. S. Rutan. *Inpatient Group Psychotherapy: A Psychodynamic Perspective*. New York: Macmillan, 1987.

von Bertalanffy, L. *General Systems Theory: Foundations, Development, Applications*. New York: George Braziller, 1968.

7

Lessons in Leadership and Conflict Resolution: Working with Palestinians and Israelis in a Conjoint Educational Effort

Hala Taweel

INTRODUCTION

This chapter addresses the following questions: Can leaders in a "changing world" detach themselves from political realities on the ground? Can they keep working with the "other" even during a state of war? Should leaders put their identity, feelings, and political affiliations on hold and act normally in a situation that is anything but normal? And how do these factors shape the leader one becomes?

To do this, I first examine the conditions under which the University of the Middle East project (UME), an educational program initiated at Harvard University, aimed at bringing together Israelis, Palestinians, and students from other Arab nations, was born. Then I review the history of the project and later reflect on how my personal history and the conflicts I lived through created the leader I became as a cofounder and president of UME.

THE BEGINNINGS

The founders were a passionate group of individuals brought together by the simple and powerful idea just noted. They had diverse backgrounds, political affiliations, and experiences of moral suffering in the face of conflict, as well as a love of adventure. The Oslo agreements (1993), which offered hope for durable peace in the Middle East, helped stimulate this visionary group of graduate students in Boston.

However, the concept of creating a new university that would include people regardless of their ethnic, religious, and political background raised eyebrows in both the Arab and the Jewish communities in the Boston area and elsewhere. Thus, not surprisingly, the project faced problems from its inception. These included the deteriorating political situation in the Middle East, the failures of the Oslo agreement and subsequent Palestinian-Israeli negotiations, the suicide bombings in Israel, the repercussions of Sharon's election, the second Palestinian Intifada followed by the bombings of Ramallah and Gaza, the war in Iraq, the events of 9/11, the election of Hamas, the war between Hizbullah and Israel, and the loss of hope on both sides. Tense moments arose when the UME leaders and students experienced the loss of loved ones during bombings in Israel or those related to the Israeli invasion of the West Bank and Gaza proved difficult to both students and leaders. Factors as varied as political views, interpersonal relations, management styles, gender, and age differences exacerbated these conflicts. These I will elaborate on later.

THE DREAM

Behind each organization, there is a personal story and events that shape its existence and which explain how and why there was a need to create it in the first place. What drives individuals to do something that they believe is so crucial and central to their lives, and which is often seen by some as "senseless," "naïve," "disloyal," "unrealistic," and by others as "courageous," "patriotic," or "visionary," to cite only a few characterizations that I have heard over the years of the organization I founded ten years ago.

I always questioned my involvement in the project I have helped build. I questioned how individuals continue to live and work together when everything around them seems to be rapidly collapsing. The constant feeling of confusion, sorrow, despair, and hope characterizes the process of our daily lives. I asked myself many times: when do you stop believing in what you do, or should you at some point stop doing what you strongly believe in? How do you deal with your feelings toward your country when everything is falling apart and you are constantly faced with the media images of death, bodies of innocent men, women, and children being lifted by angry and desperate countrymen, day after day, for the last sixty years? How do you deal with your mission of giving hope to others as a leader when you find yourself tormented or doubting your capacity to continue suffering in silence in order to carry on with your idealistic goals? Beyond sadness, how are you supposed to control your own anger and deal with what you strongly perceive as injustice while giving hope to others? As I write these words, too many of my questions remain unanswered. This chapter attempts to find answers to the most prominent ones that have affected my work. This is my story and the story of the University of the Middle East project, and this is how it all began.

MY BACKGROUND

I am Palestinian. I was born in Jerusalem a couple of years before the 1967 war and raised in Nablus and Ramallah under the Israeli occupation. I had never lived under any other regime or any other authority but the occupation. Growing up in a very political household, which is quite common among Palestinians, politics was our daily bread. This is what we discussed over breakfast, lunch, and dinner on a daily basis, and this was the substance of our daily fears. My parents' worries that they would never see their children again when they sent us off to school in the morning; our constant fears of being killed on the road, perhaps only injured; or the perspective of being locked up in a small dark cell, beaten and tortured for daring to demonstrate against the occupation or for throwing a couple of stones at Israeli soldiers were our fate. But for us, children of Palestine, throwing stones is what we did best; it was our means to reject the occupation, our only way to tell the occupiers they were not welcome on our land, the land of our parents and ancestors. My mother, Raymonda Hawa Tawil, is a journalist and a writer who was placed under house arrest and jailed by the Israeli occupation on more than one occasion. Her "crime" was merely to speak out at times when Palestinians under occupation were denied freedom of speech or expression. My mother speaks perfect Hebrew, French, English, and of course Arabic, skills which made her a *de facto* spokesperson for the Palestinians. She wrote and informed foreign journalists about the realities of daily Palestinian suffering. In her writings, she covered anything from house demolitions to funerals of young men and women killed during demonstrations or simply individuals being tortured in Israeli jails for their beliefs or actions. She also collected testimonies from the injured while recording the names and ages of thousands of Palestinians jailed without trial under the preposterous cover of "security for the state of Israel." For speaking up, the Israeli military arrested my mother. Placed once in solitary confinement in an Israeli jail, she was beaten and tortured before they moved her to a prison hospital. During that ordeal, my mother suffered facial bruises, a broken nose, and uncontrolled hemorrhage. While she was lucky to survive, others did not. As a young child (I was merely eleven years of age), my mother's suffering and the fate of my own people deeply affected me; both marked my life indelibly. A couple of years after her release, she was placed under house arrest for four months. Our own home then became our prison. We had soldiers guarding our house twenty-four hours a day, and my siblings, my father, and all our visiting friends had to produce proof of identification to get in and out of our house. It took me a very long time to comprehend what my family went through, try to turn the page on the suffering that my people experienced . . . and understand the Israelis. The intensity of the injustices that my people suffered haunted me during the formative years of my life. It took a great deal of courage to be able to comprehend and then accept "the other side." During my school years in Nablus and Ramallah, like all my friends and colleagues, I demonstrated at any given opportunity against the Israeli occupation. We raised our Palestinian flag proudly and asked the Israelis and the international community to finally recognize the plight of our people and stop our suffering. We asked that the Palestine Liberation Organization (PLO) be accepted as our sole and legitimate representative, that the occupation be stopped, and for our right to establish a Palestinian state.

Unless you have lived it, it is hard to fathom how desperately hard living under an occupying army can be. All your movements are restricted, and you live in constant fear. Some of the events I experienced in my childhood still haunt me. I still panic when I cross frontiers or borders, or simply when I pass a police car. These simple facts of life are constant reminders of the brutality of the occupation. What I have lived and seen since my early age, memories of colleagues at school, my mother sent to jail, watching over my wounded colleagues, and walking in tens of funerals for young people killed during demonstrations, are my life companions. And so are memories of humiliation while being stopped for hours at a check point or at a border crossing in the steaming heat of a summer day or the bitter cold of a winter evening; waiting endlessly for an arbitrary order that would allow us to go home. This was my daily life.

THE TURNING POINT

Almost ten years ago, after studying in France and having the advantage of living abroad (when my parents decided it was urgent for me to leave the country to avoid being killed during a demonstration like many other youngsters), I came to Harvard University to continue my studies at the Kennedy School of Government. It was a time of euphoria coinciding with the Oslo agreements. People finally wanted to believe in peace and both Palestinian and Israeli leaders were ready to shake hands. I always wanted to be part of the process of building the Palestinian State and, therefore, decided to do my Masters in Public Administration (MPA). I needed to learn the process of running a country, get Palestine back on its feet, help rebuild its institutions and government, and give Palestinians their pride and sovereignty back. When I first started my MPA program, I did not know what to expect. It was an international program with more than 200 students. We were only two Palestinians among eighteen Israelis and other foreign and American students. I did not know what to think or how to deal with the Israelis, nor did they know how to deal with me. The first week of class was tough on all levels. I felt the hostility in the eyes of some of the Israelis. Perhaps I felt they were questioning what I was doing at Harvard and whether we belonged in the same place. However, it was interesting how I immediately communicated with the Israeli women in the group. All of these women came from the Israeli navy, army, and the defense department, and should have been for me like a red flag to a bull, a reminder of the suffering of my people and the symbol of arrogance of an occupation that refused to know more about us. It was not long before I became friends with one of the Israeli women in the group. Her name was Ofra. She was a lieutenant colonel in the Israeli army and a single mother with a beautiful two-year-old daughter, who reminded me of my then two-year-old niece. Her name was Inbal, and I just loved her. She was beautiful and funny and I talked to her, sang to her, and told her how beautiful she was, all in Arabic. When Ofra heard me talk to Inbal in Arabic, she started crying. She told me that she had served in the occupied territories, in Ramallah, and that the only words she knew in Arabic were cursing words. No one ever taught her or even said to her anything nice in Arabic. Of course, coming as an occupier you should not expect the occupied to treat you well; shower you with rice, as is the habit back home; or throw flowers at you. Ofra and I connected very well; we studied together, suffered over case studies, talked about life, men, love, and of course politics. We disagreed politically but we still enjoyed each other's company. I learned some time later that Ofra worked in Ramallah with Fuad (Benjamin) Ben Eliezer. When I heard the name, I was suddenly about to faint. Ben Eliezer was the brigadier general of the West Bank, the very same person who had signed the order to put my mother in jail. I called my mother at once that evening. I was crying on the phone when I told her that I had become a close friend of Ofra, who had worked with Ben Eliezer. My mother was now saying to me, "Now it is a different era, we are in a peace process with them, and we have to forgive and put our pain aside." She also said, "If you happen to see him or talk to him, give him my regards, we are in a new era, an era of peace." I could not understand my mother's reaction; I was expecting her to be outraged and angry. She is the one, who after all was tortured, suffered, and had her nose broken in jail from the beatings. And here she was today, forgiving her jailer! And if she forgave him, could I, her daughter, forgive him? Later on, Ofra happened to be talking with Ben Eliezer, and she passed the phone on to me. He spoke beautiful Arabic; he was an Iraqi Jew. He politely asked me about my mother and sent his regards to her. He told me that he had always admired her courage and asked me if I had her fiery character! Ben Eliezer is today a member of the Israeli Knesset and has held several ministerial posts in Israel including the ministry of defense. He is today the Israeli minister of national infrastructures.

THE POWER OF EDUCATION AND ITS POLITICAL ROLE IN BRIDGING PEOPLE ACROSS NATIONS

Although at the Kennedy School it took us a long time to build trust between us and to start talking about our sufferings, the topic eventually came out in our discussions, inside and outside the classroom. Some of these interactions were very difficult, but we felt that to maintain our friendships, we should talk about the difficulties. We spoke about how I would demonstrate and throw stones at the Israeli soldiers, and they spoke about shooting at the Palestinians. We had moments of truth that were important to all of us. It was a very important step for me that my Israeli friends acknowledged the harm that had been done to us, while I also talked about tactics that my fellow Palestinians used that I did not share or agree with. This extraordinary experience to study and, for the first time, sit in a classroom with Israelis and others and see and feel that we were on an equal level, as students, has literally transformed my life. Difficult as it was at the beginning, it felt natural at the end of the year. It made me grow stronger in my beliefs in the "other." It made me see that there were good Israelis on the other side of the borders that we needed to reach out to, if only to tell them who the Palestinians really are, explain to them our suffering, and ask them to open their eyes and hearts to their neighbors. Later we were able to talk about everything. Even taboo subjects for the Israelis, such as Jerusalem and the question of the Palestinian refugees, became familiar and acceptable topics for discussion. With the enrichment of this experience and the way it transformed me as a person, I felt the urge to transmit this to others by bringing people with a focus to study together and watch the transformation that this could do to their lives; no occupied or occupier, no all guilty or innocent party, no victim and victimizer, no one there to judge us or the acts of our governments. We were all on an equal basis in a higher education institution and facing issues together and not facing each other. Higher education institutions have an amazing political power and role to play (if the institution wishes to invest in them): to work on bringing and bridging people at war to dialogues, as well as bringing people together across different social, racial, gender, and religious divides.

A FORTUNATE MEETING AND THE BIRTH OF AN IDEA

In the midst of all this, I met a person who felt the same way. After the assassination of Itzhak Rabin, Ron Rubin, an American Jew wanted to make a change. He wanted to reach out to his Palestinian and Arab fellows. We met over coffee at Harvard Square, talked about our shared interests, about our love for the region, politics, education, and how we would like the Palestinians and Israelis to be reconciled with each other. At the end of the conversation, we knew that we wanted to build a university, a safe place to bring people from all over the Middle East and North Africa to study, live together, and learn from each other. We wanted to transmit what we went through, having Israeli, Palestinian, and other Arabs study together, to show people that peace is possible when people look beyond their differences and share a common goal, the betterment of their societies and region. That day, in November 1996, the concept of a University of the Middle East project (UME) was born. We started telling our friends and colleagues about our idea and soon more than twenty people, Palestinians, Israelis, Lebanese, Jordanians, Egyptians, Iraqis, and Kuwaitis joined us. We used to meet every Sunday, over dinner in one of the restaurants in Cambridge, to talk about the needs of the region and what UME would look like, what we were going to teach, what the language of instruction would be, our target student population, where to have the first campus, whether it was going to be in the region or in the United States, et cetera. We were all graduate students at Harvard, and all of us had our countries at heart. We knew our differences, our political problems, and we were there to find our shared common goals. Within a few months, we collected hundreds of letters of support from our professors and friends in support of the concept of UME as a great and timely idea. We became the focus of all the students at Harvard when a few articles, including ones in the *Boston Globe* and *New York Times*, were written about UME and the word spread about us. To our delight, the Moroccan Ambassador Mr. Ahmad Al-Snoussi, who had heard about us, invited us to the United Nations to present our project to his colleagues, other ambassadors from Egypt, Israel, Jordan, and Palestine. The ambassadors were very enthusiastic about our idea and even wanted to incorporate it in the unilateral peace process under the "people to people" section. I immediately refused this idea. People of the Middle East created our project to target the people of the Middle East without any political agenda. I certainly did not want UME to become another item on a specific political agenda. Having lived in the region and in a complex political environment, I was aware of the consequences of such a decision and the implications of getting a political stamp on an educational program; I resisted it immediately because I knew how my fellow Palestinians would react to it. Our project would have been born dead had I accepted it as be-coming part of a peace agenda related to government. I knew deep inside me that the strength of any organization at this time was to work with the people and not with any government. Sure enough, my instinct was right. All projects and agreements related to the Palestinian-Israeli agreements stopped or were weakened a few years later. Certainly, the monetary, media focus, opening channels for us in the region and many other advantages would have been great for a nascent program like ours. It took many years for my colleagues to understand my decision to refuse to be incorporated in the "people to people" program sponsored by the United States and donor countries and aimed at strengthening the relationships and joining programs. Only years later, when the peace process and all institutions related to it started collapsing, were they grateful that we did not associate ourselves with any government or peace related agenda.

CREATION OF THE UME

After the visit to the UN, we incorporated our organization officially and UME became an independent nonprofit and nongovernmental organiza-tion whose objective was to provide opportunities for higher education for all the people and communities of the Middle East and North Africa. UME's ultimate goal is "to create a system of interconnected educational centers promoting academic excellence, regional cooperation, development, and the values of equal human dignity, open inquiry and peace in the Middle East and North Africa." After researching extensively the needs of the region, UME started building the foundation to achieve this mission. We began of-fering summer institutes in vital areas, including teacher education, educa-tional leadership, sustainable development, public policy, and civil society. Also, the basis for all our programs was academic excellence in every field and on every campus. Our aim has always been to pursue not only human relationships and development but also knowledge as an instrument to build a better world community. UME emphasizes "critical thinking, open inquiry, and creative approaches to learning. UME is interdisciplinary in structure, promoting the vanguard of research in a particular field, while simultaneously developing cross-disciplinary exchanges with other fields. Curiosity is encouraged and intellectual freedom assured" (www.ume.org). UME has a broad representation of students and faculty from all communi-ties of the Middle East and North Africa. Drawing from a diverse pool of applicants, admission to UME is based solely on merit—not religion, race, nor socioeconomic background. Students and faculty have the unique op-portunity to exchange ideas in an academic setting where interaction is a daily occurrence. UME is committed to promoting mutual respect and appreciation of equal human dignity on the individual level.

THE CHALLENGES

Deeply involved in a project that brings people from the Middle East together, our group saw the hope of a better life, for our families and ourselves, for our alumni, and for our societies, disintegrating and collapsing with the political events in the region starting with the collapse of the Camp David Accords in the Fall of 2000. I could not stop thinking of UME's alumni with whom we had pledged to continue to work to bring them and others together, and to dream big that one day we could have a campus where Palestinians, and Israelis, Moroccans, Tunisians, Algerians, Lebanese, and Egyptians could study together. I had personally promised UME's participants on many occasions that the failure of the political process would not deter us from continuing our mission and had repeatedly emphasized our determination to bring people together regardless of gender, race, political, and religious affiliations. "In days of war and peace," I had pledged. How was I to keep those promises? Was I naïve to make such promises? Is it really possible to continue working with the "other" while we are literally killing each other daily on the ground. Can I look in my own people's eyes and tell them: despite your daily suffering, I believe in a better tomorrow? Am I naïve, or a dreamer? What faith and in whom would I need to have to continue to lead an organization while the context in which it was born has collapsed and the leaders who signed those agreements are at war? I was wondering not only how to continue but actually *why* we were still continuing? My thoughts were always racing to find an answer, whether to continue or abandon what we had started. My intolerable internal conflicts and doubts were always appeased by reading the email messages our alumni from the MENA region sent to each other simply inquiring about how they were doing and expressing empathy and solidarity to one another. Such messages read, for example, "I am so sorry about what is happening in Palestine [or in Israel], I hope that you and your family are well," or "I want you to know that you and your family are in my thoughts and prayers. I am glad I met you last summer. We need to make peace between our people." These messages were sincere and heartfelt. They reflected a spirit that our programs had attempted to offer our participants. They reflected what they had learned from our programs, their teachers, and most importantly, what they had learned from each other. They reflected the hope of ordinary people who were able to do extraordinary work simply by reaching out to others in times where everything looked bleak!

On the question of equality in higher education, till today, I question the equality of our relationships. I know that UME strives to make sure that our students are treated equally. But are they really equal? No doubt they stop being equal the moment they leave our program and find themselves separated, whether at the airport or at frontiers, by color and by identity. They stop being equal when they are facing each other around a fence, as occupied and occupier. My fears become exquisitely real when I talk to professors such as the wonderful Eileen De Los Reyes about my experience at UME. Eileen told me that in her experience with groups at dialogues, and when it occurs "across empire, colonial, race and gender, there is an illusion of equality that the person might be feeling that would disappear in a moment of crisis"(personal communication, Eileen De Los Reyes, March 2008). Would that imply that I am living an "illusion of equality" with the other? Is my strong desire to believe in peace and equality blinding me? Or can it be that our students are the antidote for the theory that the illusion of equality will disappear in crisis. As it turns out, our students proved to be reaching out to each other even more in crisis compared with days of peace. My concern was always how our students will be able to go back and live in a normal world after their experience with the "other" at UME. The persons who suffered more were the Palestinians, who went back to a harsh daily reality imposed on them by occupying Israelis, the same ones they just sat with, studied, laughed and broke bread with. Was UME, sheltering the participants from these daily lives, injustices and inequalities? Is UME a temporary reprieve that is different from the inhumanities of the world surrounding it? We found out throughout the years that our alumni are a very strong group. I also firmly believe in the strong academic component of our programs that allows them to become better prepared academically and cross-culturally with each other. But a strong reason is also their resilience, that they want things to change and better their own lives and their families and societies. These young women and men are committed to creating their alumni associations in the region, becoming themselves the trainers, building recently with our help a civic education workshop inside their countries, each helping his or her community. UME alumni were able to maintain the group identity that links them to each other. They communicate daily through Yahoo and Google groups. They reach out to each other as educators, as UME alumni. Without it one can argue that their individual hope for a better future and peace might be shattered.

THE DIFFICULT YEARS

My strength, and that of my colleagues at UME, did not come from the leaders of the region. They no longer inspired us. The language of hope and peace that we had heard in 1993 on the White House lawn was now an angry one: leaders were pointing fingers, blaming each other for who had started what first. Moreover, there was no honest broker who could mediate between the parties. The United States and its president blamed the Palestinians for the failure of the peace talks, which ultimately led to the escalation of the conflict, making people angry, feeling betrayed, as if they were the "children of a lesser God" (Safieh 1996).

The Palestinian economy started collapsing, the restrictions on travel and movement continued, the wall was being erected on Palestinian land and with it came the uprooting of olive trees, house demolitions, land confiscation, and so much more. Now a surreal ugly war limited, and often completely halted, the movement of students and workers to and from their schools or workplaces, sometimes only a few miles or even a few feet away. Buildings were shelled, along with schools, universities, ministries, ambulances, the seaport, the airport, the president's headquarters, and all the symbols that represented peace, autonomy, statehood, and our very own existence. The peace and justice that we had hoped for were just collapsing in front of our eyes while the entire world stood in silence, watching, and motionless. Palestinian extremists used suicide bombers indiscriminately in populated and tourist areas around Israel, killing hundreds of Israeli innocent civilians, as well as the hope of a "normal" life between us. In turn, the bombers gave the Israeli government "excuses" to blockade a whole population and apply collective punishment. Aid to Palestinians stopped, and the word "terrorist" once again was applied to us. How can you build and work with others in these circumstances? It was so hard getting to the office and dreading a day full of news about rising casualties. Trying to work on programs, applications and deal with funders to convince them that what we were doing was right! What were we thinking? Were we unfaithful to our own selves and emotions? Were we so oblivious to what was happening at home? Were we mere idealists or perhaps full of ambition for a project we wanted to bring to success regardless of the reality on the ground? And why and for whom?

UME—CONNECTING WITH OUR PEOPLE

UME has never been a casual job for us. It was indeed a passion. It was our way of connecting with our people, a way of forgiving ourselves from not being back home, but living safely among diasporas that provided everything we could not get in our own countries. Did the guilt of not living in our countries trigger our passion to help from the outside? Probably none of this. If I had been living in Palestine at this time, no one would have supported me, and this project would have been born dead. And if Ron had been living in Israel, with the war mentality going around, there is no way he could have continued either. So what is it that kept us going? Is it the fact that we have the privilege of being in the U.S., a country of opportunities . . . ?! How could this be? We were often swimming against the current and, to be sure, united but alone. Our inspiration and strength and the answers to all our questions, whether to continue or not with our programs, came from our students. How many times did I hear these words from my staff, "I am depressed, people are killing each other, it is insane"; how many times did our board say to us, "We cannot continue. . . . We have to shut down. This is war. Who is going to come to our programs anyway?" My answer was simple: as long as we have applicants, as long as people want us to work, we will continue to provide the best education. The response came always from the students, and yes they wanted us to continue. Was it the students teaching the teachers this time? Was it them telling us what to do. "Let's continue" were their words. The students continued to support and sustain the organization even when the board was willing to let go. The students, the lifeblood of the community, served as the bearers of the new group and institutional culture. In 2002 and 2003, the suicide bombings peaked in numbers, and Israel started bombing Palestinian infrastructures relentlessly, leaving nothing in place. For my colleagues and me, it was sheer despair seeing all falling apart. We were numb with fear and wondering what would happen next. I know that I am not telling you anything that is not well known, I am just citing facts that we lived, tormented by the daily incidents trying to bridge people that can no more meet in their own countries, restricted by laws and walls and so-called "security barriers"! The first year of the second Intifada, in 2002, we received the highest number of applicants from Palestinians and Israelis. Were they looking for hope or for a simple excuse to leave home and meet outside? Or were they telling us that they were here to continue the struggle with us? What about their families? Were they risking their lives coming to a program meeting the "other" and studying together? Perhaps they were desperate to get a better education. What were really their motivations? It took gigantesque efforts for us to secure their visas to come to the U.S. because of the post-9/11 laws, which made all Arabs suspects until proven otherwise. And it took our Palestinian students often more than two days to cross borders between Palestine and Israel (which would usually take less than a couple of hours) before traveling to join our program. For me, they were the ones making the sacrifice. They remain the heroes who gave us the hope for better days to come. They came to our programs with open hearts, minds, and spirits. They came to learn, talk, and get to know people who would have otherwise stayed anonymous for them. Palestinians and Israelis basically knew each other, as occupied and occupiers. We never studied together or worked together, at least as equal members of the same society. Israeli youngsters of my age were serving in the army and being sent to Palestinian cities and villages to fight, shoot, and arrest, and sometimes follow the army orders to kill. Getting to know them and befriend them was a seemingly impossible task. We knew each other as enemies and nothing else.

THE HOPE

The frustration and the failure of the peace process has only strengthened my belief that Palestinians and Israelis need to get to know each other better in order for the conflict to end, recognizing the harm that they have done to each other, and stopping dehumanizing the other. I have learned that behind every single army uniform, as bad, horrible, and ugly as it appeared from the outside for obvious reasons, there is a human face, a human story that needs to be told. The Israelis also have a distorted image of us; they have been brainwashed about what the Palestinians are, equating all of us with suicide bombers and terrorism, and never wanting to believe that, like the Jewish people, we have suffered deeply, lost our lands and homes, only to become refugees in our own land or elsewhere. Many have lost their lives. However, Israelis have always refused to try to understand the Palestinians, the desperation they are going through, the suffocating effect of an occupation imposed on 3.5 million Palestinian men, women, and children, for whom daily life, access to schools, universities, hospitals, and work are under constant control by others. These and many other things inflamed and kept alive tensions between the Israelis and the Palestinians. And in a much more civil way tension arose between members of the UME board and staff. Sometimes it was an unspoken tension, made of disappointment and anger, but it was there and you would feel it. Our board was composed of Arab Americans, Jewish Americans, as well as others, younger as well as older members. What was interesting within our board is that we disagreed politically and we were aware of it. But these disagreements, which sometimes triggered heated discussions, did not deter us from working together. It seemed always that our mission and goal would prevail over these various obstacles. This example highlights the fact that it is possible to understand (although differently) the context of war and destruction and still work together for a better future.

After all, many of the issues seemed of rather limited significance to those of us living in Europe or the U.S., busily going about our daily lives. Years later and away from the Middle East, I now understand better the circumstances influencing the region's disparate ideologies. I have come to see these issues not simply as ethnic differences based on historical enmity but instead as the struggle of two entities attempting to come to terms with themselves and their neighbors. Regrettably, efforts at reconciliation have been unsuccessful so far, as certain actors remain bent on forwarding their own interests at the expense of the common good.

That our project still exists at all bodes well for its future success. It also speaks volumes about the accomplishments that one can realize when political, social, and cultural differences are set aside to work toward a common goal. Our students are committed to fostering cooperation by looking past their differences, and this project is a first tentative step toward erasing the history of ignorance and hatred in the Middle East by creating a forum in which future generations can share knowledge and common goals. We owe the success of this institution to the students who believed in us and despite the animosities, still came together and proved that human relations are stronger than anything else, stronger than the "the wall of infamy" that the Israeli government has built, and stronger than Palestinian extremism. Each student has an individual story to tell about how he or she came face to face with "the enemy" and how they found the courage to explore the roots of this antagonism rather than play safe and back away.

A DAY AT UME

The first day of our program is always difficult. Because we accept people based on academic merit, we never know how these people will react when they face each other. It is in fact very interesting to observe how the Palestinian and Israeli students meet. They always find each other among the crowd, and they immediately connect. You feel that everyone else in the group, the Lebanese, the Jordanians, the Egyptians, are watching over them very closely while the Moroccans, Tunisians, and Algerians are less anxious and more open politically because they are relatively farther away from the conflict. The experience is extraordinary for not only the Palestinians and Israelis but also for the Arabs and Israelis as well as the Arabs and Arabs in the group. Still everyone is watching how the Palestinians behave with the Israelis before they also make the move. There is always some tension the first few days of the program. In the last few years and in the middle of the Intifada, we did not expect any of our Palestinian or Israeli students to even apply. To our surprise, it was the year that we had more applicants from both sides. For us, it was a clear sign that we needed to continue, that there is an urge for us to exist, a palpable one.

The atmosphere between the students goes from very tense, to very open and cordial. There are always lots of tears at the end of each program, people thankful for the experience, and just very worried about going back to a daily life where there is no longer any communication between people of different backgrounds. They are aware that they might never meet again despite their close geographical locations. Because of the Israeli closures and the Wall, Palestinians cannot go into Israel and vice versa. I consider our students to be the real heroes, not only based on their decision to spend a summer course with us and leave their differences behind but also because they have to go back and face their community; we remain to see how they talk freely about their feelings and suffering without offending the others. Two years ago, one of our Palestinian students in (the Teacher Education Institute) lost one of her colleagues during the summer program. He was a high school teacher like her, and he was killed in Bethlehem by the Israeli army. My colleagues and I were so worried about the group dynamics and about how this incident might affect the students and the overall program. I was concerned that all the Palestinians students would turn against the Israeli participants. Hearing the unfortunate news, I rushed to the campus only to find the students in the group all united together in one room, hugging and crying. The Israeli participants, all of whom were in tears surrounded the Palestinian student who lost her colleague. This was in stark contrast with the vengeance acts that one might have expected back home. People in our program had built enough confidence in the "other" to share their sufferings with humility. Two days after that incident, a suicide bomb struck in the middle of Tel-Aviv. All the Arab and Palestinian students were sitting with the Israeli participants waiting to hear news from their loved ones, holding their hands, telling them how sorry they felt and how much they condemned these senseless acts of violence.

In the summer of 2006, the escalation between Israel and the Palestinians especially in Gaza was again at it is highest. UME started the summer program fearing the worst. The first day was very tense and we received the Palestinian and Israeli participants with a great deal of emotion. At the opening ceremony that took place at the Irish Institute at Boston College, as it has for the last nine years, I acknowledged our students' courage to come in the worst times, and we all prayed for better days to come. I expected the situation in Israel-Palestine to get worse, but what no one expected was that within three days a war between Hizbullah and Israel would start. That year, we had four Palestinian participants, five Israeli, and four Lebanese in addition to twelve other Arabs. The Lebanese students were from the north and south of the country as well as Beirut. And as in Lebanon, they were divided between Sunni, Shia, a Druze, and a Maronite. The Israelis were mainly from the north of Israel. This was a recipe for disaster. It was an emotional time for all. The south of Lebanon and Beirut were under heavy bombardment, and missiles were hitting the northern part of Israel. The young Shia student did not know whether his wife and two young kids were dead or alive, and the young Israeli woman from Haifa learned that her husband and kids had to evacuate their home and move to another city in Israel. One of the Israelis had two of her children serving in the army and suspected that they were in Lebanon fighting Hizbullah. Another

Israeli participant learned that a missile had landed in her garden, and one Lebanese received the news that his neighbor had been killed. It was the beginning of a very long and hot summer program. Emotions were high on all levels. For me personally, living the Israel-Hizbullah war was worse than many incidents I had lived through in Palestine. Since I met my husband over ten years ago, we visit Lebanon every year. We had witnessed how this small country had been able to stand on its feet again and regain a sense of normalcy after twenty years of civil war and were proud of what the Lebanese had been able to achieve. As a Palestinian, it gave me the hope that we could do the same one day in Palestine. However, seeing it all collapsing on the TV screens, seeing my husband's family, and our friends fleeing the country yet again was just horrible. What was happening in Lebanon was very personal again.

Once again, I could not comprehend this level of violence. And once again, the strength to continue our mission came from our students. When I saw the Israeli participant whose house a Hizbullah missile hit, I told her how sorry I was and that I hoped that her family and friends were safe. She simply answered that the missile had only hit her garden and all were safe. She added that she was more worried about her Lebanese colleague whose neighbor was killed and who had no news about his wife and kids! I ran to my room where I was staying with them on campus and cried. I cried because I did not have their strength, because I could not be as forgiving, and because I was so angry at everything. But I also cried because this program was working. It showed people what they really were; these horrible times brought their humanity to daylight. In addition, I cried because I knew that none of them could go back and brag about spending the summer with an Israeli whose children were serving in the army, or a Lebanese from the south, or a Palestinian for that matter. I spent a few nights with them where they would sit, eat, talk, and even sing for hours. They all knew that the seminars would end soon. They would be going home not knowing whether they would see each other again. The last day of the program, they cried, hugged, and wished each other good luck. Everyone went home except for the Lebanese participants who could not. All accesses and roads to Lebanon were under fire. It took most of them four more weeks to go back to a country, which they barely recognized. I cannot tell you often enough how many stories we hear from our alumni who stay connected to each other and this group is one of them. The hope that others gave me a few years ago, I am now able to give to the others. The courage of looking into someone's eyes and telling them who you are and why you are here, whether your name is Mohammad, Moshe, or Issa, and to feel that we are all equal here in this program and in this setting. My hope for our students is that their experience with us will transcend all boundaries; that just two of them or perhaps many more will sit down in a coffee place one day, whether in Boston, Toledo, Jerusalem, or Casablanca, and decide together how they want the world to become a better place. It will be their turn to start their own dream.

REFLECTIONS

"The Child is the father of the Man," Wordsworth wrote. In this context, I would argue that the child is the parent of the leader. The child, her- or himself, emerges out of a network of genetic givens and social contexts. This relationship between the genes and society continues throughout life, so that to a greater or smaller degree, the group shapes the leader and the leader shapes the group. It is not a strict one-to-one ratio but requires a good enough resonance and attunement between the leader and the group—otherwise the leader and the group part company (Benson 2009). In this relationship, the group and leader regulate each other. This has significance for my development as a leader and the particular kind of group that I came to lead.

The circumstances under which I lived as a child and later as a teenager, in Nablus and Ramallah under the Israeli occupation, where I participated as all young men and women my age did in demonstrating, protesting, and throwing rocks, shaped my life and political consciousness. In the eyes of the West and of people watching from the comfort zone of their television screen, some might consider these acts of defiance as unnecessary violence. For us Palestinians, it was a natural decision to become part of the resistance against an occupying army. I pondered years later whether my path could have led me to become actively involved in more violent anti-Israeli activities, such as throwing bombs, as an act of desperation since demonstrations never failed to turn violent because of the provocative presence of the Israeli army and its implacable response to peaceful demonstrations. Such behavior would have been an understandable consequence considering my mother's torture, our daily lives under the Israeli torment, and similar personal, daily hardships that most of my fellow Palestinians experienced.

I did become a fighter, and I still am. That, I learned from my mother who was a very potent fighter. She fought with the pen and I identified with her strongly. I felt very much in tune with her, while also fearing for her life, a death that would break that bond. My mother received people in our house regardless of their political backgrounds: Palestinians, Israelis, as well as foreign personalities, activists, and media people. They spoke, discussed, and had heated political discussions in our house. My mother introduced the foreign and Israeli media to the daily hardships of Palestinians under occupation. She took them to villages and small towns to see the realities on the ground and become eyewitnesses themselves of the brutality of the occupation, a situation that the Israeli and foreign media was oblivious about. For that, she has paid the price: in prison and being put under house arrest where our house to all became our prison for over four months. Our house was guarded by Israeli police who asked people to identify themselves before entering the house. Being brought up in an active political house, with an outspoken mother has certainly affected the person I was and who I became today. My family's history and its story is one of millions. My father, Daoud, a banker, educated in Jaffa and later in Christ Church College in England, brought lots of wisdom to the family. His stories of tolerance among Jews and Arabs when he lived in Jaffa before 1948 always resonated with me. They were friends, colleagues, and good neighbors. Only wars, greed for land, and destructions separated them. As the youngest of five kids, I was the last one still living and staying with my parents in Palestine while my siblings were off to college in Europe. Fortunately, there was sufficient regularity attunement (Stern 1985) between my parents and me to carry me through the threat. My parents always feared for my life; that I might be killed by a settler or in a demonstration was a real concern and a fate eventually encountered by many of my peers. Many Palestinian youngsters from wealthy and upper-middle-class families in fact joined the resistance. A unique bond between Palestinians regardless of their socioeconomic background and level of education was active disobedience against the occupier. They were my group and helped shaped me.

Education was very important to my family, as it is important in Palestinian society as a whole, for which any price is accepted for the sake of teaching their kids and sending them later to pursue their higher education in Palestine when possible or abroad. But because my parents wished to remove me from the "battle ground" as I noted earlier, they sent me during my late adolescence to Paris, France to study. My fighting was then channeled through more peaceful means as I was now placed under different circumstances. This effectively removed me from the immediate threat of violence and placed me in a new environment where the idea of Palestinian resistance and the fight for identity received favorable echoes. Paris for the world at large is the city of lights, culture, and fashion, but for me, Paris was the city of liberty where oppressed people from all over the world received refuge, people who had suffered wars and personal threats to their lives or who were persecuted in their homelands. They all found refuge in the country of liberty and the Human Rights Declaration, where calls for helping minorities and taking a stand for the freedom of other nations would always abound. I was exposed there to other people's sufferings and heard stories of tyrannies and dispossessions. I found my identity in the sufferings of not only my people but also of many other persecuted groups that had found refuge in Paris in the 1980s and 1990s! They were new groups with which I felt varying degrees of attunement—the French Left movement, the Tibetans, the Kurds, the Iranians, the South Africans, and the Lebanese as well as many opposition movements of African and Middle Eastern countries. All would find refuge in France, while waiting for brighter days that would allow them to go back home. They was also the Jewish Left movement, the solidarity groups of the Palestinian people, the medical associations and many other France-Palestine solidarity groups that were very involved in helping shape the political and humanitarian consciousness of the French people. I strongly felt that we were no longer forgotten. As a college student in Paris, I was able to express myself freely in meetings and demonstrations. My participation did not involve running away from the soldiers and ducking bullets and tear gas grenades. The first demonstration in which I participated was a few weeks after I arrived in Paris. It was in September 1982; the demonstration was against the massacres of Sabra and Shatila perpetrated in Lebanon by Christian militias under the cover and guidance of the Israeli army. There were tens of thousands of French people, demonstrating peacefully, yelling and shouting slogans. The demonstrations included French party officials, syndicates, students, and ordinary citizens who were outraged by the massacres that killed hundreds of Palestinian civilians. We were asking for the withdrawal of Israel from Lebanon. The French police were there, but they were there to protect the demonstrators and to insure our safety. I did not need to hide stones in my pockets or put a couple of onions in my backpack (onions were used back home to protect us from the effects of tear gas!). These events made me wonder about a different kind of organized resistance that can change public opinion. I felt differing degrees of attunement with these new groups and with the ideas that emerged for me as soon as I arrived in France and struggled with being an alien far from home and felt shifts begin to take place in my identity (Rouchy 1995; Volkan 1997). Identity includes a sense of continuity, a sense of uniqueness and a sense of affiliation or belonging. The sense of affiliation or belonging was the aspect most challenged by the move.

I identified with the Palestinians of the diaspora and became involved in the student movement in France where it was possible to attend conferences and various meetings for Palestine. This freedom of expression felt good. It gave me hope that others were accepting our fight and were considering us as freedom fighters, not terrorists. But very soon I also realized that neither us nor the Israelis are at the center of the world. These tragic events happening at home, the killing of one or several civilians did not always make the headline news and sometimes barely made it to the news wires. However, my identity as a Palestinian was reinforced when I felt that

I could represent my country differently and maybe more effectively by talking about our suffering and our daily lives.

My emerging role as leader came to a head in Cambridge, Massachusetts, USA. The variety of friends that I noted earlier, numbers of whom would have been enemies at home, in this context, became friends. The ideas and budding identity shifts in Paris moved apace in this new context. The story I told earlier reveals the nature of the attunement between my group and me that led to the University of the Middle East Project. Maintaining that connection between the group and me, their leader, has not always been easy to sustain, nor even within the leadership itself, occasionally creating major stress between the group, the rest of the leadership, and me. (The leadership in this context refers to those who worked in other leadership roles with me.) The following is an instance of such stress. The stress was quite significant during the first years of the second Intifada. The few thousand Palestinians who were able finally to be home, and all Palestinian infrastructures were under constant attack. Israel itself was living under the threat of daily suicide bombings, and we at UME were trying to continue to survive as a group! The invasion of Iraq also had created an unspoken tension in the group, especially because some members had supported the invasion while I was vehemently opposed to it. In that instance, it was easier for me to remain silent about the events to avoid any friction with my group.

Last, it is important to note that the University of the Middle East Project resides in the United States and not in the Middle East, at least for now. One may think of this as simply fortuitous. However, another possibility is that the degree of misattunement between the various nations and ethnic groups in the Middle East may have made it difficult for me to lead effectively in that context. It would have required a different kind of leadership and a different kind of organization to create any effective connection and trust, possibly a less effective one.

In brief, my effectiveness as a leader, while finding its roots in my family and my society, needed to move beyond those roots to create and lead a group with which I could find reasonable trust while waiting and working actively for the creation of a Palestinian state alongside with the state of Israel.

REFERENCES

Benson, J. F. "The Northern Ireland Conflict and Peace Process: The Role of Mutual Regulatory Symbiosis between Leaders and Groups." In *Leadership in a Changing World: Dynamic Perspectives on Groups and Their Leaders*, edited by R. H. Klein, C. A. Rice, and V. L. Schermer. Lanham, Md.: Lexington Books, 2009.

Rouchy, J. C. "Identification and Groups of Belonging." *Group Analysis* 28 (1995): 129–41.

Safieh, A. *Children of a Lesser God*. London: Palestinian General Delegation to the United Kingdom, 1996.

Volkan, V. *Blood Lines: From Ethnic Pride to Ethnic Terrorism*. Boulder, Colo.: Westview Press, 1997.

8

"When Hatred Is Bred in the Bone": Terrorist Group Dynamics and the Psycho-cultural Foundations of Contemporary Terrorism[1]

Jerrold M. Post

If, as Alford asserts, the group is the fundamental unit of political life, then it is assuredly true that the major determinant of terrorist psychology and behavior is group dynamics (Alford 1994). It is the most powerful lens through which to survey the terrain of terrorist psychology and behavior. At the 2005 International Summit on Democracy, Terrorism and Security held in Madrid, Spain, on the first anniversary of the Madrid train station bombing, the Committee on the Psychological Roots of Terrorism[2] produced a consensus document (Post 2005c). Two principle findings were:

> **1. Explanations of terrorism at the level of individual psychology are insufficient in trying to understand why people become involved in terrorism.** Indeed, it is not going too far to assert that terrorists are psychologically "normal" in the sense of not being clinically psychotic. They are neither depressed, severely emotionally disturbed, nor are they crazed fanatics. Indeed, terrorist groups and organizations screen out emotionally unstable individuals. They represent a security risk. There is a multiplicity of individual motivations. For some, it is to give a sense of power to the powerless; for others, revenge is a primary motivation; for still others, to gain a sense of significance. Within each group there will be motivational differences among the members, each of whom will be motivated to different degrees by group interest versus self-serving actions as well as those inspired by ideology.

While to be sure some emotionally disturbed individuals have carried out acts of violence in the name of a cause, severe psychopathology is incompatible with being a member of a terrorist group. Indeed, terrorist groups regularly screen out individuals who are emotionally unstable. Just as the Delta Force and British Special Air Service (SAS) commandos would not wish to have an emotionally unstable individual in their ranks because they would pose a security risk, for the same reason, neither would a terrorist action cell wish to have an emotionally unstable member in its ranks.

> 2. **It is not individual psychology, but group, organizational, and social psychology, with a particular emphasis on "collective identity," that provides the most powerful lens to understand terrorist psychology and behavior.** For some groups, especially nationalist-separatist terrorist groups, this collective identity is established extremely early so that "hatred is bred in the bone." The importance of collective identity and the processes of forming and transforming collective identities cannot be overemphasized. This in turn emphasizes the sociocultural context, which determines the balance between collective identity and individual identity. A clear consensus exists that it is not understanding individual psychopathology but understanding group, organizational, and social psychology that provides the greatest analytic power in understanding this complex phenomenon, a phenomenon where collective identity is paramount. Terrorists have subordinated their individual identity to the collective identity so that what serves the group, organization, or network is of primary importance.

But there is a broad spectrum of terrorist groups, with widely differing causes. This is illustrated in figure 8.1.

This matrix reflects a great diversity of terrorist groups and organizations, with a great diversity of causes. We can distinguish among terrorist groups that have broad social support, antiregime terrorist groups, and terrorism arising from diaspora/émigré populations. Given how different their social history and causes, there is no reason to assume they would have similar group psychologies. Thus we should be speaking of terrorisms—plural— and terrorist psychologies—plural.

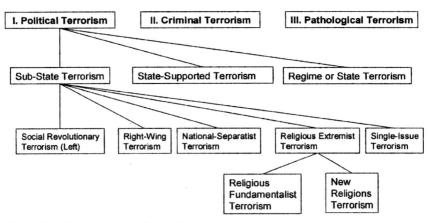

Figure 8.1.   New typology of terrorism.[3]

Given how different their causes and their perspectives, nationalist-separatist, social revolutionary, and religious fundamentalist terrorists would be expected to differ markedly in psychology. As there is a diversity of terrorist causes, the typology of terrorist groups also reflects a diversity of generational provenance. The X in figure 8.2 indicates that individuals who are at one with families who are at one with the regime do not become terrorists. Generational issues are particularly prominent for the two types of terrorism that dominated the scene at the onset of the modern era of terrorism in the early 1970s: social-revolutionary terrorism and nationalist-separatist terrorism.

As figure 8.2 reflects, in many ways, the generational dynamics of social-revolutionary terrorists and nationalist-separatist terrorists are polar opposites. Steeped in Marxist-Leninist ideology, the social-revolutionary terrorists included such groups as the Red Army Faction in West Germany, the Red Brigades in Italy, the Weather Underground in the United States, the Shining Path in Peru, and the FARC, the Revolutionary Armed Forces of Colombia. Their generational dynamics are represented in the lower-middle cell; they are are striking out against the generation of their parents that is loyal to the regime. Their acts of terrorism are acts of revenge for hurts, real and imagined. A member of the German terrorist group Red Army Faction declared, "These are the corrupt old men who gave us Auschwitz and Hiroshima." Jillian Becker (1978) addresses this dynamic with the German social-revolutionary terrorists in her aptly titled book, *Hitler's Children*.

For the most part, since the implosion of the Soviet Union in 1989, these groups have disappeared from the political scene, but the dynamics identified are those of Osama bin Laden! When he criticized as apostates the

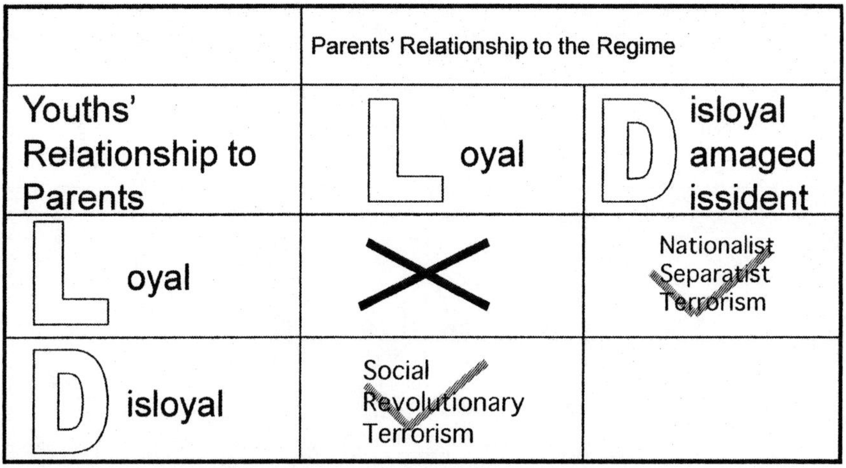

	Parents' Relationship to the Regime	
Youths' Relationship to Parents	L oyal	D isloyal amaged issident
L oyal	✕	Nationalist Separatist Terrorism
D isloyal	Social Revolutionary Terrorism	

Figure 8.2. Generational pathways to terrorism.[4]

leaders of Saudi Arabia from Sudan for permitting infidels to occupy "the land of the two cities" (Mecca and Medina), referring to the U.S. military bases in Saudi Arabia since the Gulf War, he was criticizing the royal family which had enriched his family, the regime to which his family was intensely loyal, and for his troubles bin Laden was both expelled from Saudi citizenship and his family turned their backs upon him. Thus, in addition to being a militant Islamist, he has the dynamics of a social revolutionary.

In contrast, the nationalist-separatist terrorists, represented in the upper-right-hand cell, are loyal to parents and grandparents who are disloyal to the regime and were damaged by the regime. They are carrying on the mission of their parents and grandparents, who were damaged by the regime, are dissident to the regime. Whether in the pubs of Northern Ireland or the coffeehouses in Gaza and the occupied territories, they have heard of the social injustice visited upon their parents and grandparents, they have heard their parents complaining of the lands stolen from them, and they have been raised on this bitter gruel of victimhood. It is time to stop talking and start acting.

For nationalist-separatist terrorist groups in particular, their collective identity is established extremely early so that from early childhood, "hatred is bred in the bone." The importance of collective identity and the processes of forming and transforming collective identities cannot be overemphasized. This fact in turn emphasizes the sociocultural context, which determines the balance between collective identity and individual identity. Terrorists have subordinated their individual identity to the collective identity so that what serves the group, organization, or network is of primary importance.

This subordination to the cause, in turn, gives the leaders of these terrorist groups who frame the cause a major role in creating the dominant terrorist psychology. As my committee at the Madrid summit on terrorism noted: "It is important to distinguish leaders from followers. The role of the leader is crucial in drawing together alienated, frustrated individuals into a coherent organization. The leader provides a 'sense-making' unifying message that conveys a religious, political or ideological justification to their disparate followers." Portraits of terrorist leaders, as a result, offer windows into the psychology and motivations of the followers who are attracted to their hate-mongering messages.

MOHAMMAD REZAQ:
THE GENERATIONAL TRANSMISSION OF HATRED

In the spring of 2006, the Department of Justice asked me to assist them with the trial of Mohammad Rezaq for his role in the skyjacking of an EgyptAir airliner over Malta; I spent some three days extensively interviewing him concerning his background and motivation (Post 2000). His case exemplified the generational transmission of hatred.

Rezaq's mother was eight years old in 1948 when the War of Independence occurred. They were forced to leave their home in Jaffa, an Arab suburb of Tel Aviv, and fled to her grandfather's farm on the West Bank. There they lived in relative harmony until 1967, when our terrorist-to-be, Mohammad Rezaq, was eight years old, and he and his family were forced to flee their comfortable home on the West Bank, ending up in a refugee camp in Jordan. As they were fleeing, his mother bitterly complained, "This is the second time I have been forced by the Israelis to leave my home."

In the UNICEF-supported school in the refugee camp, Rezaq was taught by a member of the PLO who told him the only way for him to become a man was to join the revolution and regain the lands stolen from his parents and grandparents. He had reading, writing, and arithmetic in the morning and paramilitary training in the afternoons from age nine on. He was not being trained to be a terrorist, but from his point of view, he was being taught to be a soldier for their cause. He moved from violent group to ever-more violent group, ending up in the Abu Nidal Organization. He was taught to blame all of the difficulties in his life on the Israelis, whom he saw as enemies in the war in which he was a heroic soldier. When he carried out the skyjacking, it was the proudest moment of his life, a dream fulfilled. At last, he was carrying out an action that would contribute to regaining his parents' land. But the dream turned into a nightmare, with tragic consequences. More than fifty people lost their lives in the hijacking and botched SWAT team attack. Rezaq is now serving a life sentence in federal prison.

PALESTINIAN SECULAR NATIONALIST
TERRORISTS IN THEIR OWN WORDS

One of the best ways of learning about the psychology of terrorists is, simply put, to ask them. In a sample of incarcerated secular Palestinian terrorists from al-Fatah and the Palestinian Front for the Liberation of Palestine, General Command, interviewed during the lull between the two *intifidas*, a major finding was that painful early background experiences shaped identity and steered Palestinian children and youth onto the path of terrorism (Post, Sprinzak, and Denny 2003). More than 80 percent of the secular group members reported growing up in communities that were radically involved.

Family Background and Early Life

As with most of the other Palestinian terrorist organizations, there was a dichotomy between how families felt in theory about their sons joining organizations and how they felt in reality. Publicly, families supported the organization and were proud of their sons for joining. Privately, they feared for their sons as well as for what the security forces might do to their families. Members were seen as heroes, but *on the other hand, families who had paid their dues to the war effort by allowing the recruitment of a son tried to prevent other sons from enlisting too.*

While most Fatah members reported their families had good social standing, their status and experience as refugees was paramount in their development of self-identity: *"I belong to the generation of occupation. My family are refugees from the 1967 war. The war and my refugee status were the seminal events that formed my political consciousness, and provided the incentive for doing all I could to help regain our legitimate rights in our occupied country."*

For the secular Palestinian terrorists, enlistment was a natural step, a step that increased social status.

> Enlistment was for me the natural and done thing. . . . In a way, it can be compared to a young Israeli from a nationalist Zionist family who wants to fulfill himself through army service.

> My motivation in joining Fatah was both ideological and personal. It was a question of self-fulfillment, of honor and a feeling of independence . . . the goal of every young Palestinian was to be a fighter.

> After recruitment, my social status was greatly enhanced. I got a lot of respect from my acquaintances, and from the young people in the village.

Decision-making and Military Hierarchy

Soldiers in the revolution exhibited a stark absence of critical thinking, with no questions concerning instructions and carrying out actions: *"There was no room for questioning. The commander got his orders from his superiors. You couldn't just take the initiative and carry out an armed attack without the commander's approval."*

View of Armed Attacks

In addition to being motivated to cause as many casualties as possible, it was our impression that armed action provided a sense of control or power for Palestinians in a society that had stripped them of it. Inflicting pain on the enemy was paramount in the early days of the Fatah movement.

> I regarded armed actions to be essential, it is the very basis of my organization and I am sure that was the case in the other Palestinian organizations. An armed action proclaims that I am here, I exist, I am strong, I am in control, I am in the

field, I am on the map. An armed action against soldiers was the most admired . . . the armed actions and their results were a major tool for penetrating the public consciousness.

KILLING IN THE NAME OF GOD: RELIGIOUS EXTREMIST TERRORISM

In the beginnings of the modern era of terrorism, the nationalist-separatist terrorists and social revolutionary terrorists regularly sought to call public attention to their cause. There were often competing claims of responsibility for their terrorist acts. Then in the late 1980s and early 1990s, the situation gradually changed; no responsibility was claimed for more than 40 percent of terrorist acts. These were the acts of religious fundamentalist terrorists. They were not trying to influence the West but to expel the West, with its secular, modernizing values. And they did not need a *New York Times* headline or a CNN story to claim responsibility, for they were "killing in the name of God," and God already knew. In addition to religious fundamentalist terrorists, the category of religious extremist terrorists also includes millenarian or new religions terrorists, exemplified by the Aum Shinrikyo terrorists responsible for the first major chemical weapons terrorist attack, the sarin gas attack on the Tokyo subways in 1995.

In the same interview study cited above, we also had the opportunity of interviewing religious extremist terrorists from Hezbollah and Hamas. The early exposure in the mosque to sermons concerned with the suffering of the Palestinian people identifying the cause as the actions of the government of Israel and the justification for defensive jihad was regularly cited by the interview subjects:

I came from a religious family which used to observe all the Islamic traditions. My initial political awareness came during the prayers at the mosque. That's where I was also asked to join religious classes. In the context of these studies, the sheik used to inject some historical background in which he would tell us how we were effectively evicted from Palestine.

The sheik also used to explain to us the significance of the fact that there was an IDF (Israel Defense Force) military outpost in the heart of the camp. He compared it to a cancer in the human body, which was threatening its very existence.

At the age of sixteen, I developed an interest in religion. I was exposed to the Moslem brotherhood and I began to pray in a mosque and to study Islam. The Koran and my religious studies were the tools that shaped my political Consciousness. The mosque and the religious clerics in my village provided the focal point of my social life.

Community support was important to the families of the fighters as well:

> Families of terrorists who were wounded, killed or captured enjoyed a great deal of economic aid and attention. And that strengthened popular support for the attacks.

> Perpetrators of armed attacks were seen as heroes, their families got a great deal of material assistance, including the construction of new homes to replace those destroyed by the Israeli authorities as punishment for terrorist acts.

The Emir blesses all actions:

> Major actions become the subject of sermons in the mosque, glorifying the attack and the attackers.

Joining Hamas or Fatah increased social standing:

> Recruits were treated with great respect. A youngster who belonged to Hamas or Fatah was regarded more highly than one who didn't belong to a group, and got better treatment than unaffiliated kids.

> Anyone who didn't enlist during that period (intifada) would have been ostracized.

The hatred socialized toward the Israeli was remarkable, especially given that few reported any contact with Israelis:

> You Israelis are Nazis in your souls and in your conduct. In your occupation you never distinguish between men and women, or between old people and children. You adopted methods of collective punishment, you uprooted people from their homeland and from their homes and chased them into exile. You fired live ammunition at women and children. You smashed the skulls of defenseless civilians. You set up detention camps for thousands of people in subhuman conditions. You destroyed homes and turned children into orphans. You prevented people from making a living, you stole their property, you trampled on their honor. Given that kind of conduct, there is no choice but to strike at you without mercy in every possible way.

Decision-making and Military Hierarchy

There is a clear hierarchical structure, with orders passed on down to unquestioning members of the organization. The leaders made the key decisions:

> And the rank and file were ready to follow through fire and water. I was subordinate to just one person. My relations with him were good, as long as I agreed to all that was asked of me. It was an organization with a very clear hierarchy,

and it was clear to me that I was at the bottom or the ladder and that I had to do whatever I was told.

Commanders in the Hamas are commanders in every way. A commander's orders are absolutely binding and must not be questioned in substance.

View of Armed Attacks

Armed attacks are viewed as essential to the operation of the organization. There is no question about the necessity of these types of attacks to the success of the cause:

> You have to understand that armed attacks are an integral part of the organization's struggle against the Zionist occupier. There is no other way to redeem the land of Palestine and expel the occupier. Our goals can only be achieved through force, but force is the means, not the end. History shows that without force it will be impossible to achieve independence. Those who carry out the attacks are doing Allah's work. . . .The more an attack hurts the enemy, the more important it is. That is the measure. The mass killings, especially the martyrdom operations, were the biggest threat to the Israeli public and so most effort was devoted to these. The extent of the damage and the number of casualties are of primary importance.

The Justification of Suicide Bombings

The Islamist terrorists in particular provided the religious basis for what the West has called suicide terrorism as the most valued technique of jihad, distinguishing this from suicide, which is proscribed in the Koran. One in fact became quite angry when the term was used in our question, angrily exclaiming, *"This is not suicide. Suicide is selfish, it is weak, it is mentally disturbed. This is istishhad* (martyrdom or self-sacrifice in the service of Allah)."

Several of the Islamist terrorist commanders interviewed called the suicide bomber holy warriors who were carrying out the highest level of jihad. Hassan Salame, perhaps the most notorious Palestinian suicide bomb commander, now serving forty-six consecutive life sentences, was eloquent in his interview:

> Every young Moslem understood the importance of our armed actions and we never needed ideology to justify them. . . . A martyrdom operation bombing is the highest level of Jihad and highlights the depth of our faith. The bombers are holy fighters who carry out one of the more important articles of Islam.

Another suicide bomb commander similarly explained:

> It is attacks when their member gives his life that earn the most respect and elevate the bombers to the highest possible level of martyrdom.

Defending himself against the notion that he was a murderer, he explained:

> *I am not a murderer. A murderer is someone with a psychological problem; armed actions have a goal. Even if civilians are killed, it is not because we like it or are blood-thirsty. It is a fact of life in a people's struggle—the group doesn't do it because it wants to kill civilians, but because the jihad must go on.*

The following extended quote from a suicide bomb commander sentenced to twenty-six consecutive life terms is interesting in revealing the aspiration to be a suicide bomber:

> *I asked Halil what it was all about and he told me that he had been on the wanted list for a long time and did not want to get caught without realizing his dream of being a martyrdom operation bomber. He was completely calm and explained to the other two bombers, Yusuf and Beshar, how to detonate the bombs, exactly the way he had explained things to the bombers in the Mahane Yehuda attack. I remember that besides the tremendous respect I had for Halil and the fact that I was jealous of him, I also felt slighted that he had not asked me to be the third martyrdom operation bomber. I understood that my role in the movement had not come to an end and the fact that I was not on the wanted list and could operate relatively freely could be very advantageous to the movement in the future.*

It is the normality of the aspiration that is particularly chilling. I am an intermediate tennis player, not terrible, not terrific, reflecting my intermediate athletic abilities. I still remember with shame the time in the sixth grade during recess when I was the last person chosen on the pick-up baseball team. Here the subject's feelings are hurt that he was not chosen to be on the pick-up suicide bomb team!

Commenting on the ubiquity of this attitude within Palestinian society, Ariel Merari, a noted Israeli terrorism expert, who teaches at Harvard Law School each fall, observed to me four years ago that "teenagers are teenagers the world around." "How do you mean, Ariel?" I asked. "Well," he responded, "as I walk around Harvard Square, and go into a pizza parlor, the kids are gossiping about their favorite team, the New England Patriots, their heroes on the team, such as Tom Brady, the quarterback, and when they grow up, they want to be a professional football player, like their heroes. Same thing in the refugee camps—only their favorite team is Hamas, their heroes are the *shahids* (the martyrs), and when they grow up, which they won't, they want to be *shahids* like their heroes.

DIFFERENTIATING GROUP DYNAMICS

For the underground, the psychology within the group is particularly powerful. Isolated from contact with the outside world, the member is extremely dependent upon the leader and fellow members for his sense of security, and challenging the group consensus is a risky matter. Consider the new member to the Heidelberg cell of the Red Army Faction Baeyer-Kaette interviewed. After a long and tedious process, he finally was accepted by the group and made Der Sprung (the leap), which meant he was committed to the underground life within the group, to being on the run, hunted by security authorities. He had always admired the Red Army Faction. Its attacks on industrialists and security forces all were designed to undermine the capitalist system. But at his first meeting as a new member, he heard of their next planned action, a firebombing of the KaDeWe department store. (The KaDewe chain is noted for its opulence, with its least expensive woman's frock costing some $400.) "Gott in himmel," he blurted out, "there will be all of these innocent victims." A chill fell over the room, as he recognized he had challenged the group consensus. He might lose his long coveted and only recently acquired membership in the group. Worse, he might be killed, for it was said that "the only way out of a terrorist group is feet first, by way of the graveyard." "Hans," the group leader coldly addressed him, "have you been to a KaDeWe store?" When Hans tremulously indicated that he had, the leader went on, "then surely you know that the people who shop there are not innocent victims, they are capitalist consumers. They are the enemy, and they deserve to die."

The underground cells with their leader present, with all of his warts and blemishes in plain view, are hothouses of tension. But when society retaliates, as ultimately it must, all internal dissension disappears, and it becomes "us versus them." At these times, the status of the group is elevated, for it confirms to them they are indeed the vanguard of the revolution, fighting against the illegitimate government. This differs from the terrorist organization with decision-making separated from the action cells.

But the nationalist-separatist and religious fundamentalist organizations described above are not underground but represent sentiments widely held within the broader society. These organizations can be considered to embody large group dynamics. Rather than being underground, the members are known within the society and are ascribed higher status than those within society at large who may admire them but have not as yet committed themselves to the path of terrorism. Given that entry to the path of terrorism and martyrdom may be in early childhood, the challenge for counterterrorism is challenging indeed.

LARGE GROUP PSYCHOLOGY AND
CHARISMATIC LEADER-FOLLOWER RELATIONS

A number of these movements embody charismatic leader-follower relationships. Charisma is not a characteristic of a leader but of a special bond between a leader and his followers (Post 1986). In these movements, psycho-culturally besieged individuals, feeling under threat and unable to succeed on their own, are drawn to a leader who identifies the outgroup as the cause of their frustrations and in effect promises a return to their rightful stature by striking out at and eliminating the identified enemy. This was the dynamic of "the true believer" Eric Hoffer (1951) so brilliantly articulated in *The True Believer* in which he sought to identify how Hitler drew so many to his cause, observing that Hitler "manipulated the slime of discontented souls."

While it is understandable how a distorted interpretation of scripture can be used to justify, indeed give sacred significance to, suicide terrorism, how individuals in a secular nationalist-separatist cause can be persuaded to give their lives for the cause is not immediately self-evident. The answer lies in the dynamics of the large group, where devoting oneself to the nationalist cause as articulated by the charismatic hate-mongering leader has been ac-cepted as the major—indeed sole—identifier by the member, so that he or she is persuaded that the act of martyrdom will benefit the group cause. The individual's life is not of concern, for individuality has been subordinated to the group cause, almost as a matter of religious faith. The all-encom-passing group is paramount. This is true of the PKK, the Kurdish separatist group under Abdullah Ocalan, and the Tamil Tigers, under Prabhakaran. Where the dominant society has engaged in a process of "identicide," this facilitates the emergence of a power leader-follower charismatic group rela-tionship. This was true in Turkey where in his pursuit of consolidating Tur-kic identity Mustafa Kemal Atatürk, the founder of Turkey, referred to Kurds as mountain Turks and made protest in the service of promoting Kurdish nationalism and even the Kurdish language illegal. This was true for Basque nationalism and language as well, where Franco made political action in the service of promoting Basque identity and the use of the Basque lan-guage *etarra* illegal. And in Sri Lanka, the Sinhala majority did not recognize the rights of the Tamil minority and sought to eliminate their participation in society. These acts of "identicide" gave force to pursuing nationalism as a faith, justifying defensive aggression in preserving their threatened identity. The leaders identify acts in the service of preserving their threatened nation as heroic, of sacred significance. And these acts of martyrdom are engraved in the threatened nation's history.

GROUP DYNAMICS OF
TERRORIST GROUPS AND ORGANIZATIONS:
IMPLICATIONS FOR COUNTERTERRORISM[5]

Given the power of the group in influencing and determining terrorist be-havior, it is critical that counterterrorist strategy embody knowledge of terrorist group dynamics (Post 2005b). If for every terrorist killed or captured, ten more are waiting in line, counterterrorism strategy that does not counter this ever-replenishing dynamic is bound to fail. Terrorism is a vicious form of psychological warfare, with violence against innocents as the instrumental act designed to win the attention of the audience to the cause. One does not counter psychological operations with smart bombs and missiles. One counters it with psychological warfare.

And that psychological warfare must embody a group focus. In particular, it should:

1. Inhibit potential terrorists from joining the group in the first place.
2. Produce dissension in the group.
3. Facilitate exit from the group.
4. Marginalize and reduce support for the group and delegitimate its leader.

I will now expand on these four elements of a comprehensive counterterrorism strategy that is group oriented in its focus.

1. Inhibit potential terrorists from joining the group in the first place.

The group dynamics are so powerful, that once in the group, it is very difficult to alter the member's mind-set for all of the group's rhetoric is designed to consolidate an "us vs. them" psychology (Post 1987). In the al Qaeda training camps in Afghanistan, fully half of the day was spent in ideological indoctrination. Given the natural movement into the terrorist group, perceived to be a valued action within the community, combating such widespread deeply engrained attitudes will obviously be extremely challenging. Yet unless these attitudes are combated, an ever-growing stream of potential terrorists will replace those killed or arrested.

In research on Middle Eastern terrorists, considerable ambivalence was found within the family, despite public support for the martyrdom of their children. One mother, who had already lost a son, reported to Nasr Hassan, a Pakistani Muslim who is on the UN staff and has interviewed "the human bombs," that if she could, she would cut a hole in her heart, take her remaining son and place him in her heart where he would be safe, and sew it up.

A particular problematic issue is schooling potential terrorists. The virulent anti-West brand of Islam being taught in the radical madrassahs of Pakistan is a case in point. What steps might be taken to ameliorate the poison to which these children are being exposed? How can moderate Muslim clerics be encouraged to help moderate the curriculums in the madrassahs? A friend reported a program of the Department of Labor recently funded in

Pakistan to combat child labor, a grant establishing secular schools. It turns out that for only $80, a student can receive a year's education. Each child educated in such a school is one not exposed to the anti-Israel, anti-West hatred propagated in the radical madrassahs.

So many dispirited youth, encouraged by hate-mongering leaders, seeing a bleak future, are encouraged and feel impelled to strike out violently out of despair. What can be done to open pathways so that ambitious youth can look forward to a future within their society? Support to programs that encourage economic development and the opening up of these societies, be it in Egypt, Pakistan, or the West Bank and Gaza, can be of major assistance in shrinking the reservoir of dispirited youth.

Both of these suggested measures—educational support and economic programs—require government agencies or NGOs funding these programs, but I believe such investment would go a long way toward reducing the population that sees no path other than the path of terrorism.

2. Produce dissension within the group.

My understanding of the group dynamics in terrorist groups is that they are virtual hothouses of tension. When they are attacked, internal tensions and disunity disappears, and it becomes "us against them." What could be done to magnify tension within the group? To sow distrust within the group? To recast the image of the group leader, of pretenders to the throne? To weaken the already stressed climate of trust and paralyze the group with distrust? Injecting such ideas into a closed group is by no means easy, but I suggest not impossible, and could be extremely helpful in reducing group cohesion and efficiency.

3. Facilitate exit from the group.

One of the difficulties in becoming a terrorist is that once one has made that choice, it is very hard to turn back, for an early hurdle to full acceptance is to carry out a terrorist action, which in turn can lead to a criminal sanction. Yet a number of governments countering terrorism have instituted creative amnesty programs akin to the protected witness program in the United States, where in return for cooperation and provision of information, amnesty is given to the cooperating terrorist, as well as financial support in entering their new life, in some cases extending to resettling in other countries and even provision of plastic surgery, as was the case with Spanish authorities and some ETA defectors. The *pentiti* program instituted by the Italian government was instrumental in breaking the back of the Red Brigades. Moreover, information developed by the defectors can then be fed back to the group and strengthen option two, Producing Dissension within the Group.

4. Marginalize and reduce support for the group and delegitimate its leaders.

Finally, and of extreme importance in information operations directed against the group, Reduce Support for the Group and Its Leaders. This is crucial. Let us consider as an important exemplar of this goal al Qaeda and bin Laden. For years he has been engaged in the arena of marshalling opinion to his view of Islam and the West, in which pursuit he has been unchallenged. The virulent brand of Islam that he has championed, the violence and destruction that he has found justification for in his extreme interpretation of the Koran—these views, which of course are consistent with those of leaders of Hamas and Islamic jihad, have not been countered. Becoming a member of al Qaeda and supporting its cause has been found to be attractive to alienated Muslim youth who were sensitized in the madrassahs and had their enmity focused in the mosques.

In the trial during the spring and summer of 2001 in federal court in New York of the al Qaeda bombers of the U.S. embassies in Tanzania and Nairobi, I served as expert witness during the death penalty phase and had the opportunity of spending some seventeen hours with one of the lower-level participants of the bombing in Dar es Salaam as well as one of the seniors in the organization. What was compelling was the role of the madrassah and the mosque, particularly the mosque. In the madrassah in Zanzibar, he was taught to never question learned authorities, especially those with religious credentials. In the mosque in Dar es Salaam, where he felt welcomed as a member of the *uma*, the community of observant Muslims, he heard of the obligations of Muslims to help other Muslims, wherever they were. He was shown films of Muslim mass graves in Bosnia and the bodies of Muslim women and children in Chechnya. Alone and isolated except for the mosque, he vowed, in his words, to become a soldier for Allah and defend these innocent victims against the soldiers of Serbia and Russia. When he gave voice to these sentiments, a man whom I infer was a spotter for al Qaeda informed him that to be a soldier for Allah, he must get training, and using, his own money, he went to Pakistan, was screened, and sent to an Osama bin Laden training camp in Afghanistan. After seven months of training, when he was offered only participation in Kashmir but could not fight the soldiers in either Bosnia or Chechnya, he returned to Dar es Salaam, isolated, aimless, as an assistant grocery clerk, but still participating in the mosque, until three years later when he received a call and was asked if he wanted to participate in a jihad job. Without further question, he responded yes, and entered the pathway of terrorism. His pious wish to defend Muslim victims was bent into participating in an act of mass casualty terrorism. As he was confronted with the consequences of the bombing in which he had participated, in contrast to other terrorists, he was overwhelmed emotionally with the death of innocents, that what he had done was inconsistent with his views of jihad. "Their jihad," he said, "is not my jihad." Nor however is it the jihad of the majority of mainstream Muslims, yet they have been remarkably mute, giving free rein to bin Laden and his colleagues to steer alienated youth into this extremist path in the name of Islam. Bin Laden's justifications, as spelled out in the al Qaeda Terrorism Manual, are inconsistent with the Koran, and yet to the unquestioning alienated youth, they are taken as religious justification for killing in the name of God (Post 2005a). How to counter these religiously based arguments? This will take moderate Islamic clerics and moderate Islamic leaders engaging in the task of reclaiming their hijacked religion, depicting bin Laden and his ilk as distorting the meaning of the Koran, as violating the spirit of Islam in the service of self-aggrandizing motivations of the leaders. The goal is to make the group not a mainstream path for alienated youth, but a deviant path, and to not have the leaders be seen as romantic heroes, but as preachers of a perverted Islam. This requires activating voices not now heard, for these changes must come from within Islam, and at the present the voices of extremism are not contested.

VIRTUAL GROUP DYNAMICS

This chapter would be incomplete were it not to call attention to a special emerging type of group dynamics of increasing relevance to terrorist recruitment and group dynamics—virtual group dynamics. According to Gabi Weimann (2006), author of *Terror on the Internet*, there are now some 4,800 radical Islamist websites. Youths increasingly have incorporated review of favorite websites into their daily routines. What role do these radical websites play in consolidating radical political identity in the youth whose psychology is in transition? Do they become members of a virtual community of extremist hatred? How to counter this powerful—and growing—influence? These questions are raised not to provide answers but to emphasize that virtual group dynamics is emerging as an area of great importance requiring applied research.

NOTES

1. This chapter draws on several major sources: J. Post, *The Mind of the Terrorist: The Psychology of Terrorism from the IRA to al-Qaeda* (New York: Palgrave-Macmil-

lan, 2007); J. Post, "When Hatred Is Bred in the Bone: Psychocultural Foundations of Contemporary Terrorism," *Political Psychology* 26(4) (2005d): 615–36; J. Post, E. Sprinzak, and L. Denny, "The Terrorists in Their Own Words: Interviews with 35 Incarcerated Middle Eastern Terrorists," *Terrorism and Political Violence* 15(1) (2003): 171–84; J. Post, "Psychological Operations and Counter-terrorism," *Joint Force Quarterly* 37 (2005b): 105–10.

2. Jerrold M. Post, M.D., Chair; Members of Committee: Scott Atran, Ph.D.; Dipak Gupta, Ph.D.; Nasra Hassan; John Horgan, Ph.D.; Ariel Merari, Ph.D.; Marc Sageman, M.D.; Alex Schmid, Ph.D.; Chris Stout, Ph.D.; Jeff Victoroff, M.D.; and Stevan Weine, M.D.

3. This graphic is a modified version of a typology of terrorism first introduced by A. Schmid, *Political Terrorism: A Research Guide* (New Brunswick, N.J.: Transaction Books, 1983).

4. This generational matrix was first introduced by the author in J. Post, "Notes on a Psychodynamic Theory of Terrorism," *Terrorism* 7(3) (1984): 241–56.

5. These ideas were first advanced in a paper prepared for Countering Terrorism through Strategic Psychological Operations presented to the International Conference on Counter-Terrorism in Democracies, University of Haifa, December 30, 2002–January 2, 2003. This paper was published as J. Post, "Psychological Operations and Counter-terrorism." *Joint Force Quarterly* 37 (2005b): 105–10.

REFERENCES

Alford, F. *Group Psychology and Political Theory.* New Haven, Conn.: Yale University Press, 1994.

Becker, J. *Hitler's Children: The Story of the Baader-Meinhof Gang.* London: Panther Books, 1978.

Hoffer, E. *The True Believer: Thoughts on the nature of Mass Movements.* New York: HarperCollins, 1951.

Post, J. "Notes on a Psychodynamic Theory of Terrorism." *Terrorism* 7(3) (1984): 241–56.

———. "Narcissism and the Charismatic Leader-Follower Relationship." *Political Psychology,* 7(4): 675–88.

———. "Hostilite, Conformite, Fraternite: The Group Dynamics of Terrorist Behavior." *International Journal of Group Psychotherapy* 36(2) (1986): 211–24.

———. "Murder in a Political Context: Profile of an Abu Nidal Terrorist." *Bulletin of the Academy of Psychiatry and the Law* 28 (2000): 171–78.

———, ed. *Military Studies in the Jihad Against the Tyrants: The Al-Qaeda Training Manual.* Maxwell Air Force Base, Ala.: USAF Counter-Proliferation Center, 2005a.

———. "Psychological Operations and Counter-terrorism." *Joint Force Quarterly* 37 (2005b): 105–10.

———. "The Psychological and Behavioral Bases of Terrorism: Individual, Group and Collective Contributions." *Addressing the Causes of Terrorism: The Club de Madrid Series on Democracy and Terrorism* 1 (2005c): 7–12.

———. "When Hatred Is Bred in the Bone: Psychocultural Foundations of Contemporary Terrorism." *Political Psychology* 26(4) (2005d): 615–36.

———. *The Mind of the Terrorist: The Psychology of Terrorism from the IRA to al-Qaeda.* New York: Palgrave-Macmillan, 2007.

Post, J., E. Sprinzak, and L. Denny. "The Terrorists in Their Own Words: Interviews with 35 Incarcerated Middle Eastern Terrorists." *Terrorism and Political Violence* 15(1) (2003): 171–84.

Schmid, A. *Political Terrorism: A Research Guide.* New Brunswick, N.J.: Transaction Books, 1983.

Weimann, G. *Terror on the Internet: New Arena, and New Challenges.* Washington, D.C.: United States Institute of Peace Press, 2006.

9

The Northern Ireland Conflict and Peace Process: The Role of Mutual Regulatory Symbiosis between Leaders and Groups

Jarlath F. Benson

"It's a case of I am the leader, there is the mob. I must follow" (Moloney 2008, p. 293).

This chapter examines the deeper underlying needs that seek expression and fulfillment through political conflict. It is asserted that leaders and groups resonate with the deepest causes of these conflicts and that the dynamics between these partners can prolong or transform intractable conflict. The Northern Ireland conflict and peace process is explored because the author is most familiar with that circumstance and also because it offers striking examples of an essential process of attunement and misattunement between leaders and their groups.

THE NORTHERN IRELAND CONTEXT

At one minute to midnight on July 31, 2007, the British army terminated the longest running operation in its military history, and life in Northern Ireland officially returned to normal. A simple one-line sign-off on the Military Radio network announced, "Operation Banner is terminated" (*Newsletter*, August 2007, p. 10).

This military intervention, which had dominated social, political, and psychological life for four decades, was driven through in 1969 by the British government in Westminster over the wishes of the local partisan Stormont parliament as policing in the province collapsed amid large-scale street riots, interfactional clashes, bombings, assassinations, and the fear of anarchy. Thirty-eight years later the ending of Operation Banner in what was intended at the outset to be a "limited operation" marked the completion of a quite remarkable change in the security situation and in the everyday life of the province and its strife-torn peoples.

Two questions immediately spring to mind: First, how has four decades of intractable conflict been resolved in a peace process and made amenable to politics; and second, what were the factors and dynamics that made the situation intractable in the first place?

I argue in this chapter that the answer to both questions has to do with a complex relationship in the local system of leaders and groups in which leaders created and inspired groups and groups created and followed leaders, so long as they channeled, reflected, and expressed the deepest feelings, images, needs, and aspirations of the participants. Alderdice has similarly argued that "the personality of the leader is a representation of some key elements of the psychology of the group s/he leads, as well as mirroring particular qualities and providing an inspiring role model" (2007, p. 202). This assertion derives from the work of Bion (1961) on "basic assumptions" or collective defense mechanisms that has clearly illustrated how groups in situations of real or imagined crisis are able to unconsciously select particular members with distinct psychological predispositions in an attempt to lead them out of danger and manage the heightened emotional anxieties of the group. Hopper (1997) has added a fourth basic assumption to Bion's original three and asserts that traumatized and regressed groups oscillate between a tendency to mass and merge to deny differences and maintain sameness and togetherness and an opposing tendency to feel alienated from each other, indifferent, and aggressively withdrawn. I demonstrate later how regressed groups operating in either polarity seek out leaders who mirror and endorse the groups' belief systems and fantasies.

An attempt to explain the phenomenon of intractable conflict in Northern Ireland might offer a three-part schema beginning with loss and grievance (material or ideational) moving to a demand for justice and reparation before culminating in violence in the absence of redress. The grievance would involve disputed and contested territory, the status of violence as a recursive cultural and political institution in a controversial state, and the corrosive effects of civil, economic, and electoral deprivations which are perpetuated by sectarian institutions (Bew 2007; Bowyer Bell 1993; McKittrick and McVea 2001; Tonge 2005).

Such an analysis would be linear and clear but would not help us get to grips with the "deep structure" of unrelenting and decivilizing nature of violence here and its mutation into permanent sectarianism, tribal feuding, rioting, and gangsterism. We should also require an explanation of how such primitive and inarticulate passions were gradually transformed into a peaceful verbal and mental process.

I suggest that we need to elaborate a psychosocial perspective—one that views the conflict and the peace process as both a social and psychological phenomenon that constructs novel as well as regressive forms of enactment and performance between the groups and their leaders who inherited the historical problem and who were eventually to go on and create the solution. Such a psychosocial perspective would assert that violence became detached from its initial context and became the condition of its own repetition and reproduction because of pathological and regressive narcissistic dynamics (Benson 1992, 1995). Healthy group relations, functional leadership, and mutual collaboration and exchange were corrupted and replaced with meaningless and symptomatic communication at the level of action and ritual.

The failure of group relations and of thoughtful and articulate leadership resulted in a disastrous and divisive subgrouping characterized by a malign and violent mimetic reciprocity that in turn triggered a de-differentiation and de-individuation in society. It is a fact that in a small country of one and a half million people, tens of thousands of men and women became involved with violent republican and loyalist groups. One observer commenting on how deeply society was permeated by paramilitarism estimates that more than 30,000 people served terms of imprisonment, and it follows that the numbers involved in servicing the conflicting groups must have been correspondingly greater (McKittrick and McVea 2001, p. 150).

At the psychic epicenter of this dissonant society, a dangerous and recidivist narcissism rejected dialogue and relationship and was malignantly self-absorbed and self-fulfilling. Only gradually and painfully with the patient construction of new emotional and mental maps and relationships has an eagerness for political activity and unarmed struggle replaced a centuries-old tradition of armed rebellion and counterviolence.

The initial and prolonged intercommunal strife and the gradual transformation of this enduring conflict has to do with how groups and their leaders continuously redefined and co-created each other in what I shall term a "mutual regulatory symbiosis." I mean by this term is that groups and their leaders will create, select, and relate to each other not simply on rational grounds but on the basis of an emotional resonance and attunement. This resonance and attunement enables each partner in the interaction to participate in each other's state of mind, reflect and express what they care about most deeply, and thereby predict what they will do and say. This ensures cohesion for the group, affirms identity, and provides security for all.

I contend that groups and leaders search each other out so that they might share, confirm, and shape each other's experience and provide opportunities for a reciprocal resonance of their deepest feelings and desires and view of the world. The result is a cyclical process of constant mental and emotional influence—an interactional synchrony between the partners. Groups and their leaders symbiotically participate in a mutual regulation of their emotional states and aspirations and this serves to maintain self-cohesion and identity and reinforce historically resonant views and expectations of the world or conversely enable people to manage change and transition with creative and healthy strategies.

In addition, every group and leader partnership is emotionally connected to every other group and leader partnership in the social system, even though previously they may have often refused to recognize each other or interact in any way. Thus, they are reciprocally determined so that how one leader or group behaves affects how another leader or group behaves, and the subsequent behavior then influences the original leader-group partnership in a positive or negative spiral phenomenon. This dynamic was emphasized at the annual party conference of the constitutional nationalist Social and Democratic Labour Party (SDLP) in November 2007. At that time, the party leader, Mark Durkan, asserted that his party had "changed the politics of every other party on the island without changing a single principle of our own or sacrificing a single value" (Clarke 2007).

The recent work of the political psychologist Drew Westen supports my assertion of a deep emotional basis in complex group and political phenomena. Based on of the latest cognitive neuroscience and his own research using magnetic resonance imaging to monitor the development of political attitudes, Westen asserts that "the political brain is an emotional brain" (2007, p. xv). He overwhelmingly concludes that what matters most in politics is how partisans feel toward their parties and their principles, how people feel toward their leaders, and how they feel about their leaders' policy positions (2007).

Truth and progress depends of course on how much information and relationship leaders and their groups are willing or can bear to include or exclude to maintain group cohesion and identity. Inevitably in polarized societies, several possible truths and a primitive group consciousness will generate contradiction and conflict whereas a more evolved and sophisticated group consciousness can sustain plurality and paradox and generate creativity and a hopeful way forward.

An infamous example of the emotional upheaval generated by irreconcilable truths occurred in the early 1980s when the Reverend David Armstrong, the Limavady First Presbyterian Church minister, was forced to flee the province following a bitter controversy that enraged religious hard-liners. It generated insults and ultimately death threats and sparked a political war of words that even reached government level in the regional Assembly. The Reverend Armstrong fell afoul of his own congregation and church and transgressed their beliefs and values by simply exchanging pulpit greetings on Christmas morning 1983 with the local Catholic cleric (*Belfast Telegraph,*

Dec. 24, 2000). As a leader, he was no longer attuned to the values and beliefs of his parishioners in terms of what his group could bear emotionally and was ultimately exiled from Londonderry. As Steve Bruce comments in a recent work, "it was his own people who drove him out" (2007, p. 63).

I believe this is what Brendan Behan meant when he famously quipped "that the first item on the agenda at any group meeting in Ireland is the split!" Certainly the psychological dynamics of splitting and malign projective identification are, as we shall observe, most important factors contributing to the poisonous and vituperative political factionalism here. Where once Unionism, for example, at least in its own estimation, stood for the interests of the majority political and ethnic bloc, interpreted their wishes, and confirmed their security and right to rule, that party eventually fragmented into some six competing and hostile groups. Consequently, leaders as individuals and factions quarreled over whom most truly represented traditional values and directions. Similarly, the minority Nationalist and Republican interests diverged and fractured into fissiparous groups and leaders. Equally, the murderous and confusing alphabet of paramilitary factionalism came about not least because of various groups defining themselves as ideologically purer than previous comrades whom they were only too willing to kill or have their political enemies assassinate. Northern Ireland degenerated into a place full of aggrieved people whose rage and humiliation found expression in feuds and retaliation and whose self-esteem was measured in terms of enviously depriving and begrudging others.

Groups and their leaders here have long had to engage in a continual wary and vigilant mutual interaction and search for emotional resonance if authority is not to be undermined and deposed and subgroups splinter off to join the nearest extreme position. A recent dramatic example of this was the 2004 defection of the Ulster Unionist Party (UUP) MP Jeffrey Donaldson to the more extreme Democratic Unionist Party (DUP) led by the Reverend Ian Paisley. Donaldson had long been a critic of the UUP party leader David Trimble's decision to operate the local Assembly without complete and verifiable IRA arms decommissioning and was a long-time standard-bearer for the hard-line right wing within the UUP. After a protracted and acrimonious public wrangle, which brought the party into disrepute, Donaldson finally split from his political group, taking colleagues with him to join with his former political enemy Paisley. The UUP vote collapsed in the local government and Westminster elections of the following year as large numbers of party faithful followed Donaldson into the DUP ranks (Bruce 2007, pp. 129–30).

What was evident was that David Trimble as a leader was unable to regulate the emotional conflicts of his group in the way that the republican leadership is able to (publicly at least) regulate its own emotional conflicts and maintain party and communal morale. The chief negotiator for the British Government has attested to "Trimble's poor people skills and the bad management of his party" (Powell 2008, p. 111). The emotional trauma to the UUP cannot be overstated. For the first time in its history, a majority of the people it claimed to know and represent had rejected the UUP.

THE SYMBIOTIC NATURE OF THE SELF AND SOCIETY

I want to turn now and consider the important question of how individual and group identity become intertwined at local and national levels. The starting point of such a psychosocial approach must elucidate the nature of the self and identity. Identity is what marks us out and stamps us as a particular and unique individual. The etymological root of the word *identity* is derived from a Greek word *idio* which means distinct, personal, particular, private and gives us such English words as idiom—one's own particular way of speaking; idiosyncrasy—one's own particular way of behaving—and of course idiot—one who is inexperienced or lacks an identity. To have an identity is to manage the paradox of multiplicity and oneness; we live in many and contradictory worlds and are aware of many aspects and sides to ourselves and yet there is an enduring sense of being a person, of having a core identity or essential self.

We can delineate four dimensions and characteristics of this self that have importance for our study. The self that I am has a body, has a psychology, is a social being, and is preoccupied with existential, ethical, and transcendental questions (Benson 2001, p. 253). Leaders and their groups are constantly engaged in a mutual work of cementing and protecting these dimensions of self and ensuring their coherence and expression, and the implicit contract is that leaders mirror safe self-images to the group, regulate and manage unbearable feelings while promoting positive feelings and providing opportunities for inspiration and idealization—or are deposed!

This contract between leaders and their groups must first acknowledge and address a psychophysical context, which has to do with embodiment and being related to a particular environment. The body can become a vehicle for exchanging secret communications or a weapon of war as in a hunger strike and issues of physical territory so vital in the Northern Ireland context. These can range from the painting of wall murals and the daubing of street pavements with partisan colors to contentious flying of flags and emblems and hostile assertion of the right to march disputed routes.

The interrelationship of the body, psyche, and society has long been an observable feature of the social psychology of Northern Ireland. In the early days of the "Troubles," young women in Republican areas who fraternized with British soldiers had their heads shaved and were publicly tarred and feathered. As the conflict persisted, kneecappings and other grotesque physical assaults were used to punish community offenders, discipline wavering partisans, advertise and propagandize paramilitary presence, strength, and righteousness as alternatives to despised traditional and now ineffective authority. Republican prisoners used mass starvation in an attempt to persuade the Westminster government to grant them prisoner-of-war status. Lethal anorexia and hunger was politicized as a sacrificial act to purify and decriminalize the prisoner and subvert the state. Earlier, the same prisoners had embarked on the "Dirty Protest" in which they smeared their feces on the walls of their cells, thus using their bodies and even their waste products as weapons to attack and humiliate their enemies (Rice and Benson 2005).

Second, the contract between partners includes a careful monitoring of the psychological context where subjective experience and responses emanating from feelings deep within of which we are hardly aware are given voice and confirmation. Leaders are adept at appealing to the deepest emotions of their groups for both positive and negative outcomes and are able to inflame as well as soothe anxious and suspicious followers.

Third, leaders and groups must pay attention to a psychosocial context, which maintains interpersonal relations and subgroupings and maintains involvement in a social medium of meanings, customs, culture, and politics. The calendar is littered with commemorations of past triumphs such as successful gunrunning escapades, glorious battles, loss of brave warriors, and the triumphs of wise leaders. The litany is endless, and leaders and groups use these psychosocial events to maintain self-cohesion, affirm identity, and sniff out weakness or treachery. Recently, the Irish language has become a means of identifying, affirming, and cohering a republican and at times militant self-expression to the exclusion and rage of opponents. This has been reciprocally mirrored by funding and insistence on the establishment of the Ulster-Scots language as an expression of a unionist and loyalist cultural identity. The war of tongues caused heated exchanges in the local Assembly in October 2007.

Finally, a psychospiritual dimension to human life provides leaders and groups with self-awareness, purpose, meaning, values, ethics, and choices. In a discussion of individuals and groups prone to violence, Alderdice acknowledges that "they espouse transcendent values such as 'justice for their people' which are regarded as higher than issues of normal individual morality" (2007, p. 202). Commenting on prayer and protest in political life, Bew records how during the hunger strikes wall murals in republican ghettoes depicted the hunger strikers as Christ-like figures with rosary beads being frequently displayed and comments how "young activists on public demonstrations switched seamlessly from political chant to deal out a decade at the rosary" (2007, p. 528). Unresolved issues of nationality, religion, and power laden with historical baggage have immense significance for the contesting groups and most leaders recognize the need to resonate with these deep values and guiding principles in their groups. Groups can be volatile and are prone to fission around these sensitive values and purposes and disputes about purity and lineage have been lethally common.

How do these four contexts and dimensions of identity mesh and interrelate, and how are they transmitted and maintained? Rupert Sheldrake provides an intriguing biological theory that is helpful to our inquiry. His theory of Morphic Resonance asserts that individual and group behavior is shaped by informational fields, which extend through space and time and represent the collective and cumulative memory of a particular species, race, or culture. These morphic fields structure human thought, language, customs, culture, and society, and they organize the interrelationship of these component parts. They are stabilized by resonance with the society or group's own past and inculturate the developing individual.

In the Irish preoccupation with history and how it defines identity, we see evidence for Sheldrake's (1988) thesis that "through repetition the nature of things becomes increasingly habitual." And of course "things are as they are because they were as they were." The loyalist battle of the Boyne, the Siege of Derry, and the republican "Blood Sacrifice" of 1916 continue to be fought out in the psyche of Northern Irish groups and communities. A large part of the popular culture, custom, and mythology of the major traditions here derives from the suffering and longings of the past and is given enormous valency by the continued sufferings and longings of the present. The pain of the past gives legitimacy to the struggles of the present, and one must endure the pain of the present if one is to affirm or redeem past sacrifice. These potent sadomasochistic and aggressive themes and impulses permeate the psychological life of all traditions in the province for good and ill, and enduring leaders are sensitive to the tenderest feelings of their groups.

Effective and transformative leaders are those who can resonate with and express the deepest feelings, images, and aspirations of their constituent groups and can in time slowly micromanage and channel historic self and group narratives and images into new directions. An example of this occurred in October 1993 when an IRA attempt to bomb a loyalist paramilitary Ulster Defence Association (UDA) headquarters on the Shankhill Road in Belfast killed nine innocent Protestant civilians and the IRA bomber. When Gerry Adams, the president of Sinn Fein, who at the time was engaged in the beginning peace process, was photographed carrying the coffin of the dead IRA bomber in the traditional republican funeral there was a huge cry of popular outrage and the fragile peace process was almost derailed. What only a very few observers realized at the time was that Adams was obliged to perform this public ritual to maintain his own credibility with the physical force Republican movement and continue to be able to nudge recalcitrant people along the path to peace. Adams was walking the narrow tightrope of affirming traditional cultural values while at the same time engaging in a process designed to transform them. Adams was too astute a politician and too attuned to the emotional requirements of his group to go beyond what they could bear, unlike the unfortunate but well-meaning Reverend Armstrong.

Another example of how historical and cultural emotional resonance can influence and even generate a relationship between leaders and their groups occurred as a consequence of the first of the infamous Drumcree marches in 1995 that propelled militant loyalism into national and international consciousness. Drumcree was a traditional loyalist Orange march and demonstration, but when the police, the Royal Ulster Constabulary (RUC), attempted to reroute the march away from a Catholic district and a potential confrontation, thousands of outraged Orangemen congregated over the following days demanding the right to walk their traditional route and affirm and preserve their Ulster-British culture. Many Orangemen and loyalists saw the sudden and novel refusal of Catholic and Nationalist residents to let them march through Drumcree as a manifestation of the IRA's post cease-fire strategy of "Tactical Use of Armed Struggle" (TUAS)—a strategy by which republicans would seek to heighten street tensions, provoke Orange reprisals, and then enter the fray as defenders of the embattled Catholic community.

Eventually, the march was forced through in what was seen by many as a triumph for militant and recalcitrant loyalism. David Trimble, who at the time was only the local MP for the area, celebrated the success of the march by walking with another participant, Ian Paisley, hands joined aloft through cheering and ecstatic crowds of supporters. Trimble's show of determination reinforced his previous hard-line credentials, and when James Molyneaux who had led the Unionist party for the past sixteen years was ousted just two months after Drumcree, Trimble was elected as the most implacable and trustworthy of the five candidates to replace him.

Trimble's election seemed to indicate that many Unionists viewed the peace process as hazardous and not as an opportunity for progress and now turned to him as their obvious spokesman. However, as Trimble's biographer makes clear, at Drumcree the normally rational Trimble was in fact "swept along by the emotion of the occasion, which was bound up with such hallowed loyalist concepts as the right to "'walk the Queen's highway' to which he heartily subscribed" (Godson 2005, p. 142).

While on this occasion Trimble's emotional resonance with his political and religious group swept him into power, his subsequent "dismissive approach towards aspects of the unionist communal mood, because certain institutional arrangements had been settled to his satisfaction, was one of his greatest weaknesses as UUP leader." It contributed to his own increasing isolation and rejection as leader and the collapse of the Unionist party in 2005 (Godson 2005, p. 818). Indeed, the more extreme DUP led by Paisley was able to successfully make Trimble, who played a huge role in the evolving peace process, not least by going into government with Sinn Fein, into a hate figure. They potently and symbolically connected him to the traitorous Colonel Robert Lundy of historic dread and contempt who had betrayed the Protestant loyalist people in the seventeenth century. It is an interesting historical resonance that like the later Reverend Armstrong Colonel Lundy was similarly obliged to flee the same area on pain of his life.

Trimble's biographer notes that there was very little affection for Trimble even within his own party and that "He was simply not that interested in other people or their problems" (Godson 2005, p. 822). In addition, Trimble was prepared to tolerate very wide-ranging changes to the way Northern Ireland was governed as long as, for him, the essential Union with the United Kingdom was preserved. These factors meant that he could not successfully engage with or persuade party members and the wider unionist group of his argument, and thus he was obliged to deal with a series of challenges to his leadership and the slow hemorrhaging of support for his party to the next extreme grouping. Despite the emotional tide that swept him into power, Trimble never satisfactorily established that mutual regulatory symbiosis with his group that would have allowed them to influence him more or allowed him to soothe their deeply felt anxieties, and as we shall see, he was eventually undermined as leader and obliged to give way.

This idea that the individual reflects not just a personal but also a collective and historical identity is further strengthened by Jean Claude Rouchy's (1982) concept of "incorporated culture." Rouchy asserts that in child-rearing activity a cultural and social conditioning force permeates the physical relationship of the mother and baby and becomes the basis of character and behavior. Rouchy believes that cultural identity is actually inscribed into the body of the child and then later communicated by the individual to the outside world through certain habits, gestures, ways of looking, corporal attitudes, and linguistic stereotypes. Thus, in any society it is possible to recognize and place a person's class and group by observing and decoding these culturally derived signals.

In her work to integrate the new neuroscience with the tenets of psychoanalysis, Sue Gerhardt (2004) has demonstrated how the infant brain is "customized" or tailored to fit the culture and circumstances it finds itself in. She describes how the orbitofrontal cortex, which is the part of the brain that plays the key role in emotional and social life, only develops after birth and only in response to social experiences. This is a powerful insight into how the norms, narratives, and worldviews of particular subcultures can be transmitted between generations and suggests clearly how intractable conflict can be sustained in a society. It provides the physiological basis for the elegant psychological assertion describing how a traumatized group transmits its psychological experience through the generations to its descendants which Vamik Volkan (2004, pp. 47–52) has described.

Volkan asserted that what he calls "chosen glories" and "chosen traumas" are the two elements that play the most important role in particularizing a group's identity and connecting it to its past. He suggests that groups tend to hold onto mental representations of events, which generate a shared feeling of success and triumph among members, and in times of crisis or in war-like situations, leaders and groups frequently reactivate chosen glories to bolster group solidarity and rally around the flag. One can only too easily call to mind the litany of triumphalist chosen glories of groups in Northern Ireland and every history and media telling of the "Troubles" revels in them so that even most outsiders can recall a few of the more extravagant and significant events.

Volkan describes the more complex phenomenon of the chosen trauma as the collective representation of an event that causes the group to face drastic common losses, to feel helpless, victimized, and humiliated by another group. By sharing the mental representation of the original tragedy, a new generation of the group is unconsciously bonded and the event becomes a crucial marker of group identity. The Maze Hunger Strike referred to earlier is an astonishing example of cultural identification with the aggressor and resymbolization of starvation as sacrificial victimhood and reconstruction of the historical narrative of politicized hunger.

Just as previously the great famine had threatened the extinction of certain groups in Irish society, so now the iconography of starvation was again employed to threaten the extinction of a disputed grouping a retrograde mimetic reproduction of cultural and historic significance. The psychosocial performance of the "sacrificial rite" central to the Hunger Strike sought to legitimize IRA violence and connect it with deep roots in the folk memory while at the same time reconstructing and annexing historical reality (Rice and Benson 2005).

Another interesting angle on the intertwining of individual identity with group life and the role of the leader is found in Freud's (1921) early group psychology paper. He believed that the mechanism of identification is basic in group formations and put forward the idea that group members identify with the leader whom they view as a father surrogate and that they identify with one another and relate to each other through their tie to the leader. A second important mechanism at work in the group is empathy or projective identification, which enables the group members to experience their group life through one another. It is clear that some of the self-love or healthy narcissism of members is projected onto the group so that it becomes very special.

The political Democratic Unionist Party (DUP) led by the charismatic Ian Paisley, who also founded his own Free Presbyterian Church and the diametrically opposed Sinn Fein led by the equally charismatic Gerry Adams, are two obvious groupings in Northern Ireland. Both groups actively promote a sense of their historic and special destiny led by talismanic leaders intimately attuned to the feelings, needs, and aspirations of their members. Paisley has been a central figure in Northern Ireland politics for fifty years and has an undeniable appeal for a large proportion of Protestants. Gerry Adams has been important in republicanism for thirty years and has been central in guiding Sinn Fein and the IRA away from violent militarism into a new model of republican politics.

These groups and their leaders are hugely valued and idealized within their own circles whereas other groups can become the recipients of unbearable hatred and devaluing. Both of these groups clearly fulfill many of the criteria advanced earlier in a discussion of Hopper's fourth basic assumption of massification. The groups appear unified and present enmeshed characteristics in which difference is abhorred and an illusion of sameness and togetherness is highly valued. These dynamics as we shall see have been hugely influential in the intergroup relations of Northern Ireland and have resulted in both the DUP and Sinn Fein becoming majority electoral winners and eclipsing traditional political parties to the point that no government is possible without the consent and active cooperation of these former enemies.

The work of Heinz Kohut (1977) confirms and reinforces the idea that the self can become conflated with the group. Through the school of Self Psychology Kohut and his circle developed musters compelling theoretical and clinical evidence to demonstrate that personal well-being is the result of an empathic environment in early childhood that has the two principal and crucial functions of providing the developing self with appropriate mirroring and opportunities for idealization.

Kohut asserts that empathic maternal attention and caring provide the infant with a mirror in which it gradually comes to recognize and experience itself as a total entity—as a self. This mirroring is crucial for the gradual emergence and development of an enduring sense of identity and a self, which may eventually mature into adequate ambitions and competence and realistic self-esteem. Because of failures or inconsistencies in empathic mirroring, the individual's self may become unstable or disturbed, and there can be a tendency to narcissistic vulnerability and disorder.

In a second line of maturation during the formation of the self, not only does the infant want to be admired by its caretaker, it wants to psychically fuse with the caretaker whom it experiences as omnipotent and perfect and therefore soothing because of the parent's ability to regulate the infant's troubled emotions. In other words, the parent is idealized, and the infant wishes to merge with this powerful and perfect other to preserve its own cohesion and security.

Kohut and his colleagues believe that we continue to need throughout life and search for empathic mirroring and idealizing objects and situations to maintain healthy psychological well-being. From this perspective, we can see how many people would be attracted to various political movements or spiritual traditions to create a context for living. The major religions and political movements mirror important self-images that are essential for a meaningful sense of self, identity, belonging, and acceptance and also importantly provide opportunities for self-identification with and idealization of revered secular, political, and saintly figures. Alderdice (2007) makes the point that many individuals in Northern Ireland who joined terrorist groups did so because they admired significant people in their community who for generations had maintained a tradition of using physical force to resolve political problems. Kohut's work is crucial for understanding the psychological, social, and political dynamics in Northern Ireland and explicating the dynamics involved in the mutual regulatory symbiosis of leaders and groups. Firstly, individuals and groups need and seek out people and experiences, which will mirror and reflect their self-esteem and ambitions, and secondly individuals and groups need and seek out people and experiences, which will inspire and motivate them. Appropriate mirroring and healthy inspiration were sadly lacking for decades in Northern Ireland. After partition of the island of Ireland in 1921 and the setting up of what was in effect a permanent Unionist Protestant state, politics atrophied in the two communities in the North. Many Catholics did not bother to vote believing that Unionist domination was irreversible and unopposed elections became a feature of the Stormont system. The Catholic Nationalist party was disorganized and divided and usually boycotted Stormont. It provided no leaders as ideal models or opportunities for inspiring its natural constituency and instead negatively mirrored the powerlessness and poor self-esteem of a socially excluded and despised people.

For fifty years, the continuously Protestant government mirrored itself grandiosely on an English Westminster model, and when the illusion was shattered in 1972 with the imposition of Direct Rule from Westminster, the Loyalist Protestant community experienced a profound narcissistic humiliation in the form of the loss of its parliament and powers. The Unionist and loyalist community regressed into mass action (Ulster Workers Council Strike) and lobbied unsuccessfully for merger or union with the idealized Westminster government that showed no desire to accommodate the Unionist fantasy. That it was the "Mother of Parliaments" in London that rescinded the local parliament was a particularly shameful and infantilizing wound to the once mighty unionist peoples.

The Nationalist minded Catholic community in Northern Ireland tended to look to Dublin to satisfy its desires for primary identity and to assuage the sense of loss generated by enforced separation. But here again one can see a theme of intense frustration since the Irish government gained its own independence at the cost of the partition of the island in 1921 and the northern nationalists were surrendered to the Protestant Unionist majority and obliged to await the time *"their day would come."* The acute sense of loss is a traditional and resonant theme for generations of Nationalists and republicans. A later leader of the major Nationalist political party, while under its leader John Hume, did succeed in fostering a symbiotic relationship with successive Dublin governments much to the fury and dread of Unionist and Loyalist groups who accused the Nationalists of precisely what they themselves aspired to do in relation to Westminster. The inevitable presence of malign projective identification meant that each leader and group system in the North mirrored its own treachery and disregard for the well-being of the whole as the chief desire of the other.

In the 1960s, the political and cultural climate in Northern Ireland began to change. The dominant majoritarian Unionist party had a new leader, Terence O'Neill, who believed that moderate reforms and modernization were called for and that Catholics could be involved in supporting Unionist government and the state. Hard-line Protestant fundamentalists such as Ian Paisley opposed him in this, and within the Unionist party, intransigent factions led by William Craig and Brian Faulkner as well as by institutions such as the Orange order were steeped in an emotional mind-set in which Catholics were putative enemies of the state. O'Neill however was unable to provide an inspiring figure who could mobilize his group's support and was seen as distant and aristocratic and not at all an ideal leader. He lacked the social and personal skills that could allow him to participate in or generate the mutual regulatory symbiosis that binds leaders and groups and soon fell from power, leaving an agitated and increasingly divided unionist political culture behind him.

As monolithic unionism seemed to be cracking, Nationalists and Catholics were just beginning to find new possibilities and instruments for political expression. A growing civil rights movement attracted figures such as John Hume, Gerry Fitt, and others as a means of coordinating the majority of Catholics who belonged to no organizations and encouraged them to move away from political isolation into political participation. The Northern Ireland Civil Rights Association was an umbrella organization that had a largely middle-class leadership and agitated for political reforms by the discriminatory unionist regime. Reforms did come in due course, but the real legacy of this radicalization of Catholics was the later formation of the Social

Democratic Labour Party (SDLP), eventually led by John Hume who would come to be the most prestigious politician of the "Troubles" and indeed in Ireland. The SDLP was created as a response to the sterile and uninspiring defeatist politics of the old Nationalist Party. It cohered around an agenda that is now largely accepted by other parties including the DUP and Sinn Fein who both bitterly opposed it throughout the conflict.

Hume and others took the view that it was possible for Catholics to engage with a modified Stormont and was successful in mirroring to alienated Catholics a positive and dynamic self-image in which they could see themselves as competent and valuable (Hume 1997). Later, as the architect of the vitally important 1985 Anglo-Irish Agreement, he helped to internationalize the Northern Ireland conflict, redefining the relationship among London, Belfast, and Dublin and drawing in American and European commitment to ending the conflict. The recontextualizing and internationalizing of the problem engineered by Hume, which eventually led to a definitive peace process, made him an inspiring and idealized figure for many. His political analysis of the conflict meant that one no longer saw Britain as an imperialist presence the IRA asserted but as a neutral party involved only because of Unionist insistence on the preservation of partition. Irish unity could only come about by Protestant consent. Hume insisted that the real border was not geographical but mental and emotional. He thus redefined conventional Irish nationalism and was successful in creating a new constitutional nationalism that appealed hugely to the pacifist sentiments and historical, cultural, and ideological values of his own group and enhanced their self-esteem and sense of identity.

Hume played yet another key role in developing the peace process through his internationalist engagement with Gerry Adams, which was instrumental in weaning the IRA away from violence and consolidating electoral and peaceful politics (Hennessy 2001). The IRA was a militant organization wholly committed to securing unity of the two parts of Ireland through physical force. They were largely based in southern Ireland and increasingly more left-wing than militant. A tiny and ineffectual force throughout the greater part of the Stormont regime, the IRA really only came to prominence in the early 1970s after a northern group that included the charismatic young Gerry Adams split from southern command in 1969 to form the Provisional IRA. For the next thirty years, republican paramilitary action operated alongside its deadly loyalist twin to provide the violent backdrop to the stuttering stop start political environment. Both republican and loyalist paramilitary groupings were prone to split endlessly because of deadly and murderous feuds and involved the rest of the population in their fearful machinations and intrigues.

It was inevitable that in a society such as Northern Ireland, where language and thought and dialogue were deficient, men and women of action would seize the bloody initiative. But, painfully and only gradually it became evident that violence was not working and some paramilitaries began looking for alternatives. An event occurred in 1981 that was to prove hugely transformative in the history of violent republicanism, and some observers even regard it as the genesis of what would eventually become the peace process (McKitterick and McVea 2001, p. 143).

Republican prisoners initiated a second hunger strike to the death, and the election of the doomed Bobby Sands as a Sinn Fein candidate proved to be a key moment in the development of Sinn Fein as a political force. The decision to enter the electoral arena in support of the prisoners "was a combination of fortuitous circumstance and the determination of the prisoners rather than any strategic planning by Sinn Fein" but did convince most republicans that electoralism could offer another way of prosecuting their war (Murray and Tonge 2005, p. 110). The 30,000 votes Sands polled convinced the republican political elite that here was a grassroots group that could be carefully cultivated and the massive vote was clearly telling the leadership that people would support talking and politics rather than withdrawal and violence. Here we see yet more evidence for the assertion of a mutual regulatory symbiosis between groups and their leaders. An emotionally charged group of Nationalist and Republican voters seized the opportunity of a traumatizing event to speak with one voice, and a startled but skillful and attuned leadership was quick to see the possibilities and move rapidly in the direction of a mass electoral and political strategy that would come to replace violence. Many republican sympathizers who would not countenance joining the IRA were prepared to work for its objectives politically, so it made sense to the astute leadership to broaden and expand the political party.

Over the next decades, Gerry Adams and the republican political elite would mirror, shape, and inspire the growing Sinn Fein movement to the point where it would eventually eclipse and overtake the SDLP as the major nationalist party. Adams and his cohort would come to practice as a very high art the emotional processes and dynamics which make for electoral success.

Westen has identified four essential strategies for political and electoral success. He asserts that "The first goal transcends any given candidate: to define the party and its principles in a way that is emotionally compelling and tells a coherent story of what its members believe in and to define the other party and its values in a way that undermine its capacity to resonate emotionally with voters" (2007, p. 137).

Other strategies include maximizing positive feelings toward the candidates and encouraging negative feelings toward opponents as well as managing positive and negative feelings about the candidate's policies and positions. Westen's central point is that "managing positive and negative feelings should be the primary goals of a political campaign" (2007, p. 138). Adams and Sinn Fein are recognized widely as absolute masters of these political-emotional arts and that they were very mindful of the need to always pay attention to their grassroots was evident at every step along the peace process and a major factor in why it took so long.

Adams's counterpart on the loyalist side is the hugely influential Ian Paisley who is equally adept at telling a compelling emotional narrative to his DUP party faithful and increasingly growing numbers of Protestants. Ian Paisley "has built a career on claiming continuity with the glorious past" (Bruce 2007, p. 257). He mirrors a self-image for his group that is persistently backward looking and traditionally rooted in simple rural and religious values and beliefs. He presents to his people an identity grounded on heritage and nostalgia. Throughout his political and religious career, he has vehemently opposed all attempts at accommodation and deal making and has consistently stood on his version of core unionist values and principles.

Paisley has been spectacularly successful in inflaming and channeling the most negative feelings in his group toward his unionist opponents and has brought down every unionist politician or leader who dared stand against him from O'Neill through Trimble. He has made himself the object of idealization within his grouping with his seeming omnipotence and omniscience, often appearing to know of backdoor deals and betrayals before they happened.

However, even so idealized a figure cannot exceed what his group will tolerate. In the Free Presbyterian Church, which he founded and has led unopposed since 1951, Paisley has been savagely attacked by members who have been astonished and traumatized that he has entered government with the traditionally reviled and hated Sinn Fein particularly after his persistent refusal to countenance them over the years. In January 2008, hard-line dissidents in his church calling themselves Concerned Free Presbyterians forced the once omnipotent Paisley to resign as moderator after fifty-six unopposed years to prevent a potential ecclesiastical split. In March 2008, Paisley was also obliged to announce his resignation as leader of the political party that he had founded after "weeks of internal pressure at every level of his party" (*News Letter*, March 2008, p. 4). This began when Jim Allister, a long-standing supporter, quit the DUP in protest at Paisley going into an executive power-sharing coalition with Sinn Fein in March 2007. With other disaffected DUP members, Allister set up the oppositional Traditional Unionist Voice (TUV) political party, which contested the Dromore by-election in February 2008. The DUP, which prided itself as the representative of Ulster unionism, lost the by-election. According to the Lagan Valley Member of Parliament Jeffrey Donaldson, who had earlier deserted the Unionist party to defect to the DUP, "The Dromore by-election has given the DUP food for thought . . . the fact that over 700 traditional DUP supporters chose this time to switch their vote to the TUV reflects a concern in a significant section of the Unionist community that cannot be ignored. . . . (electors) chose this by-election to make a protest with their vote and the message they are sending to the Party will not be ignored" (Dromore Leader, Feb. 19, 2008).

The TUV party leader Jim Allister said the Dromore election result for his party represented a "phenomenal achievement from a standing start." He asserted that "a loss of 44% of the DUP vote is unparalleled and betokens the gross loss of confidence by grassroots unionists in Ian Paisley's leadership" (BBC News, 24 Feb. 14, 2008). Allister was to prove prophetically correct.

This unprecedented rejection of Paisley by his own people again illustrates the delicate attunement of the mutual regulatory symbiosis that exists between leaders and their groups. Like the unfortunate Reverend Armstrong, it appears that Ian Paisley has exceeded what his group could emotionally bear and relations have ruptured. It has been traumatic and just too much for many of Paisley's supporters that the man who defended them against terrorists and their supporters should have gone into government with those he reviled for decades. The ubiquitously invincible Paisley has been deposed as leader, and the political party and church groups have sought out new, and one suspects, more amenable and attuned leaders.

Until this time, Paisley and his group, like Adams and Sinn Fein, have represented a model of mutual regulatory symbiosis between the leader and the group. As leaders, Paisley and Adams have mirrored a self-image and identity to their groups that members have found entirely reassuring and satisfactory and have inspired their groups with values and beliefs and a worldview that was to their mind the purest possible as a basis for living. Adams and Paisley have been able to rouse their people emotionally, shape their beliefs and behavior, and soothe them in times of distress. As leaders, they have in turn relied on the powerful cohesion of their groups whose shared religious and political beliefs cemented their social identity.

Paisley was a vibrant figure throughout the "Troubles" and grew his power base with frightening assertions of betrayal by others and personal claims to integrity and tradition. He was attractive to many Protestants alarmed at the passivity and inertia of James Molyneaux who led the Unionist Party for sixteen years and under whose leadership the party drifted and atrophied. Adams was an equally attractive and charismatic ideal for many urban working-class nationalists and republicans who felt the middle-class SDLP with its elderly leadership represented a more accomodationist approach and was not attuned with their experiences and values. However, it is Paisley who has paid the price for not educating his people and who, in going beyond what they can tolerate, has broken the mutual regulatory symbiosis and been deposed from power.

CONCLUSIONS

I noted at the beginning of this chapter that there had been four decades of intractable conflict in Northern Ireland that was eventually resolved in a peace process and made amenable to politics. This conflict reveals important insights about the relationship between leaders and groups because of the political longevity and evolution of the successful leader-group partnerships and the volatile nature of other group and leader systems. I have indicated the major factors and dynamics that made the situation intractable and have asserted in this chapter that the key to understanding the conflict and its transformation has to do with the dynamics of idealization and mirroring in generating a complex relationship between leaders and groups, which I have called a mutual regulatory symbiosis.

I have demonstrated that successful and transformative leaders are emotionally attuned to their groups and that groups will remove leaders who are unempathic or forfeit their trust. I have illustrated how individual and group identity become intertwined at local and national levels and shown how four dimensions of this fusion of individual and national self-image become the basis and medium for the mutual regulatory symbiosis of leaders and group partnerships. Essential to this mutual regulatory symbiosis are the dynamics of idealization and mirroring.

In conclusion then I assert that those leaders and their groups that have done best in political power in Northern Ireland represent the current, most perfectly attuned models of mutual regulatory symbiosis. The older and traditional political parties have atrophied and are in danger of extinction. They have failed to emotionally resonate with and be attuned to the deepest fears, needs, and aspirations of their members and to provide leaders who can channel and maintain self-cohesion and identity and reinforce historically resonant views and expectations of the world while simultaneously enabling people to manage change and transition with creative and healthy strategies.

REFERENCES

Alderdice, J. "The Individual, the Group and the Psychology of Terrorism." *International Review of Psychiatry* 19(3) (2007): 201–9.

Benson, J. F. "The Group Turned Inwards: A Consideration of Some Group Phenomena as Reflective of the Northern Irish Situation." *Groupwork* 5 (1992): 5–18.

Benson, J. F. "The Secret War in the Dis-United Kingdom: Psychological Aspects of the Ulster Conflict." *Group Analysis* 28 (1995): 47–62.

Benson, J. F. *Working More Creatively with Groups.* 2nd ed. London: Routledge, 2001.

Bew, P. *Ireland: The Politics of Enmity 1789–2006.* Oxford: Oxford University Press, 2007.

Bion, W. *Experiences in Groups and Other Papers*. London: Tavistock, 1961.

Bowyer Bell, J. *The Irish Troubles: A Generation of Violence 1967–1992*. Dublin: Gill and McMillan, 1993.

Breuer, J., and S. Freud. *Studies in Hysteria* (vol. 3, Pelican Freud Library). Harmondsworth, England: Penguin, 1893.

Bruce, S. *Paisley: Religion and Politics in Northern Ireland*. Oxford: Oxford University Press, 2007.

Clarke, L. "If Fianna Fail Marries the SDLP It Will Be No Party for Sinn Fein. *The Sunday Times*, April 11, 2007.

Foulkes, S. H. "Problems of the Group from a Group-Analytic Point of View." In *The Large Group: Dynamics and Therapy*, edited by L. Kreeger, 33–56. London: Constable, 1975.

Freud, S. *Group Psychology and the Analysis of the Ego* (vol. 12, Pelican Freud Library). Harmondsworth, England: Penguin, 1921/1985.

Gerhardt, S. *Why Love Matters: How Affection Shapes a Baby's Brain*. East Sussex, England: Brunner Routledge, 2004.

Godson, D. *Himself Alone: David Trimble and the Ordeal of Unionism*. London: Harper Perennial, 2005.

Hennessy, T. *The Northern Ireland Peace Process: Ending the Troubles?* New York: Palgrave, 2001.

Hopper, E. "Traumatic Experience in the Unconscious Life of Groups: A Fourth Basic Assumption." *Group Analysis* 34(1) (1997): 439–70.

Hume, J. *A New Ireland: Politics, Peace and Reconciliation*. Boulder, Colo.: Roberts Rhinehart Publishers, 1997.

Kohut, H. *The Restoration of the Self*. New York: International Universities Press, 1977.

McKittrick, D., and D. McVea. *Making Sense of the Troubles*. London: Penguin Books, 2001.

Moloney, E. *Paisley: From Demagogue to Democrat*. Dublin: Poolbeg Press, 2008.

Murray. G., and J. Tonge. *Sinn Fein and the SDLP: From Alienation to Participation*. Dublin: The O'Brien Press, 2005.

Powell, J. *Great Hatred, Little Room: Making Peace in Northern Ireland*. London: The Bodley Head, 2008.

Rice, C. A., and J. F. Benson. "Hungering for Revenge: The Irish Famine, the Troubles and Shame-Rage Cycles and Their Role in Group Therapy in Northern Ireland." *Group Analysis* 38(2) (2005): 219–35.

Rouchy, J. C. "Archaic Processes and Transference in Group Analysis." *Group Analysis* xv(3) (1982): 235–60.

Sheldrake, R. *The Presence of the Past*. London: Fontana, 1988.

Tonge, J. *The New Northern Irish Politics*. Hampshire, England: Palgrave (Macmillan), 2005.

Volkan, V. *Blind Trust: Large Groups and Their Leaders in Times of Crisis and Terror*. Charlottesville, Va.: Pitchstone Publishing, 2004.

von Bertalanffy, L. *General Systems Theory*. New York: George Braziller, 1968.

Westen, D. *The Political Brain: The Role of Emotion in Deciding the Fate of the Nation*. New York: Public Affairs Books, 2007.

Index

Contributors

Jarlath F. Benson, M.Soc.Sc., M.Med Sc. is a group analyst and psychotherapist in private practice in Northern Ireland for the past twenty-three years. Benson is past director of the Northern Ireland Institute of Human Relations and was academic director of the Institute of Psychosynthesis London for ten years. Benson is author of the best selling text, *Working More Creatively with Groups* (London: Routledge, 1997 (2nd edition, 2001) about to go into its third edition and has published a number of articles on the psychology of the Northern Ireland "Troubles."

Harold S. Bernard, Ph.D., A.B.P.P., C.G.P., D.F.A.G.P.A. is clinical associate professor of psychiatry at New York University School of Medicine. He is past president and distinguished fellow of the American Group Psychotherapy Association. He is coeditor of three volumes: *Handbook of Contemporary Group Psychotherapy, Basics of Group Psychotherapy,* and *Psychosocial Interventions for Medical Conditions: Principles and Techniques,* as well as author of numerous journal articles and book chapters. He maintains private practices in Manhattan and in Westport, Conn.

Richard M. Billow, Ph.D. A.B.P.P. is director of the Group Program and clinical professor at the Derner Institute, Postgraduate Programs in Psychoanalysis and Psychotherapy, Adelphi University, Garden City, New York. He is a frequent contributor to the psychoanalytic and group literature. His book, *Relational Group Psychotherapy: From Basic Assumptions to Passion* (Jessica Kingsley Press, 2003), won the Alonso Award of the American Group Psychotherapy Association. He maintains a private practice in Great Neck, N.Y.

Jean Lau Chin, Ed.D., A.B.P.P. is professor and dean of the Derner Institute of Advanced Psychological Studies at Adelphi University in Garden City, New York. Her prior executive management positions include: systemwide dean, California School of Professional Psychology at Alliant International University; president, CEO Services; Regional Director, Massachusetts Behavioral Health Partnership; executive director, South Cove Community Health Center; and co-director, Thom Child Guidance Clinic. She is a licensed psychologist with almost forty years of clinical, educational, and management experience in health and mental health services. Dr. Chin has published extensively with ten books and over two hundred presentations in the areas of cultural competence in health, education, and mental health; ethnic minority and Asian American mental health issues; and women's issues including leadership. Her most recent book is: *Women and Leadership: Transforming Visions and Diverse Voices* (2007) published by Blackwell Press.

Zachary Gabriel Green, Ph.D. is a senior scholar at the Academy of Leadership, University of Maryland through which he offers seminars on negotiations, psychology of decision-making and group behavior worldwide. A clinical psychologist in private practice for two decades, Dr. Green applies this professional lens and his organizational analysis background to his role as an executive coach for the World Bank. He is a fellow of the A. K. Rice Institute for the Study of Social Systems and co-founder of Group Relations International. Through the latter organization and in his writing, Dr. Green gives focus to the theory and practice of transforming social justice issues. He is author of numerous popular and scholarly articles on identity, culture, leadership, and group behavior. Zachary is married with two sons and resides in the Netherlands.

Peter Gumpert, Ph.D., C.G.P. is a clinical and organizational psychologist who practices individual and couple psychotherapy in Brookline, Mass. He founded and for twenty-five years was president of an organizational consulting firm located in Massachusetts. He consults on work culture change and collaboration to major manufacturing and technology companies as well as public sector organizations. Prior to his work as a clinician and consultant, Dr. Gumpert was an academic psychologist, principally Associate Professor of Psychology and Education at Teachers College, Columbia University, where he taught in the doctoral program in social and organizational psychology. He continues to teach in the group psychotherapy training program at the Northeastern Society for Group Psychotherapy, and is a senior clinical supervisor at the Boston Institute for Psychotherapy. Dr. Gumpert has co-authored a book based on his research in social and personality psychology, entitled *The Success-fearing Personality: Theory and*

Research, published in 1978 by Lexington Books, D.C. Heath & Co. He has also contributed many articles and chapters related to issues in social, organizational, and clinical psychology.

Robert H. Klein, Ph.D, A.B.P.P., C.G.P., D.L.F.A.G.P.A. is a clinical faculty member at the Yale School of Medicine, New Haven, Conn. A fellow of the American Psychological Association and diplomate in Group Psychology, he is past president of the American Group Psychotherapy Association (AGPA), member of the board of directors of the Group Psychotherapy Foundation, founding member of the National Registry of Certified Group Psychotherapists, and a distinguished life fellow of AGPA. Following 9/11 he served as the Co-Chair of the AGPA Disaster Outreach Task Force. A recognized expert in the area of group psychotherapy, he lectures, consults, and supervises both nationally and internationally. He is the author of numerous publications, including co-author of *The Termination Process in Individual and Group Psychotherapy*, and co-editor of *Group Psychotherapy for Psychological Trauma, Handbook of Contemporary Group Psychotherapy* and *Public Mental Health Service Delivery Protocols: Group Interventions for Disaster Preparedness and Response*. Dr. Klein maintains a private clinical practice with offices in Westport and Milford, Conn. He may be contacted at 88 Noble Avenue, Milford, CT 06460. Email: drrklein@aol.com.

Joseph V. Montville is chair of the Center for World Religions, Diplomacy, and Conflict Resolution at George Mason University and distinguished diplomat in residence at American University. In July 2008, he was awarded the Nevitt Sanford prize for "distinguished professional contribution to political psychology" by the International Society of Political Psychology at its annual meeting in Paris.

Jerrold M. Post, M.D. is professor of psychiatry, political psychology, and international affairs and director of the political psychology program at The George Washington University. Dr. Post has devoted his entire career to the field of political psychology. Dr. Post came to George Washington after a twenty-one-year career with the Central Intelligence Agency where he was the founding director of the Center for the Analysis of Personality and Political Behavior. He played the lead role in developing the "Camp David profiles" of Menachem Begin and Anwar Sadat for President Jimmy Carter and initiated the U.S. government program in understanding the psychology of terrorism. He served as expert witness in the trial in the spring of 2001 for the al Qaeda terrorists responsible for the bombing of the U.S. embassies in Kenya and Tanzania, and, since 9/11, has testified on terrorist psychology before the Senate, the House of Representatives, and the United Nations. In addition to numerous journal articles and book chapters, Post has written or edited ten books, his most recent being *Leaders and Their Followers in a Dangerous World* (Cornell) and *The Mind of the Terrorist: The Psychology of Terrorism from the IRA to al-Qaeda* (Palgrave-Macmillan). He is a frequent commentator on national and international media on such topics as leadership, leader illness, treason, the psychology of terrorism, suicide terrorism, weapons of mass destruction, Saddam Hussein, Osama bin Laden, Hugo Chavez, Mahmoud Ahmadinejad, and Kim Jong Il.

Cecil A. Rice, Ph.D. C.G.P., F.A.G.P.A. is associate editor of the *International Journal of Group Psychotherapy*, a co-founder and president of the Boston Institute for Psychotherapy, established in 1970 as a mental health clinic serving the Greater Boston area and providing postgraduate training for mental health professionals. He has a particular interest in the long-term after effects of civil war on the community of Northern Ireland where he co-founded the Northern Ireland Group Psychotherapy Conference serving the professional needs of mental health workers in that community. He also co-founded the Rice Fund at the Northeastern Society for Group Psychotherapy, of which he is a past president, funding projects addressing violence and trauma in society. He has a private practice in group, individual, marital, and family therapy in Needham, Massachusetts, and teaches psychiatric residents for Harvard Medical School at Massachusetts General and McLean hospitals. He has lectured widely and led numerous workshops throughout the USA and Ireland. He has written many articles and book chapters on groups and group therapy including co-authoring *Inpatient Group Psychotherapy: A Psychodynamic Perspective*, 1987. Dr. Rice's email address is cecil.rice@comcast.net.

Victor L. Schermer, M.A., L.P.C., C.A.C., C.G.P., F.A.G.P.A. is a psychologist in private practice and clinic settings in Philadelphia, Penn. He is executive director of the Study Group for Contemporary Psychoanalytic Process and founding director of the Institute for the Study of Human Conflict. He has maintained a sustained interest, published papers, and conducted conferences on the application of psychology and psychoanalysis to social and political issues. Schermer has served on the Faculties of the Continuing Education Program for Social Workers at Rutgers University and the Institute for Psychoanalytic Psychotherapies. He is a fellow of the American Group Psychotherapy Association and a consultant for their Disaster Relief Task Force. He is co-editor with Robert Klein of *Group Psychotherapy for Psychological Trauma*, for which they received the Alonso Award of the Group Psychotherapy Foundation. In addition, he is co-author of *Object Relations, the Self, and the Group* and co-editor of *Ring of Fire* and of *Group Psychotherapy of the Psychoses*, and author of *Spirit and Psyche*. He has contributed numerous articles and chapters to books and journals in psychoanalysis and psychotherapy. He is a frequent presenter of lectures, seminars, and workshops both in the United States and Europe. His email address is VLScher@voicenet.com.

Hala Taweel, Ph.D. is the president and cofounder of the University of the Middle East Project, a 501c3 organization based in Cambridge, Mass. Born in Jerusalem, Dr. Taweel was raised in Nablus and Ramallah. She holds a Ph.D. degree in Higher Education Administration from Boston College, the Lynch Graduate School of Education, a Masters in Public Administration from Harvard University, the John F. Kennedy School of Government. Her first Masters degree in Computer Science and Human Science was received from Paris VIII University, Paris, France. She also holds a Diploma in Diplomatic and Strategic Studies from the Center for Law and Defense at Paris V University. Dr. Taweel's interest is in international higher education with special focus on the Middle East. She is also a member of the Board of Trustees of Roger Williams University in Bristol, R.I.

Vamik D. Volkan, M.D., D.L.F.A.P.A., F.A.C.Psa is an emeritus professor of psychiatry at the University of Virginia, Charlottesville, Virginia; an Emeritus training and supervising analyst at the Washington Psychoanalytic Institute, Washington, D.C.; and the Senior Erik Erikson Scholar at the Austen Riggs Center in Stockbridge, Massachusetts. He holds honorary doctoral degrees from Kuopio University, Finland, and from Ankara University, Turkey. He has served on the editorial boards of sixteen professional journals including the *Journal of the American Psychoanalytic Association*, authored or co-authored thirty books, and was the editor or co-editor of ten more. He has published more than four hundred scientific papers or book chapters. Since 1979, he has been involved in a series of unofficial diplomatic negotiations between influential enemy representatives. Currently he is involved in bringing together representatives from the Western and Islamic worlds to examine the existing perceptions and feelings concerning the so-called Western-Islamic world split. He was a president of the International Society of Political Psychology, Virginia Psychoanalytic Society and is president-elect of the American College of Psychoanalysts.   •